EU and US Banking in the 1990s

To our parents

EU and US Banking in the 1990s

Alfred Lewis

School of Management
Binghamton University
State University of New York
Binghamton, New York, USA

Gioia Pescetto

Department of Economics
Brunel University, West London
Uxbridge, Middlesex, UK

ACADEMIC PRESS LIMITED
24–28 Oval Road
LONDON NW1 7DX

U.S. Edition Published by
ACADEMIC PRESS INC.
San Diego, CA 92101

This book is printed on acid free paper

332.1094
L67e

A catalogue record for this book is available from the British Library

KH

ISBN 0-12-446640-0

Typeset by WestKey Ltd., Falmouth, Cornwall
Printed in Great Britain by Hartnolls Limited, Bodmin, Cornwall

Contents

List of Figures

List of Tables

List of Abbreviations

BCCI	Bank of Credit and Commerce International
BIF	Bank Insurance Fund
BIS	Bank for International Settlements
CD	Certificate of Deposit
DIDMCA	Depositary Institutions Deregulation and Monetary Control Act
EC	European Community
ECB	European Central Bank
EFTA	European Free Trade Association
EMI	European Monetary Institute
EMS	European Monetary System
EMU	European Monetary Union
ERM	Exchange Rate System
EU	European Union
FBSEA	Foreign Bank Supervision Enhancement Act
FDIC	Federal Deposit Insurance Corporation
FDICA	Federal Deposit Insurance Corporation Improvement Act
FIRREA	Financial Institutions Reform Recovery and Enforcement Act
FRN	Floating Rate Notes
FRS	Federal Reserve System
GDP	Gross Domestic Product
HC	Holding Company
IBF	International Banking Facilities
IMF	International Monetary Fund
LDC	Less Developed Country
NOW	Negotiable Order for Withdrawal
OBHC	One-Bank Holding Company
OECD	Organization for Economic Co-operation and Development
OPEC	Organization for Petroleum Exporting Countries

Preface

This book was conceived the first time we met, on one of those UK conference evenings which always end with a drink in the pub. It seemed like an excellent idea that night. As often happens, the next morning we panicked. How could we possibly trust each other and be certain that we would stand by our promises? Neither of us, however, had the courage to break the previous night's agreement. Whether we were right is for you to judge, but what follows is the result of our labour.

This book was written in a period of important changes in the world financial scene, changes which have affected banking deeply. Both the European and the US banking sectors are undergoing deep transformations brought about by different events. However, similarities between the experience of these two areas make a comparison worthwhile and useful in identifying future trends. With the creation of a single European market, banking in the European Union has become more integrated and the history of the US federal system provides insights into the problems faced by an integrated financial area. Similarly, as US banks face deregulation and interstate integration in retail banking, they may well learn a few useful lessons from their European colleagues. The globalisation of financial services calls for a joint analysis of the banking sectors in two economic areas which are so strongly related, both economically and politically. Moreover, recent events in both areas lead to the conclusion that not only competition within these two areas, but also competition between US and EU banks will increase.

More than ever before, the strategic behaviour of EU and US banks is expected to converge. The banking industries on both sides of the Atlantic are facing intensified competition at home, both within the industry and from non-banking institutions which are now allowed to offer a wider array of financial services, including some traditional banking services. This is most likely to lead to changes in the industry structure, its competitive posture, and the type and size of banking institutions; it is also likely to change their foreign policy, depending on whether market integration will bring about more trade creation or more trade diversion. Globalisation of financial services means that it is a must for large banks to participate in both markets. This implies that the restructuring of the EU and US banking industries will create opportunities for European banks to consolidate their presence in the US market, and vice versa.

One ought to be careful, however, not to go too far with the similarities. The US experience is very different from the recent developments in Europe, and dissimilarities between the two systems are also quite important. Thus, the analysis of the two banking systems will be kept separate at first and the similarities drawn subsequently. The effects of economic integration on EU banking and of deregulation on US banking represent challenging topics of study, since at the theoretical level financial intermediation is still not very well understood and competition among financial intermediaries is impeded by the existence of market failure and asymmetric information. In this book, the recent developments in the two industries will be discussed in the light of the economic theory of financial intermediation, integration and industrial structure. The traditional theory of oligopoly is not really adequate to explain the possible structural changes in the two banking industries, since it usually refers to markets where there is no entry. Instead, the theory of contestable markets seems to be particularly relevant, since potential competition from outside the industry is the key element and it is applicable to multiproduct firms.

This book is divided into three parts. Part I provides an analysis of the changing environment since 1980, both in the EU and the US. Developments in banking regulation, marketing strategies and industry structure are related to the growing globalisation of the banking sector. The second part discusses the nature of banking in relation to three main areas in economic theory: market failure and the need for regulation; the effects of deregulation and integration on competition; market entry and contestability. The third part discusses the future prospects for EU and US banking.

It has been our intention to write this book for a wide audience. Although we have applied recent developments in economic theory to the analysis of banking intermediation, we hope that financial practitioners and policy makers will find this book both useful and appealing. To them this book will provide a broad perspective of the changes occurring in European and US banking. We also hope that it will be a source of stimulating ideas to our academic colleagues and researchers in the field. Although not a textbook, students attending courses on financial markets and banking, or financial integration, will find here an example of modern applied analysis of banking.

Acknowledgements are in order. We are grateful to all those colleagues who read and commented on early drafts. Our special thanks go to Phil Holmes and Mansoob Murshed for their insightful comments and to Chris Newnham for her patience in typing some rather lengthy and complex tables. Finally we must thank our friends and families for enduring the occasional frustrations and bad moods which are usually caused by projects of this kind.

Introduction

The banking industry is experiencing profound and discontinuous changes globally. Several factors contribute to this status of flux, including increased economic instability in international markets, globalisation, disintermediation and deregulation in the main industrialised countries and the introduction of new information technologies. In addition, and as a consequence of these factors, a process of financial innovation has also been taking place which in turn has had an impact upon the regulatory, structural and marketing changes occurring in the industry (Canals, 1993).

While all these factors are present in both the US and Europe, the creation of a unified European market in financial services has affected the European banking sector in particular. And, of course, the opening of Eastern Europe to the influence of Western economies has added yet another factor of interest.

International financial instability

In the last two decades, the development of international financial markets has been characterised by growing globalisation and integration. These phenomena have brought with them increased efficiency of financial intermediaries and a greater volume of international capital flows. In this environment, instability arises from the lack of consistency between the economic policies of the major industrialised countries and the existence of a system of floating exchange rates.

The 1992 crisis of the European Monetary System (EMS) is an example of this type of instability problem. Before capital movements were liberalised, capital controls protected central banks' reserves against speculative attacks, and inflation differentials were reconciled with pegged but adjustable exchange rates. After 1990, however, the new EMS of no realignments and no controls became unstable in the presence of independent monetary policies. Eliminating realignments, in fact, although it had anti-inflationary benefits in weak-currency countries, made relative price changes more difficult to effect. Eliminating capital controls, although it is thought to contribute to a better resource allocation, left central banks powerless to counteract speculative attacks.

The developing countries' external debt problem of course aggravated the consequences of international financial instability and hit the banking sector in particular. Unlike previous debt crises, the developing countries' debt crisis of the 1980s was mainly related to commercial bank debt and thus accentuated the needs for the changes in organisation, services and financial product specifications which we have observed over the last decade. These changes have been greatly facilitated by deregulation. Exchange rate volatility and high interest rates have forced central banks to approve deregulatory measures, and the private financial sector to innovate.

Deregulation

The financial regulatory systems which were in place in the US and in Western Europe until a few years ago originated from the measures approved by President Roosevelt after the financial crisis at the beginning of the 1930s (Kennedy, 1973). Four main groups of measures were included: a federal insurance system; measures designed to avoid price competition and in particular payment of too high rates of interest by individual banks, with the consequent increase in the risk of bankruptcy; regulation of the geographic expansion of credit institutions; and the separation of activities of commercial banks from those of investment banks.

These measures were gradually introduced in Western Europe, until, at the beginning of the 1980s, a general trend towards deregulation started to reverse the regulatory process. Already in the 1960s European and US banks had found ways to evade the legislation regarding interest rates and geographical location. This trend was consolidated in the 1970s, when high inflation rates encouraged the design of new high interest rate financial products which were not recognised as deposits. For example, in 1977 Merrill Lynch introduced the Cash Management Account, with which investors had access to a current account, a credit card and a money fund with immediate access to a loan up to a maximum of 50% of the account-holder's balance. Regulation of interest rates was abolished in the US in 1986 and more recently in the major European countries.

The same fate occurred to regulations on geographical restrictions, finally abolished in 1990 in the US. In Western Europe, the creation of a single market for financial services as part of the 1992 programme has abolished barriers among member states. Technological innovation was a major cause of the erosion of the geographical barriers and also accelerated the penetration of non-banking firms into activities which had previously been exclusive to commercial banks, especially lending (Ballarin, 1985; Pavel and Rosenblum, 1985; and US Congress, 1984). In the area of consumer credit, savings banks have increased their activity; in commercial credit, companies have increasingly relied upon the issuing of commercial paper and medium-term debt issued in the capital markets; banks have even lost some of their traditional capacity to attract savings deposits.

This deregulatory process was further supported by the economic literature on the effects on economic efficiency of regulatory restrictions. Whenever regulation is introduced, the best that we can achieve is a 'second best' solution. It is thus very difficult to determine whether welfare has been improved as a consequence of introducing the regulation (Vives, 1991).

Finally, the changes in the international financial system, with the introduction of floating exchange rates, the globalisation of financial markets and the subsequent increase of capital flows between countries, increased competition and thus accentuated deregulatory pressures within national financial markets. This competition was mainly based on price differentials and close customer-bank relationships in the design of new financial products.

An important consequence of these forces is that commercial banks have sought regulatory approval to expand their activities beyond the boundaries of traditional banking, with the main objective of boosting profitability. In fact, the net rate of return on banks' operations had been slowly but steadily falling since the beginning of the 1980s (Danker and McLaughlin, 1985). The placement and exchange of share titles was, for example, one of the banks' new activities which had a positive influence on their operating results. In 1986–87 the London capital markets were opened to foreign firms and fixed commissions on stock market transactions were abolished. These regulatory changes encouraged banks to become more active in the London capital markets and other European countries to initiate similar reforms.

A new competitive environment

The development of international financial markets, which could operate outside the constraints of domestic market regulation, increased competition at every level. The nature of international markets made them highly competitive from the onset. With many participants from different countries, concerted action was unlikely to occur and price competition kept transaction costs low, relative to those prevailing in domestic markets. Furthermore, the participation of financial institutions with different backgrounds created a highly innovative environment, with institutions competing also through product differentiation. A good example in this respect is the increasing international influence of Japanese banks.

International financial markets were not just competitive internally and between themselves, but they were also in competition with domestic markets. This in turn affected profoundly the competitive behaviour of domestic financial markets. In the 1960s and 1970s, competition in most national financial markets was limited by agreements and restrictions, some official such as controls on interest rates and credit, some based on mere conventions. However, as business became more and more international and banks' customers were increasingly able to choose where to invest and to borrow, banks started to face international competition and monetary authorities had to give way to the demand for deregulation. Also stock exchanges came under increased pressure to deregulate and participate in the international securities trade: New York was open to international competition in 1976, London in 1986 and other European stock exchanges have followed since then.

* * *

As a result of these forces, the structure of the United States and European Union banking industries are expected to look different by the end of the 1990s. Large European banks in particular are trying to become more competitive with respect to the large US and Japanese banks. An example of this type of policy is provided by the Deutsche Bank which in recent years has diversified its activity geographically all over the EU, buying the Italian branch of the Bank of America, Morgan Grenfell in the UK and the Sociedad de Investimentos in Portugal, and taking majority positions in other banks. Mergers have also taken place within individual countries to increase the degree of concentration in the banking sector; examples are the merger between Banco di Roma, Cassa di Risparmio di Roma and Banco di Santo Spirito in Italy and the creation of the new Banco Bilbao Vizcaya in Spain. Other forms of collaboration among banks have also been adopted, such as mutual share exchanges between Commerzbank and Banco Hispano Americano, and between Istituto Bancario San Paolo di Torino and Compagnie Financière de Suez.

Part I

The Changing Environment: 1980–1993

1

Banking in the European Union

1.1 Regulatory and institutional
    environment
1.2 Marketing strategies
1.3 Structural adjustment
Appendix: The structure of EU banking

1.1 Regulatory and Institutional Environment

Banking is still one of the most heavily regulated economic activities, in spite of continuous attempts in several countries to free the industry from the inefficiencies and distortions which often accompany regulation.[1] The integration of the European financial services industry is an interesting case of the regulatory issues involved in the creation of a single financial market. The main issue is the need for centralised regulation, together with the harmonisation of national regulations and the allocation of responsibility between central and national regulators and supervisors.

Since the 1957 Treaty of Rome, the European Commission has been taking steps towards deregulation and harmonisation in the supply of financial services in the European Community (EC). In the period 1957–73, the Community focused on the deregulation of entry in domestic markets, culminating in June 1973 with the adoption by the Council of a directive on the abolition of restrictions on freedom of establishment and freedom to provide services in respect of self-employed activities of banks and other financial institutions. This directive was based on the principle of national treatment, which ensures the equal treatment of national EC financial institutions with respect to their entry on foreign markets and the conditions in which they conduct their activities (Walter, 1988). In 1973, however, the presence of restrictions on capital flows and the lack of coordination in banking supervision were still impeding international competition (Clarotti, 1984).

In the period 1973–85, the efforts of the European Community turned

---
[1] The need for banking regulation in relation to problems of market failure and the effects of regulation on competition and economic welfare are analysed in Chapters 5 and 6.

towards the harmonisation of financial regulation. In 1977 the First Directive on the Coordination of Laws, Regulations and Administrative Provisions Relating to the Taking Up and Pursuit of Credit Institutions was adopted. This directive established the principle of home country control: credit institutions operating in foreign markets within the EC should be under the supervision of the monetary authorities of their home country, rather than the host country. Further, it required member countries to have a system for the authorisation of new banking institutions based on two main criteria: minimum capital requirements and adequate management. Thus this directive paved the way to the more recent harmonisation of banks' liquidity and solvency ratios. However, no specific regulation was provided for in the First Directive.

In practice, member countries had stricter regulations than those laid down by the First Banking Directive and thus the harmonisation process appeared to exist only on paper. At the beginning of the 1980s the European banking markets were still rather fragmented. The differences in the regulation of banking and financial services and in the restrictions on capital flows among European countries were major obstacles to the integration of European financial markets. This problem was attested to by the publication of a White Paper in 1983 recommending more integrated European financial markets and the 1985 proposal presented by the European Commission at the Council of Ministers held in Milan of a detailed timetable for the completion of the internal market. The principle of home control had not been actually applied and a bank wishing to operate in another EC country still needed the authorisation of the foreign country's supervisors. In its operations abroad, the bank was under the supervision of the host country's authorities. Also, there were still restrictions on capital flows which severely impaired the supply of international services. In 1984, for example, the market share of foreign institutions in France and Germany was 16% and 4% respectively, but export of financial services represented only 2% of total output in both countries.

At the 1985 Council of EC Ministers in Milan, a White Paper on the Completion of the Internal Market by 1992 called for a single banking licence, home country control and mutual recognition. These were the principles later incorporated in the Second Banking Directive. In the pursuit of full financial integration in the Community, the European Commission has had as its main objective the promotion of fair competition. This means free entry of foreign banks into national markets and non-discriminatory supply of services, at the same time ensuring the protection of consumers through an appropriate regulatory framework.

Once the goal of financial integration had been accepted, in April 1989 the Delors Committee went further by making public recommendations for a European Economic and Monetary Union (EMU). These recommendations led to two intergovernmental conferences in December 1990 on EMU and political union. The expected outcome was an agreement on the form and pace of the EMU and in particular on the statutes of a European central bank.

The Second Banking Directive

Following the 1987 Single European Act, the European Community was committed to completing a single market in goods and services, including financial services, by the end of 1992. Table 1.1 summarises the major binding directives and non-binding recommendations concerning banking and more generally the financial sector.

Table 1.1   The European single market: financial services.

Directives
1. **Capital Liberalisation Directive**
    Issued: 1988
    Implemented: mid-1990
    Ref.: OJ no. L178, 8 July 1988
    Aim: to achieve free movement of capital within the EC
    Action: all member countries removed exchange controls by July 1990, with the exception of Spain and Ireland which removed them by the end of 1992, and Greece and Portugal which have until the end of 1995 to do so
2. **Directives for Credit Institutions**
    (i)   **First EC Banking Directive**
        Issued: 1977
        Implemented: 1979
        Ref.: OJ no. L322/30, 17 December 1977
        Aim: to establish authorisation procedures for deposit taking institutions
    (ii)   **Consolidated Supervision Directive**
        Issued: 1983
        Implemented: 1985
        Ref.: OJ no. L193/18, 18 July 1983
        Aim: to bring supervisory arrangements in the EC in line with the 1983 Basle Concordat
    (iii)   **Bank Accounts Directive**
        Issued: 1986
        Implemented: 1 January 1993
        Ref.: OJ no. L372/1, 31 December 1986
        Aim: to harmonise accounting rules and reporting requirements
    (iv)   **Own Funds and Solvency Ratio Directives**
        Issued: 1989 (Amendments: 1991)
        Implemented: 1 January 1993
        Ref.: OJ no. L124/16, 5 May 1989; OJ no. L386/32, 30 December 1989; OJ no. C186 Vol. 34, 18 July 1991; OJ no. L339/33, 11 December 1991
        Aim: to adopt a common definition of capital and common risk-related capital adequacy requirements, consistent with the 1988 Basle Capital Adequacy
    (v)   **Second EC Banking Directive**
        Issued: 1989
        Implemented: 1 January 1993
        Ref.: OJ no. L386/32, 30 December 1989
        Aim: to provide a 'single passport' for banks to provide services across the EC
        Action: banks must be allowed to provide a broad list of banking services across borders subject to home country control and under uniform standards (see Table 1.2)

(Continued)

(*Table 1.1 continued*)

   (vi)   **Bank Branches Directive**
          Issued: 1989
          Implemented: 1 January 1991, to apply to annual accounts for the financial
          year beginning on or after 1 January 1993
          Ref.: OJ no. L44/40, 16 February 1989
          Aim: to specify reporting requirements for bank branches whose head offices
          are outside the EC member country where the branch is established
   (vii) **Second Consolidated Supervision Directive**
          Issued: 1990
          Implemented: 1 January 1993
          Ref.: OJ no. C315, 14 December 1990
          Aim: to extend the range of circumstances under which credit institutions
          have to be supervised on a consolidated basis
3. **Directives for Investment Services and Capital Adequacy**
   (i)   **Undertakings for Collective Investment in Transferable Securities
          Directive**
          Issued: 1988
          Implemented: 1989
          Ref.: OJ no. L375, 31 December 1985
          Aim: to allow EC-wide marketing of unit trusts and similar investment
   (ii)   **Second Non-Life Assurance Directive**
          Issued: 1988
          Implemented: 1990
          Ref.: OJ no. 172, 4 July 1988
          Aim: to establish authorisation requirements and supervisory and regulatory
          frameworks
   (iii) **Insider Dealing Directive**
          Issued: 1989
          Implemented: 1992
          Ref.: OJ no. L334, 18 November 1989
          Aim: to make insider dealing unlawful and establish cooperation between
          member countries to facilitate enforcement
   (iv)   **Third Motor Insurance Directive**
          Issued: 1990
          Implemented: 1992
          Ref.: OJ no. L129, 19 May 1990
          Aim: to further harmonise laws on compulsory motor insurance
   (v)   **Motor Insurance Services Directive**
          Issued: 1990
          Implemented: 1992
          Ref.: OJ no. L330, 29 November 1990
          Aim: to extend to motor liability insurance the freedom of services provisions
          of the Second Non-Life Insurance Directive
   (vi)   **Annual Accounts of Insurance Undertakings Directive**
          Issued: 1991
          Implemented: 31 December 1993, but only applying to annual accounts
          commencing on or after 1 January 1995
          Ref.: OJ no. L374, 31 December 1991
          Aim: to establish a framework for a common standard of accounting
          disclosure for insurance undertakings
   (vii) **Third Non-Life Insurance Directive**
          Issued: 1992

Implemented: 1994
Ref.: OJ no. L228, 11 August 1992
Aim: to provide a single licence system whereby an insurer with a head office in an EC member country can provide direct non-life insurance throughout the EC on the basis of its home country authorisation

(viii) **Third Life Assurance Directive**
Issued: 1992
Implemented: 1 January 1993
Ref.: OJ no. L360, 9 December 1992
Aim: to establish authorisation requirements and supervisory and regulatory frameworks

(ix) **Investment Services Directive**
Issued: 1993
Implemented: 1995
Ref.: OJ no. L141/27, 11 June 1993
Aim: to establish a 'single passport' for investment firms
Action: liberalise access to stock exchanges across Europe; establish an investor compensation scheme; etc.

(x) **Capital Adequacy Directive**
Issued: 1993
Implemented: 1995
Ref.: OJ no. L141/27, 11 June 1993
Aim: to establish harmonised capital adequacy requirements for investment firms consistent with the Solvency Ratio Directive for banks

Recommendations

1. **Credit Institutions**

(i) **Recommendation on Deposit Guarantee Schemes**
Ref.: OJ no. L33/16, 4 February 1987
Aim: to establish depositor compensation schemes

(ii) **Recommendation on Code of Conduct on Electronic Payments**
Ref.: OJ no. L365/72, 24 December 1987
Aim: to establish a voluntary code of conduct between issuers, traders and consumers

(iii) **Recommendation on Payments Systems**
Ref.: OJ no. L317/55, 24 November 1988
Aim: to establish a code of conduct between bank card issuers and card holders

(iv) **Recommendation on Transparency of Cross-Border Bank Charges**
Ref.: OJ no. L67/39, 15 March 1990
Aim: to make more transparent the information supplied and the invoicing rules to be observed by banks in connection with cross-border payments

(v) **Recommendation on Insurance Intermediaries**
Ref.: OJ no. L19, 28 January 1992
Aim: to facilitate freedom of establishment and services for insurance agents and brokers

Some 20 of the directives in the 1992 programme directly affected banking and capital market activities. The Commission's aim was not simply that banks should have the right to establish in any Community state and provide services subject to host country regulation, but that they should be free to have branches in other countries and to provide services across borders. These cross-border

Table 1.2   Scope of the EC Second Banking Directive

1   Deposit-taking and other forms of borrowing
2   Lending (consumer credit, mortgages, factoring, trade finance)
3   Financial leasing
4   Money transmission services
5   Issuing and administering means of payment (credit cards, travellers' cheques and bankers' drafts)
6   Guarantees and commitments
7   Trading for own account or for the account of the customers in:
    (a) Money market instruments (cheques, bills, CDs, etc.)
    (b) Foreign exchange
    (c) Financial futures and options
    (d) Exchange and interest rate instruments
    (e) Securities
8   Participation in share issues and the provision of services related to such issues
9   Money broking
10 Portfolio management and advice
11 Safekeeping of securities
12 Credit reference services
13 Safe custody

Source: Second Banking Directive, COM(87) 715.

services should be regulated mainly by the authorities in their home country.[2] The Commission adopted the universal banking model, allowing banks to undertake investment banking activities, with national supervisors regulating the links between insurance, commercial and industrial companies and banks. This approach gave rise to differences between EC countries, with some countries like Britain opposing the ownership of banks by industrial companies, and other countries like France or Belgium allowing it.

The most important directive is the Second Directive on the Coordination of Credit Institutions (more simply and usually referred to as the Second Banking Directive) which was issued by the Commission on 13 January 1988. This directive proposes that approved banks should be allowed to provide a broad list of banking services across borders subject to home country control (Table 1.2). This principle of mutual recognition simply states that if a banking service can be legally performed under some conditions, in one country, it cannot be forbidden under the same conditions in another country.

More importantly, this directive also establishes a single banking licence, valid across the EC. It is enshrined in the principle that once a bank is authorised to undertake activities in its home country (according to the rules prevailing there), it may conduct the same activities in any member country, irrespective of whether or not these activities are allowed in the host country and without the need to obtain local authorisation. In fact, the implementation of this principle amounts to the mutual recognition of regulatory bodies, for the list of activities

[2] With regard to non-EC banks, subsidiaries authorised in one EC country are treated as EC banks; however, branches do require national authorisation.

covered by the directive. The implications of this principle are wide-ranging: a foreign bank might be able to gain some competitive advantage by supplying domestic customers with products that domestic banks cannot offer.

Of course, the regulatory body of the domestic market has an incentive to change its own regulation in order to put local banks on the same level as the foreign bank. As a result, some harmonisation of the regulations across countries has occurred, as the various national regulatory bodies have attempted to 'level the playing field'. Moreover, it is reasonable to expect that the national regulatory agencies could use their power to provide their domestic banks with a competitive advantage abroad. Indeed, it would suffice for these agencies to allow a banking product which is forbidden in other countries (or allow an existing product under weaker conditions). Since one could expect all regulatory agencies to respond by relaxing their own regulations, a process of competitive deregulation ensues; that is, a process in which regulatory agencies compete through their rulings to provide their domestic banks with some competitive advantage. In order to avoid the extreme outcome of ending up with too little regulation, the Commission has recognised that some basic rules should be harmonised. These basic rules include the process of prudential supervision (size and composition of funds, solvency and liquidity coefficients, concentration of credit risks) and the definition of common standards of investor protection.

So as to permit mutual recognition, the directive proposes further harmonisation of the conditions for authorising credit institutions. First of all it sets uniform standards for criteria already included in the First Coordination Directive, such as adequate initial funds, harmonised capital adequacy rules, repute and experience of managers (Dermine, 1990a and 1990b). It also introduces new requirements on the supervision of major shareholders. Regulation of banks' equity participations in the non-financial sector will also be harmonised, with a limit of 10% of own funds on holdings in individual companies and a limit of total equity participation of 50% of own funds.

Thus, this directive follows the principle of home country prudential supervision except in respect of securities business, where the host country still maintains an influence over capital requirements for foreign banks trading in its domestic markets. Host countries of course continue to operate monetary policy measures which affect the domestic currency business of foreign and domestic banks alike.

The directive does not oblige all national authorities to apply the same regulations. For example, it does not require them to abolish restrictions and demarcations on the activities of domestic banks. But it does require them to allow foreign banks to do those things which they are permitted in their home country. The assumption of course is that national authorities do not wish to place domestic institutions at a disadvantage and will therefore deregulate of their own volition. However, this aspect of the proposals is inevitably worrying banks whose field of activity is at present constrained by domestic regulations.

The Delors plan

In 1989, the Delors Report proposed the progressive realisation of the Economic and Monetary Union (EMU) in three stages. In Stage I, all EC currencies would join the ERM on equal terms. At this stage, capital movements among member states are fully liberalised and exchange rate realignments still permitted, although economic policy coordination is expected to improve. In Stage II, a federal system of central banks would be set up around a central institution, eventually to become the European Central Bank (ECB). This central institution is in charge of the transition to a Community monetary policy and the margins of fluctuation within the ERM are narrowed, with exchange rate realignments only taking place under exceptional circumstances. In Stage III, the ECB would replace the national central banks in formulating and implementing common monetary policy. Exchange rates are locked and eventually a single European currency is adopted.

Stage I began in July 1990 with a target closing date of December 1993. The completion of Stage I, however, is conditional upon progress in economic convergence, implying sustained non-inflationary growth and a low level of unemployment. From here, the proposal recommends a fast implementation of the EMU. Specific proposals for the implementation of Stages II and III were submitted to the Intergovernmental Conference by the European Commission, the governors of the national central banks and governments of member states. At the time of writing, the latest draft proposals were based on the beginning of Stage II in 1994, when an autonomous European Monetary Institute (EMI) was to be set up to coordinate the monetary policies of the member states. After two years, by the end of 1996, the EMI and the European Commission will assess the progress made towards economic convergence by means of the following indicators of convergence: convergence of inflation and interest rates to the lowest EC levels; contained budget deficits of member countries; and stability of currencies within the EMS. On the basis of these indicators, the European Council will then decide by unanimous vote whether and when to move on to Stage III. By majority vote, the council of finance ministers will decide which countries should join the currency union, at what exchange rates, and the terms and conditions for countries still not in shape to join. In this final stage the EMI will become the European Central Bank.

At Maastricht in 1991 it was decided that a European Central Bank would be set up in either 1997 or 1999, and a European single currency created.

The future of the EMU and the European Central Bank

The Delors plan and later proposals confirm that the EU intends to implement an approach to monetary integration in which the central administrative arrangements play a vitally important role. Its view is that, if a stable single currency monetary union has to be finally achieved in Europe, it is essential that monetary policy should be centrally controlled and coordinated at EU level. However, what role should be played by national central banks in implementing these pan-European policy decisions and what voting rules should be used to resolve conflicts are still matters for debate.

The present Delors plan is that a ECB Council, consisting of the 12 governors of the existing national central banks and six executive directors appointed by the European Council, will decide the policy of the new ECB (Committee of Governors, 1990). Voting will usually follow a simple majority rule, although there might be weighted voting on some financial matters. The idea is that governors' and directors' decisions should not be influenced by national governments or the European Council, and that eventually national central banks will simply become branches of the ECB, losing their present autonomy.

Much of the debate on these institutional central arrangements in based on personal political views. However, keeping this in mind, there are three main lines of argument which emerge from the various official and private proposals for transition to EMU:

1. Central planning and administration are essential for a smooth transition from the EMS to a single currency EMU (Gros and Thygesen, 1990).
2. Market forces are sufficient to achieve a single currency EMU from the present EMS structure (Vaubel, 1990).
3. The present EMS structure is inadequate and must be reformed before moving on to a single currency EMU.

These three views will be discussed in Chapter 6. All that the Delors Report proposed was a gradual transfer of decision-making power over monetary policy from the national authorities to the new federally structured central monetary institution, the ECB. The three fundamental principles for the ECB should be:

1. the main objective of price stability;
2. independence from both national governments and EU authorities;
3. democratic accountability.

The ECB's tasks would be the formulation and implementation of a single European monetary policy, the management of exchange rates and reserves and banking supervision.

The text of the Maastricht Treaty is full of sweeping generalisations and thus leaves room for differing interpretations. This can be viewed as a weakness of the Treaty, but seen against the 1992–93 crises of the ERM, it can also be seen as a merit, since it leaves scope for interpretation in the light of changing circumstances (Briscoe and Johnson, 1993). There is no doubt that there cannot be a proper single market without EMU, given the costs imposed by changing exchange rates. This is particularly obvious in the financial market sector, where interest rate differentials are mainly due to expectations regarding exchange rates, rather than the degree of competitiveness of financial institutions.

Capital adequacy

In the early 1980s, a global capital shortage and some evidence that capital inadequacy was a growing problem in the international banking market re-emphasised the importance of capital adequacy regulation. Bank supervisors in the Group of Ten countries observed a substantial deterioration in the quality of banks' loans to developing countries, at a time when rapid financial liberalisation was increasing competition among banks and providing incentives to take on high-risk assets. Moreover, bank leverage ratios were at historically high levels in some countries. As a consequence of this situation, bank supervisors' main concern became to strengthen banks by raising capital standards.

After initial efforts by individual countries, some based on simple leverage ratios, others on balance-sheet risk asset ratios, it became clear that more coordination of individual countries' supervisory bodies was needed both to define a more sophisticated measure of capital adequacy and to standardise capital definitions and requirements across countries. Historically, capital adequacy requirements have always shown a cyclical pattern, in the sense that they have tended to increase at times when the perceived banking risk was growing. This is not surprising, since the purpose of capital adequacy regulation is to maintain the stability of the banking system, and thus in periods when that stability is threatened, regulation is tightened. Throughout the past two decades, capital adequacy has been redefined several times, culminating in 1988 in the new BIS (or Basle) rules on capital adequacy and the EC Solvency Ratio, Own Funds and Capital Adequacy Directives.[3]

The Basle convergence agreement establishes a common framework among the Group of Ten countries for measuring the size of a bank's capital and setting minimum standards for its adequacy in relation to the bank's credit exposure. The agreement applies only to internationally active banks from the Group of Ten countries and Luxembourg. However, it is expected that national supervisory bodies will adopt similar measures and thus the principle will apply to a wider range of countries. Certainly the United States and all EU countries have already declared their intention to apply the basic principles of the agreement to all banks. In Japan, only 35 banks with subsidiaries and branches overseas will be required to comply with the agreement, while for other banks it will be optional.

In defining bank capital, the agreement makes a distinction between 'core capital', comprising shareholders' equity and disclosed reserves, and 'supplementary capital', comprising other types of reserves and various debt instruments. Core capital is the highest quality capital, since it has a relatively stable

---

[3] For details on the Own Funds Directive, see the *Official Journal of the European Communities* (OJ), no. L124/16, 5 May 1989, and subsequent amendments in OJ no. C186 Vol. 134, 18 July 1991, p.14, and OJ no. L339/33, 11 December 1991. On the Solvency Ratio Directive, see OJ no. L386/32, 30 December 1989. On the more recent Capital Adequacy Directive, see OJ no. L141/1, 11 June 1993.

nominal size and can absorb losses while a bank continues to operate as a going concern. According to the Basle agreement, core capital must account for at least half of a bank's total recognised capital. The ratio of core capital to total funding is an important variable, since it affects the shareholders' decision with respect to the trade-off between portfolio risk and return. The credit exposure of a bank is assessed by weighting, according to weights specified in the agreement and which reflect the perceived credit risk of the exposure categories, and then summing up various categories of asset and off-balance-sheet exposure. A bank's capital adequacy is then measured by the ratio of its recognised capital to its aggregate risk-weighted credit exposure. According to the agreement, a ratio of 8% should have been achieved by the end of 1992. Table 1.3 shows the average BIS capital ratio of banks in EU countries and other major countries. Although not all the banks in the top 1000 have disclosed their BIS capital ratio, the figures suggest that the target of 8% has been comfortably achieved.

Capital adequacy is defined in relation to a bank's credit risk exposure: the higher a bank's credit risk exposure, the more capital is required. It must be emphasised, however, that the convergence agreement does not cover market risk, such as interest rate or foreign exchange position risk. Moreover, although the measurement of capital is mainly based on book valuations of assets and liabilities, the possible inclusion of some of the unrealised capital gains on equity holdings in supplementary capital means that fluctuations in the market value

Table 1.3   Average BIS capital ratio in major countries (1992)

Country (no. of banks considered)	%
Belgium (6)	10.5
Denmark (4)	15.0
France (13)	9.4
Germany (13)	10.4
Greece	n.a.
Ireland (2)	9.9
Italy (18)	15.1
Luxembourg (2)	11.6
Netherlands	n.a.
Portugal (6)	13.8
Spain (14)	12.0
UK (18)	16.1
Total EU	12.9
Japan (73)	9.1
USA (59)	12.8
Canada (8)	8.5
Australia (10)	10.2
Switzerland (3)	8.4

Source: The Banker, Top 1000, July 1993/own calculations.

of assets may in some cases have a significant impact on the size of recognised capital.

Also, on the issue of capital adequacy, the EC directive of March 1993, although based on the same principles, sets out more detailed requirements than the BIS convergence agreement and applies to credit institutions and investment firms. It specifies initial capital and own-funds requirements. It also takes into consideration foreign exchange risk by specifying that if an institution's overall net foreign exchange position exceeds 2% of its total own funds, this excess should be multiplied by 8% in order to calculate the institution's own-funds requirement against foreign exchange risk. In calculating the foreign exchange position, the following elements have to be considered: net spot position, net forward position, irrevocable guarantees that are certain to be called, net future income/expenses not yet accrued but already fully hedged, net delta equivalent of the total book of foreign-currency options, plus the market value of other options, and any positions which an institution has taken to hedge against the adverse effect of the exchange rate on its capital ratio.

The pressure to meet the capital adequacy rules might have had a number of effects on banks' behaviour. The main pressures have come from the need to find new methods of raising funds and maintain or increase profitability. In fact, when capital adequacy requirements are increased, the effect is similar to an increase in profit tax. It has been argued that, to increase capital, adequacy requirements may impose a competitive tax on banks and that this may be as risky as to allow them to operate with a lower capital ratio (Gardener, 1992). The argument here is that banks could become less competitive and lose market share to other institutions and other markets. As they lose traditional intermediation business, they may be forced into lower-quality, more risky business, and problems of adverse selection and risk underpricing could occur.

New sources of fee and commission revenue needed to be found, at the same time restoring lending margins and cutting costs. In particular, costs had become far too high in the bubble years of the early and mid-1980s and thus unnecessary expenditures were trimmed. Some banks had to reconsider their growth policy, turning their efforts towards strengthening their capital position rather than towards mere asset growth. In an attempt to avoid regulation, banks created new forms of tier one and tier two capital. Examples of this behaviour are the use of variable rate notes, perpetual preferred stock and repackaged perpetual debt. Already in 1987, when the committee was still discussing the BIS convergence agreement, Japanese banks were allowed to raise new equity capital through domestic convertible bonds. Japanese and French banks were also facilitated in securitising certain types of assets and in 1988 the issue of asset-backed securities by US banks rose by more than 50%. Japanese banks in particular were actively seeking ways of increasing the capital adequacy ratio by phasing out the system of compensating balances, channelling increasing proportions of funds into government bonds which receive a zero-risk weight and making a greater use of government guarantee programmes.

Although it is possible to calculate a theoretically optimal capital ratio, and various capital adequacy rules are expected to have certain specific effects on banks, in practice it is rather difficult to determine the impact of capital adequacy rules. However, the theoretical and empirical studies conducted on this issue can help us to understand the practical significance. The theory of finance can be applied to model the trade-offs inherent in banks' value maximisation between the advantages of a high debt to equity ratio, when debt interest is tax-deductible, and the increased risk of bankruptcy associated with high leverage (Buser *et al.* 1981). There is also some evidence that equity capital is, when risk-adjusted, more expensive than debt. A recent study, for example, found that bank merger prices are higher for banks with a low equity–capital ratio (Adkisson and Fraser, 1990).

With respect to the regulatory impact, some of the literature suggests that constraining the portfolio composition of a bank or specifying a minimum capital requirement cannot generally be seen as decreasing the probability of bankruptcy (Kahane, 1977; Di Cagno, 1990). However, a combination of these regulatory instruments may achieve the desired effect. Some evidence also exists that different capital adequacy rules have different effects on bank portfolios and that the risk–assets ratio method, which inspires both the Basle convergence agreement and the EC Capital Adequacy Directive, is comparatively better than others (Lackman, 1986; Kim and Santomero, 1988).

1.2   Marketing Strategies

In the last few years, most European banks have shifted the emphasis of their marketing strategies from a demand-pull approach to a supply-directed orientation. Under the competitive pressure of more unified and deregulated European financial markets, banks have become more concerned with adjusting the structure of their business to the new environment, rather than with innovating into new products or markets. However, some interesting changes in banks' marketing strategies have also become evident.

Two basic strategies have prevailed in the recent past: market-oriented strategy versus bank-oriented strategy. The market-oriented strategy stresses the importance of reacting quickly to changing demand conditions and market opportunities. Institutions need to become flexible so that the adjustment of supply to demand can occur smoothly. This approach was quite fashionable in the 1980s, when being profitable was more important than gaining market shares. Product marketing was replaced by customer marketing, trying to reap the profits from market segmentation; intermediation was replaced by the supply of services, based on the search for the most profitable market niches at international level; interest margins were replaced by fees; and in general the belief was that domestic markets in Europe were saturated and thus banks should go international in search of a 'global' dimension.

This market-oriented strategy has been difficult to implement and in practice supply has not always followed demand as smoothly and quickly as required. Many banks experienced problems in launching new products, mainly due to a lack of professional expertise. The demand for experienced people pushed upwards the cost of professional labour, and the consequent reallocation of resources within the institutions from the more traditional banking activities to the development of new products created instability and affected staff morale. Although the turnover was rising, it was also becoming more unstable. In some cases, the increased innovative activities and the capital markets and fee business did not generate enough earnings to compensate for the loss of traditional intermediation business and the reduction in interest margins. Fees plummeted under the increased competitive pressure following the Big Bang. The stock market crash of October 1987 and the milder crises of October 1989 and, to a lesser extent, August 1990 showed how unstable investment banking activities can be and how over-estimated prospects on some of the new markets had been (Lafferty Business Research, 1990). The reform of the gilt market in London was not as attractive as expected and by 1990 only 19 market makers remained active; in 1990 the London market for US bank debt was closed, due to the poor ratings of debtors and the consequent increase in spreads and decrease in volume; the secondary market for equity and the market for medium and long-term debt did not live up to expectations, either.

As a consequence of this unstable environment, some banks have moved to a more bank-oriented strategy and have shifted resources back into the more traditional banking functions. The main consequence of this change of policy has been the restructuring of human resources within banks, with inevitable redundancies.

The use of information technology

Most banking activity involves the storage, retrieval and regular updating of large amounts of data. It is thus not surprising that the use of information technology in banking has helped greatly in reducing costs, increasing speed, improving efficiency and diversifying services and products (Canals, 1993). At the beginning of the 1960s, large-scale automation was first introduced in banks, with large computers saving time and costs in performing administrative and organisational tasks. In the 1970s, telecommunications and computer technology created greater flexibility in the execution of fund transferrals, deposits and withdrawals. Although the advantages of the use of technology in banking have been great, it has also had the effect of distancing banks from customers, thus making the marketing of new products more difficult. The present wave of innovation is characterised by an effort to personalise services according to clients' individual needs by introducing the Customer Information File, which will store detailed information on each customer.

Technology has also introduced new types of risk into banking and has created the need for greater data storage. Back-office computers to store documentation need to be highly elaborate and sophisticated and they are difficult to manage. Very costly mistakes in the choice of technology have been made. Similarly, the implementation of some of the new services, as for example home banking systems, has proved costly, and not commercially viable.

The areas of banking where technology improvements are most needed are services which require the handling of large volumes of paper and the transmission of information worldwide. Examples are given respectively by cheque-handling operations, where the introduction of electronic cheques is estimated to cause a reduction in the processing costs of up to 90%, and the effort to create an integrated international framework, where specific information can be used in different locations at the same time. Furthermore, with the reduction in profit margins from traditional banking operations, banks need to diversify and offer new services and products, and they also need to personalise products. This can only be done efficiently if information technology is used both for designing and marketing these new services.

An aspect which will be discussed later, but which needs to be mentioned in relation to the use of information technology, is that economies of scale are likely to be present in the management of information equipment, allowing larger banks to enjoy a wider reach of operations.

Financial innovation

Financial innovation *per se* is certainly not new, but the pace at which new financial instruments and markets have been introduced in the last two decades has been surprising. New technology, deregulation, internationalisation and globalisation have all contributed to these changes. Technological advances have allowed financial institutions to supply an increasing number of complex financial products, which would have been impossible to manage when transactions were processed manually. Furthermore, the fact that money can now be moved around the world easily, cheaply and instantly, in 24-hour currency markets, has also paved the way for new financial products and services.

There is no doubt that the use of microelectronic technology has made international operations progressively easier. In the 1960s and 1970s, the main incentive to operate outside national boundaries came from the existence of widespread national restrictions, such as controls on interest rates, foreign exchange, credit and the range of activities of financial institutions. Thus, for example, the Eurocurrency markets gave US, European and Japanese banks and security houses the opportunity of doing business abroad which they were prevented from doing at home. Non-financial companies also expanded their activities abroad during this period and this provided a further incentive for banks to supply their clients with those services needed for their international operations. In Europe some financial centres, such as London, Zurich, Luxembourg and Paris, became the main geographical locations for international operations and cradles for the marketing of new products.

These new markets tended to be very competitive, in terms of both price and product differentiation. Since the participants were banks and security traders from many countries, concerted action was unlikely to succeed. This meant that transaction costs, both margins for banks and issuing and dealing costs for security traders, were kept low relative to national markets. Moreover, this was coupled with a very innovative environment, where financial institutions with different national backgrounds were developing new ideas and learning from one another. Eventually, international markets started to compete with domestic financial markets and this had a profound effect on domestic markets.

The intensity of the innovative process has raised several questions, particularly regarding three aspects: identification and control of the causes of innovation; the impact of innovation on interest rates, prices of financial assets and risk perception; and finally the effects of innovation on the managerial strategies of financial institutions (Zecher, 1984). While there is a wide consensus in the literature about the last two points (Cavanna, 1992), less is known about the first aspect. However, there is some agreement on at least four causes of financial innovation (Canals, 1993). Firstly, the changes in governments' financial regulation have worked as a major incentive to financial innovation in banking. Regulation creates entry barriers and imposes implicit taxes on permitted operations; as a result, banks have devised ways of getting around regulatory constraints by creating new types of assets and transactions. The subsequent deregulatory process has increased competitive pressure, through the liberalisation of domestic markets, and new financial products have thus emerged as a means of increasing the competitive power of institutions.

Secondly, the introduction of new technology in banking has contributed to the innovative process, by reducing some operating costs, improving information systems and thus allowing the introduction of new services to customers. Thirdly, the unstable international financial environment, in addition to problems in fighting off inflation in many countries, stimulated the introduction of new financial instruments to adapt to the new operating environment. Examples are provided by long-term securities with indexed interest rates and variable interest rate loans supplied in response to the growing needs of public administrations following large public deficits; the reduction of medium-term maturity for loans with fixed interest in response to increased interest rate volatility; the emergence of financial futures and options markets and the increasing use of negotiable instruments to replace loans and credits for financing; swaps of currency and interest rates, following the increase in interest rates due to high inflation. Finally, the process of disintermediation has deeply affected the structure of banks' assets and their activities, with a growth in the issue of commercial paper.

The economic analysis of financial innovation is based on the Schumpeterian distinction between process and product innovation. Examples of the two types of innovations are electronic fund transfers, which represent a process innovation, and money market mutual funds, which represent a product innovation. However, more often than in other sectors of the economy, financial product innovations are in many cases intertwined with process innovations: for example, cash management instruments permit a complete integration of current accounts, time deposits, mutual funds shares and similar, due to the widespread computerisation of the financial sector.

The main financial innovations since the 1970s have been widely discussed in the literature (Silber, 1975; BIS, 1986; Harrington, 1987; Cavanna, 1992) and to produce a full list of them would go far beyond the scope of this book. However, a few categories of innovations can be identified:

1. The first category of innovations relates to cash management procedures and the use of new information technology to reduce the opportunity costs of holding cash balances.
2. Other innovations relate to the intermediation process: they are aimed at cutting the operating costs of financial institutions and at managing assets and liabilities more efficiently. An example of a successful innovation in this category is CDs, which became very popular also because of their negotiability. Negotiable Order for Withdrawal (NOW) accounts or money market deposit accounts in the US, and similar instruments elsewhere, are example of non-negotiable successful innovations.
3. Financial innovations were also introduced in the traditional segments of capital markets, such as variable interest rate instruments, swaps, deep discount bonds, serial zero-coupon bonds and floating rate notes. Other innovations had the characteristics of both equity and debt, such as equity note units, participating loans, participating securities and certificates of investment.
4. Finally, new innovative areas of capital markets have been introduced, such as commercial paper market, financial futures, financial options and unlisted securities markets.

Cross-border trade

The Commission's objective on the completion of the internal market was twofold: it was both to remove the barriers to intracommunity trade in goods and services, and to allow for the free movement of factors of production. In the banking sector, intracommunity trade occurs if a resident of one country obtains services performed by a bank established in a foreign country. Alternatively, rather than supplying its customer from abroad, a bank could choose to open a subsidiary or a branch in the customer's country. This alternative arrangement requires the bank to make an investment abroad, to move capital, and presumably to move some labour (at least initially) to staff the subsidiary or branch.

Up to the late 1980s, cross-border lending within Europe was of little significance in relation to the banks' overall activities. For example UK-registered banks had only $51bn in claims on EC countries – just under a quarter of their total external claims. Belgium, Luxembourg and France accounted for over half of the total and most of it was inter-bank activity. Only about $10bn of British banks' loans to the EC were to private-sector non-banks, which was a tiny share of the continental EC market.

Another symptom of the lack of integration and cross-border competition was the significant variation in prices of financial services in the various Community member states. The Cecchini Report published in 1988 (Cecchini, 1988) on 'The cost of non-Europe' gave estimates of the potential fall in financial product prices through the completion of the internal market. There are obvious criticisms which can be levelled at the methodology employed in compiling these estimates, which consists of identifying one 'standard' product in each country with the average of the four lowest prices. However, taking the Cecchini Report's figures at their face value, there appeared to be wide disparities in the relative cost of different products among EC countries. For example, in the UK, consumer credit was relatively more expensive than anywhere else in the Community except West Germany, but mortgages were the cheapest. France had the cheapest credit cards but the second most expensive mortgages. Other countries such as Spain and Italy appeared generally to have more expensive financial products. These last two countries still discouraged the entry of foreign banks, and in contrasting them with a country such as the Netherlands, it could have been argued that this was the major cause of the higher prices for financial services. On the other hand, the UK banking market had been open to foreign competition for many years and yet the Cecchini Report suggested that the price of UK banking services could have been reduced by almost a fifth following EC market integration.

This last point suggests that there might have been other barriers to entry that were at least as significant as the regulatory ones, and therefore that the removal of the legal barriers to entry alone would not have produced perfect competition. In spite of these possible barriers, Cecchini's estimates suggested that after 1992 the gains in benefits to consumers were likely to add up to about ¾% of GDP. This was in fact one of the largest gains in an individual sector identified by the report. Taking into account the impact of cheaper financial services elsewhere in the economy, the result of completing the internal market in this sector could be to add about 1½% to GDP over a six to eight-year period.

The Cecchini Report certainly provided an interesting and simple benchmark. Yet, the assumption that prices will converge to some kind of 'low' level seems questionable. Presumably, a 'perfect' market for a homogeneous commodity with a large number of small profit-seeking banks might achieve such convergence. Casual observation, however, does not suggest that the EU banking industry fits the picture too well, at least in its current structure. It is well known that in Western Europe banking products are differentiated in the sense that consumers will not necessarily switch from one bank to another in response to small price differences; banks tend to be few and large, rather than many and small; some regulation will have to stay for prudential reasons; banks in some countries are notorious for their collusive behaviour. That is to say that the structure of the banking market is likely to be and to remain imperfectly competitive.

Certainly up to the late 1980s, the main constraint to the cross-border flow of banking services was the restrictions on capital movements. The Commission's action on the liberalisation of capital flows proceeded in two steps. The first wave of liberalisation (which came into force on 1 March 1987) dealt primarily with capital movements related to the flows of goods and non-financial services. The second wave of liberalisation was expected to be fully implemented by mid-1990.

The question with respect to cross-border trade is: should we expect more trade diversion or more trade creation? At present, trade within the Community in banking services is limited, at least relative to other industries. The bulk of trade takes place between EU countries and the rest of the world, rather than among EU countries themselves. Especially if as a consequence of the single market, the EU banking sector should become more and more integrated, this suggests that trade diversion towards non-EU countries could very well occur as a consequence of integration, rather than more trade creation in the Union.

The alternative to the export of services for a bank is the establishment of branches or subsidiaries in foreign countries. Access to foreign markets can take place either by establishing *ex novo* a subsidiary, or by acquiring a foreign bank.[4] There are wide discrepancies in foreign penetration between different EU countries, and in the past observers have often explained these discrepancies by the possible existence of 'hidden' barriers to entry, or the possibility that existing EU regulations were used with much discretion, particularly in Germany, Denmark, Italy and Portugal.

1.3   Structural Adjustment

The European Commission has taken some concrete steps with respect to the issue of market access, with the Second Banking Directive and its principle of mutual recognition. These regulatory changes are expected to have an effect on the banking industry's structure, depending on the implications of various types of reaction to the tremendous increase in the size of the market for the larger EU banks. Smaller local banks face no effective increase in the size of the market, but the fact that those larger banks that compete with them in local markets will probably have become much bigger and will operate in the entire EU banking market may be important.

It has been argued in the economic literature and in the press that the EU

[4] The penetration of foreign banks into different national markets will be discussed in Chapter 2.

banking sector is already fairly concentrated, and doubts have been cast on whether there remain any further economies of scale to exploit. In fact, the most striking feature of the EU banking sector, in relation to that of other country groups, is the size of the banks' assets. The figures in Table 1.4 show that, both in 1989 and in 1992, EC banks accounted for well over one-third of the total assets of the largest 1000 banks in the world. Japanese banks too accounted for approximately one-third of the world's total assets; but, during the three years in question, while the assets share of EC banks increased, that of Japanese banks declined.

Although one-third of banks in the top 1000 are from EC member countries, the average assets size of EC banks still remains much smaller, at \$28.5bn in 1992, than the average assets size of Japanese banks, at \$66.7bn. EC banks are, however, larger on average than banks in the United States, where the average assets size is \$14.8bn. Thus, compared to the Japanese banking sector, there seems to be some scope for increasing concentration in the EU, but there is even more scope in the United States.

With respect to the EU countries alone, Table 1.5 shows the distribution by country of the total assets of EU banks in the top 1000. The countries have been arranged in descending order of size of assets, and display two clear breaks in the size distribution, giving three groups of countries. In terms of banking assets, thus, we have four large countries, namely West Germany, France, Italy and the United Kingdom; three medium-sized countries, namely Spain, the Netherlands and Belgium; and five small countries, namely Denmark, Portugal, Greece, Luxembourg and the Irish Republic. In 1992, the four large countries accounted for about 76% of the EU total in terms of assets, and about 70% in terms of number of banks. These two shares had both decreased from 78% and

Table 1.4   Assets of top 1000 banks[a] by country groups.

	Total assets $bn		%		No. of banks	
	1989[b]	1992[c]	1989	1992	1989	1992
EU	7012.6	9550.0	35.4	38.0	342	336
EFTA[d]	1136.7	1441.1	5.7	5.7	75	77
Japan	6368.3	7471.0	32.2	29.7	112	112
US	2530.6	2627.0	12.8	10.5	222	178
Other countries	2748.5	4036.8	13.9	16.1	249	297
World total	19 796.7	25 125.9	100.0	100.0	1000	1000

[a]*The Banker*'s 'Top 1000' ranking includes only deposit-taking institutions that are recognised by a central bank. This excludes those institutions that are governed by legislation other than a banking law, some of which are quite large. The most important institutions that are left out of this ranking are most postal savings banks and British building societies.
[b]The figures refer to banks' assets at 31 December 1989 or 31 March 1990.
[c]The figures refer to banks' assets at 31 December 1992 or 31 March 1993.
[d]This category includes Austria, Finland, Liechtenstein, Norway, Sweden and Switzerland. Austria, Finland and Sweden joined the EU on 1 January 1995.
Source:The Banker, Top 1000, July 1990 and July 1993/own calculations.

74% respectively in 1989; most of this decline was due to the reduced share of the Italian banks.

The degree of concentration of the EU banking sector is shown in Table 1.6. Taken as a whole, the EU banking sector appears to be less concentrated than the banking sectors in Japan and the United States. In 1992, the top ten banks in the EU held only 27% of the assets of all EU banks included in the top 1000; the top five held almost 15%; and the top three almost 10%. While these figures hardly changed over the three-year period from 1989, the corresponding figures for Japan and the United States showed slightly increased concentration in both countries. In 1992, the top ten Japanese banks held more than 50% of the total banking assets, while the top ten US banks held just over 40%.

Because of the small number of banks in some countries, the data for individual EU countries in Table 1.6 need to be read with caution. However, if we look at the larger countries, we can see that the UK and the French banking sectors appear to be much more concentrated than the German, Italian and Spanish banking sectors.

More detailed information on the structure of the EU banking industry can be derived from the tables and figures in the Appendix to this chapter. Tables A1.1–A1.10 summarise the characteristics of the distribution of aggregate data on the banking sectors of EU member countries. The data refer to the size (total assets), strength (tier one capital), soundness (capital/assets ratio) and performance (profits on capital and returns on assets) of banking institutions included in the top 1000 world banks. These figures show that in terms of total assets, the 'average' French bank, with $78bn, is much larger than banks in other EU

Table 1.5 Country distribution of assets of EU banks.[a]

Country	Total Assets $ bn		%		Number of Banks	
	1989	1992	1989	1992	1989	1992
Germany	1912.5	2668.6	26.6	27.7	105	93
France	1554.2	2051.0	21.6	21.3	31	26
Italy	1234.7	1423.9	17.2	14.8	116	10
UK	939.9	1218.8	13.1	12.6	36	35
Spain	455.8	694.8	6.3	7.2	38	47
Netherlands	384.6	658.0	5.4	6.8	12	15
Belgium	310.0	446.4	4.3	4.6	11	11
Denmark	157.4	155.1	2.2	1.6	16	11
Portugal	68.0	121.5	1.0	1.3	11	11
Greece	49.9	75.9	0.7	0.8	6	8
Luxembourg	74.3	72.1	1.0	0.7	5	4
Irish Republic	46.4	54.5	0.6	0.6	2	34
Total EC	7187.7	9640.6	100.0	100.0	389	368

[a]Figures have been computed using data in *The Banker*'s 'Top 500' ranking. These include only deposit-taking institutions that are recognised by a central bank and thus exclude those institutions that are governed by legislation other than a banking law.

Source: The Banker, Top 500 European Banks, October 1990 and September 1993/own calculations.

Table 1.6   Concentration of the banking industry (% of assets).[a]

Country (no. of banks)	Three Largest Banks		Five Largest Banks		Ten Largest Banks	
	1989	1992	1989	1992	1989	1992
Belgium (11 & 11)	53.0	54.6	81.1	81.6	99.4	99.4
Denmark (16 & 11)	40.5	71.2	62.8	86.6	89.8	99.0
France (31 & 26)	44.0	45.6	64.4	68.1	88.8	90.9
Germany(105 & 93)	24.2	25.3	35.3	36.5	57.0	58.6
Greece (6 & 8)	80.5	66.4	94.5	84.8	–	–
Irish Republic (2 & 3)	–	100.0	–	–	–	–
Italy (116 & 104)	24.0	23.8	36.8	37.6	58.8	59.6
Luxembourg (5 & 4)	69.1	77.6	100.0	–	–	–
Netherlands (12 & 15)	71.3	85.7	95.2	94.9	99.2	98.8
Portugal (11 & 11)	51.1	52.9	68.6	71.3	96.2	96.6
Spain (38 & 47)	33.3	37.0	49.4	54.7	72.3	74.4
UK (36 & 35)	52.3	57.4	68.5	73.1	87.7	91.4
Total EU (500)	9.5	9.9	15.2	14.9	26.2	26.9
Japan (112 & 112)	18.0	18.2	29.3	30.0	46.9	52.4
U.S.A. (222 & 178)	17.0	20.2	23.8	28.6	36.0	41.2
Canada (8 & 11)	59.5	52.8	89.0	76.7	–	98.8
World (1000)	5.8	5.4	9.4	8.9	15.5	16.0

[a]Figures in the table have been computed using data from *The Banker*'s Top 1000 World Banks and Top 500 European Banks. The market shares are thus based on the assets of the banks included in these surveys, rather than the total banks' assets. The number of banks included in the databank for each country is specified in brackets.
Source:The Banker, July and October 1990 and July and October 1993/own calculations.

countries, such as the Netherlands ($44bn), Belgium ($40bn) and the UK ($35bn). In terms of dispersion of assets size around the mean value measured by the coefficient of variation, the UK and Italian banking sectors show the greater dispersion with a large number of smaller banks (Figures A1.15 and A1.27). Portugal, Belgium and Greece show the lowest levels of dispersion and most Belgian banks are close to the average assets size.[5]

According to the statistics in the same tables, French banks also tend to have larger tier one capital and they are not very profitable on average. Not surprisingly, the highest levels of profitability, measured by profits on capital and returns on assets, are recorded in Greece, Portugal, Spain and Italy, where the banking sectors are still relatively tightly regulated. Regulated banking markets, in fact, tend to generate significantly higher rents, when compared with unregulated markets. In regulated markets, financial margins are larger, profitability is higher and wages are well above average (Gual and Neven, 1993).

So far it is clear that, in many EU countries, the banking sector is characterised by few very large institutions and a number of smaller, local and more specialised banks. Following Buigues and Jacquemin's (1988) categorisation of structural environments which we will analyse in section 6.2, we could

[5]Belgium is the only country which shows negative kurtosis in its assets distribution. This implies a distribution with thinner tails than a normal distribution.

then argue that the banking industry has characteristics common to both an environment where volume is the main feature and a specialised environment, depending on the specific banking functions considered. In fact, for the supply of most traditional banking services, such as retail banking, size is important to compete efficiently. However, many of the functions of industrial banking have some specialised aspects which make the product non-homogeneous and the relation between supplier and customer specific, especially when the customer is a local small- or medium-sized firm.

Thus, banks involved in industrial banking should benefit from integration, which will open new markets for specialised products. However, as we will discuss later, this tends to be an area where sunk costs are high and consequently competition is not of a contestable type. This means that entry in this sector of the market may be difficult, due to the collusive behaviour of existing banks. One way of avoiding some of these problems is to enter a foreign market by acquiring an existing local operator. This could well be the theory behind some of the cross-border acquisitions which have already taken place, such as the acquisitions by Deutsche Bank of the Italian Banca d'America e d'Italia and the British merchant bank Morgan Grenfell, and the acquisition by the Swiss Bank Corporation of S. G. Warbourg.

If this proves to be the main theory behind the actions of EU banks, we could then observe the formation, not so much of pan-European universal banks, but of pan-European specialised banks with either a product group focus or a client segment focus. While their managerial task will be made somewhat easier by the fact that they will not be burdened with a complex matrix of products and/or clients, they will also have less ability to rely on profits of one business area to support another during temporary crises. Nevertheless, their very focus will also be their competitive advantage, giving them flexibility in reacting to changes in demand. Pan-European specialised banks will be able to take advantage of market integration, because a European field of operations will enable them to build scale and diversify their business risk. The main skill in doing this will be to choose the right segment of the market and define its characteristics and parameters.

Mergers

One way of achieving size is by mergers and acquisitions. Mergers within countries represent only a partial solution to the problem because geographical presence throughout the Community is required as much as sheer size. The only EU country in which mergers between large banks have been recorded in recent years is Spain. The absence of such mergers in other countries is mainly due to the small number of core banks resulting from previous industry restructuring. As our previous analysis has indicated, EU banks are already large in relation to the world ranking. Because of this situation and because of the absence of evidence that economies of scale exist at such large sizes in the banking sector, doubts can be raised over the need for higher concentration within EU countries.

With respect to cross-border mergers, the situation is more complex. There is no doubt that geographical location matters. In general, banks will prefer to operate from the home base with the least onerous supervisory regime. Given that supervisory standards have not yet been completely harmonised, this gives rise to the possibility that some relocation of financial firms could result from the single market. And a relatively quick way of relocating activities would be through mergers.

Given the above considerations, it is not surprising that merger activity among banks in preparation for 1992 was quite modest, especially when compared to other industries. There are two main merger strategies which banks can adopt. Firstly, they can become stronger by mergers and acquisitions within their own national markets; and secondly they can acquire or form alliances with banks in other EU countries. Up to now, there has only been evidence of the first form of activity among leading banks in Spain, Denmark and Holland, since the degree of concentration within most EU national sectors is already quite high. But there has also been a lack of cross-border merger activity involving large EU banks. There may be many reasons for this, but certainly there is a regulatory reason. The authorities of all EU countries have some means of preventing their banks from falling into foreign hands, and many have indicated that this power would be used in any proposed foreign takeover of a core bank. Thus the only outright acquisitions by banks from other countries that have taken place have been of small and medium-sized banks. Some minority shareholding acquisitions have also been taking place between banks in different countries.

There are possible links between industrial and bank mergers. Cross-border merger activity in several industries has resulted in the creation of holding companies with portfolios spanning different industries, rather than unified companies in particular industries. The connection between the merger activity in the industrial and financial sectors occurs at various levels. First, the holding companies that seem likely to emerge in many cases will probably include a bank or a financial service company of some kind. This was a factor in the siege laid by De Benedetti and the Compagnie Financière de Suez against Société Générale de Belgique, since this group contained one of the large Belgian banks, Banque Générale. It has also been suggested that the ownership of a bank by an industrial group can protect the group from predators by discouraging or delaying a takeover through the need to secure central bank approval of the acquisition of the bank. The links between industrial and bank mergers are even stronger in countries where banks have large holdings of shares of industrial companies, as in Spain where many of the largest industrial companies are without a stock exchange listing. In this situation, banks acquire a particular importance to those who are trying to form industrial combinations. Reciprocal equity stakes may well be the norm for acquisition activity for some time.

Other alliance strategies

At present the alliances between banks are of several kinds. A number of clubs were created in the early 1970s, mainly to fight off the American invasion of European banking. The formation of SWIFT and Eurocheque were initiatives with the same original motive; joint ventures and consortium banks provide cooperation, particularly in investment and international banking; and there are also initiatives for joint training facilities.

There are some grounds for preferring alliances to mergers, if the banks' aim is to cover the whole of the EU. The first ground is that networks of alliances, whether formed on the basis of clubs or not, could almost certainly reap all the economic benefits of size that are to be had. There are some advantages of size in certain aspects of bank operations (payments, computer systems, international banking, placing of securities and so on). These advantages could be secured, as in the existing clubs, by forming joint ventures, but it would probably aid the cohesion of the group if they were placed in the care of a central bank for the network. The network could avoid to some extent the undoubted diseconomies of scale that exist in any large organisation by leaving the national members intact for the greater part of the business, in which any economies of scale have probably been exhausted by their present size.

The second ground is that there is a positive advantage in leaving the national members intact because of the public attitude to banks. Banks always depend completely on public confidence to carry out their business, but alongside this confidence there is in every country a deep-rooted populist dislike and fear of banks and finance, which would be quite dangerous if it were allied with nationalist feelings. People can easily become accustomed to buying motor cars, electronic equipment and fast food from abroad, or from local suppliers owned by foreigners, but it would probably take much longer to become reconciled to the fact that all the big banks in the country had lost their identities within a supranational group.

Appendix: The Structure of EU Banking

In this appendix we present the characteristics of the distribution of the data relating to the banking sectors in most EU countries.

The raw data set used was published in September 1993 by *The Banker* magazine, in a special issue on the top 500 European banks. It is not comprehensive, but it does cover the main European commercial banks down to a minimum assets size of $468m, and $99m of tier one capital. To permit international comparisons, the figures are converted into US dollars, using the exchange rate at the end of the accounting year. Thus individual banks' performance is affected by their currency's performance relative to the US dollar.

As for the top 1000 world banks' rating published in July, the definition of capital used follows the Bank for International Settlements definition. It reflects only the core of a bank's strength, including common stock, preference shares which are perpetual, irredeemable and non-cumulative, and disclosed reserves. It excludes capital instruments, such as cumulative or fixed-term stock, which tends not to be affected by the ups and downs of a bank's business, and other hidden items, such as goodwill and revaluation reserves. The total asset figures exclude contra items such as acceptances and guarantees.

The capital asset ratio is calculated by simply dividing the asset figure by the tier one capital figure. This is not the same as the tier one capital ratio defined by the Basle Committee, which calculates assets by giving cash, loans, mortgages and securities different weighting, depending on the risk class of the type of asset.

The tables in this appendix summarise the characteristics of the aggregate data distributions for each country. Assuming that x_t, $t=1,2,...,n$ define observations on a random variable, the statistics in the tables have been calculated using the following formulae:

Mean = $\bar{x} = \Sigma_t \, x_t \, / \, n$

Standard deviation = $S_x = [(\Sigma_t(x_t - \bar{x})^2 \, / \, (n-1)]^{1/2}$

Coefficient of variation = absolute value of $(S_x \, / \, \bar{x})$

Skewness = $\sqrt{b_1} = m_3/m_2^{3/2}$

Kurtosis = $b_2 = m_4/m_2^2$

where $m_k = \Sigma_i \, (x_i - \bar{x})^k \, / \, n$, $k = 2,3,4$

In the tables, $\sqrt{b_1}$ and $(b_2\text{-}3)$ appear. These two measures can be used to construct different tests of departures from normality. A non-normal distribution which is asymmetrical has a value of $\sqrt{b_1}$ different from zero: a positive value indicates skewness to the right and a negative value skewness to the left, as shown in Figure A1.1. The measure of kurtosis (or curvature) is equal to 3 for the normal distribution. A positive value for $(b_2 - 3)$ indicates a unimodal non-normal distribution with thicker tails than the normal distribution; a negative value indicates a non-normal distribution with thinner tails than the normal distribution, as shown in Figure A1.2 (D'Agostino et al. 1990).

More intuitively, it is easier to understand skewness and kurtosis by looking at the frequency plots in this appendix. In each Figure A1.3–A1.29, there is a histogram and a frequency curve relating to the same set of data specified in the figure's heading. A histogram is a bar graph of a frequency distribution. The class boundaries are identified along the horizontal axis of the graph, while the number of observations (or frequencies) are identified along the vertical axis. Thus, the width of each bar in the histogram indicates the class interval while the height indicates the frequency of observations in each class. The histograms in the figures in this appendix are constructed by dividing the variable x_t range

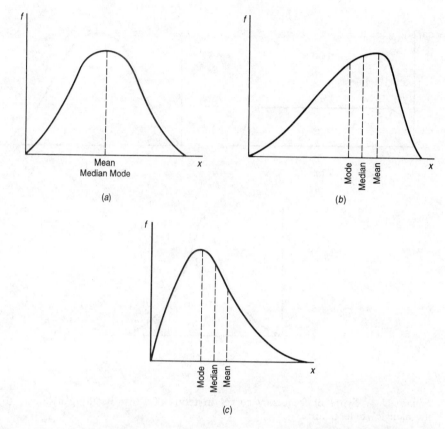

Figure A1.1 Relationships among the mean, median and mode: (a) symmetrical, (b) negatively skewed, (c) positively skewed

into n intervals of length $S_x/4$, where S_x is the standard deviation of x, centred at the mean $\bar{x}$. Then the proportion of x_t in each interval constitutes the histogram and the sum of the proportions is unity; i.e. the height of each bar may be thought of as a measure of the probability that a bank lies in a particular size range for a given country.

A frequency curve can be described as being a smoothed line graph of a frequency distribution. The form of a frequency curve can be described in two ways: in terms of its departure from symmetry, which is what we have defined as skewness, and in terms of its degree of peakedness, which is what we defined as kurtosis. Thus, if a frequency curve is non-symmetrical with the longer tail of the frequency curve to the left, it is said to be negatively skewed (Figure A1.1 (b)); if the longer tail is to the right, then it is positively skewed (A1.1 (c)). In terms of kurtosis, if a frequency curve is relatively flat, with the number of observed values distributed evenly across the classes, it is said to be platykurtic (Figure A1.2 (a)); if it is peaked, with a large number of observed values

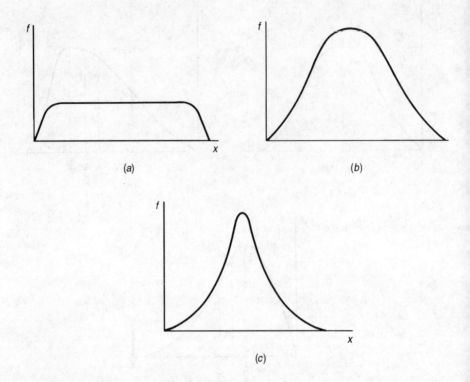

Figure A1.2 Types of frequency curves in terms of Kurtosis: (a) platykurtic, (b) mesokurtic, (c) leptokurtic

concentrated within a narrow range of the possible values of the variable being measured, it is said to be leptokurtic (A1.2 (c)); and, finally, if it is neither flat nor peaked with respect to the general appearance of the frequency curve, it is said to be mesokurtic (A1.2 (b)).

The characteristics of the distribution of the data allow us to describe the population of banks in some details by using only a few summary statistics (Tables A1.1–A1.10). For example, if the variable 'Total assets' is used as a measure of bank's size and in the sample relating to Italy we have 104 observations, we can describe this variable by means of only seven numerical values which appear in Table A1.6. The mean of the distribution of assets of Italian banks is that numeric value which represents, and is typical of, all the 104 values in the sample, while the maximum and minimum values simply describe the range of assets values. However, to interpret the mean we also need to know whether the distribution is symmetric, since in a symmetric distribution the mean is the central value, it coincides with the median and the mode, and thus gives a good representation of the distribution. On the other hand, if a distribution is positively skewed, then more observations lie to the left of the

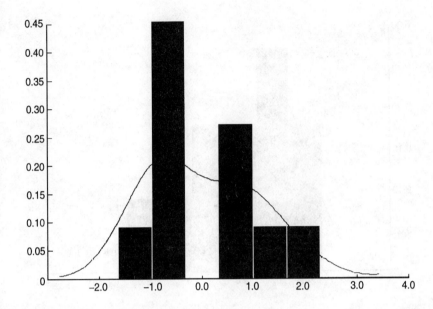

Figure A1.3   Belgian banks: frequency distribution of total assets, 1992

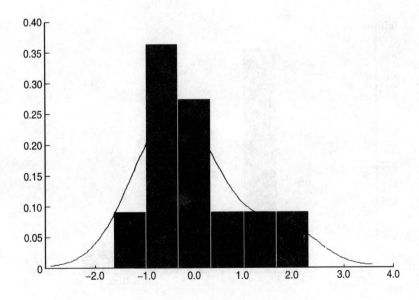

Figure A1.4   Belgian banks: frequency distribution of tier one capital, 1992

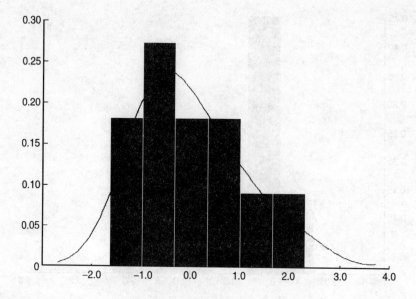

Figure A1.5   Belgian banks: frequency distribution of capital assets ratio, 1992

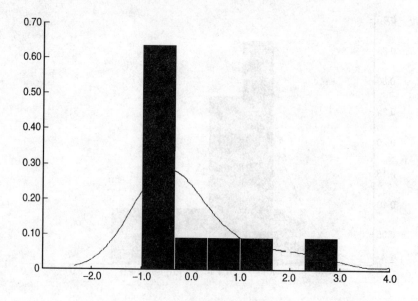

Figure A1.6   Danish banks: frequency distribution of total assets, 1992

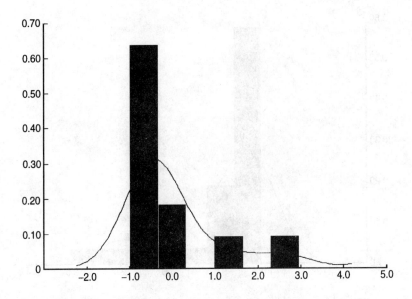

Figure A1.7   Danish banks: frequency distribution of tier one capital, 1992

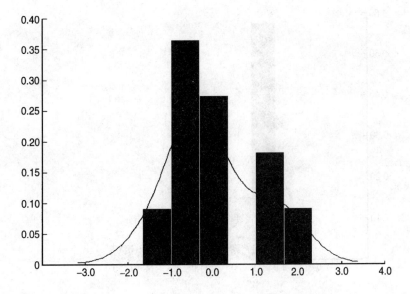

Figure A1.8   Danish banks: frequency distribution of capital assets ratio, 1992

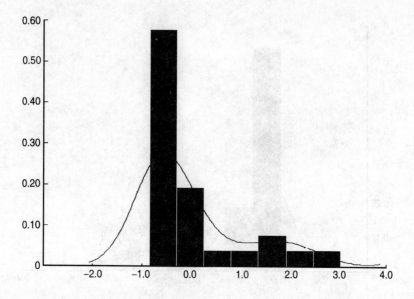

Figure A1.9   French banks: frequency distribution of total assets, 1992

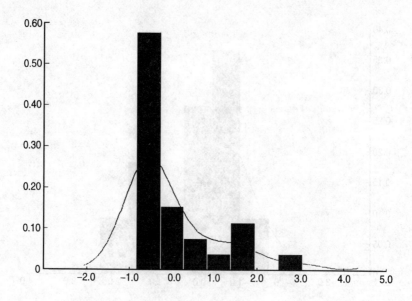

Figure A1.10   French banks: frequency distribution of tier one capital, 1992

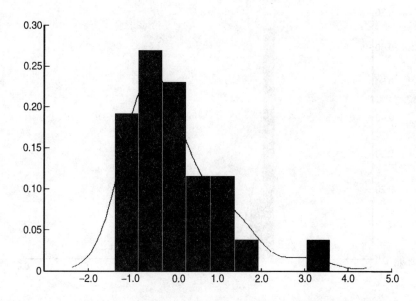

Figure A1.11   French banks: frequency distribution of capital assets ratio, 1992

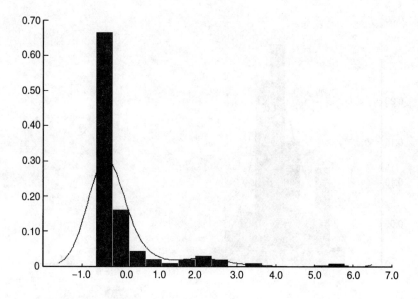

Figure A1.12   German banks: frequency distribution of total assets, 1992

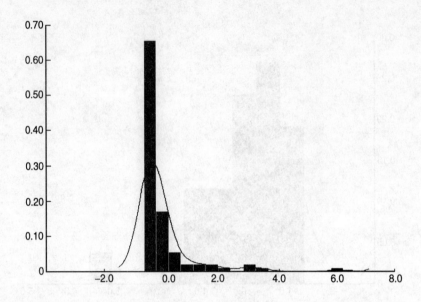

Figure A1.13   German banks: frequency distribution of tier one capital, 1992

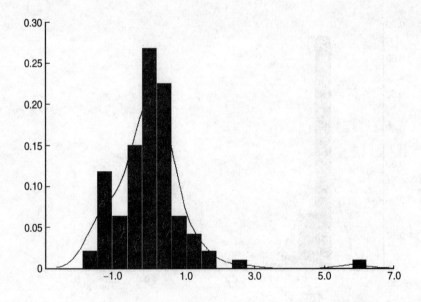

Figure A1.14   German banks: frequency distribution of capital assets ratio, 1992

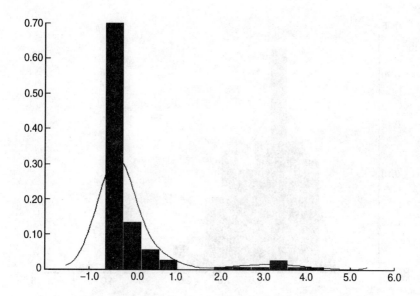

Figure A1.15   Italian banks: frequency distribution of total assets, 1992

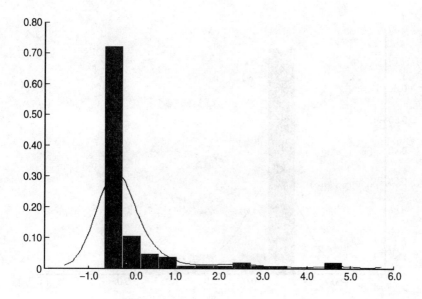

Figure A1.16   Italian banks: frequency distribution of tier one capital, 1992

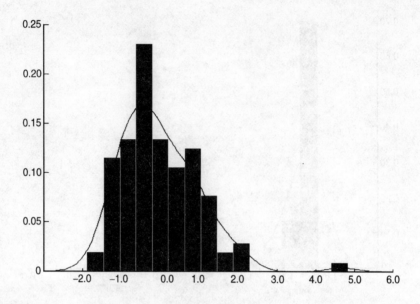

Figure A1.17   Italian banks: frequency distribution of capital assets ratio, 1992

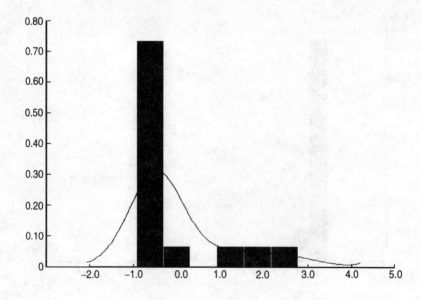

Figure A1.18   Dutch banks: frequency distribution of total assets, 1992

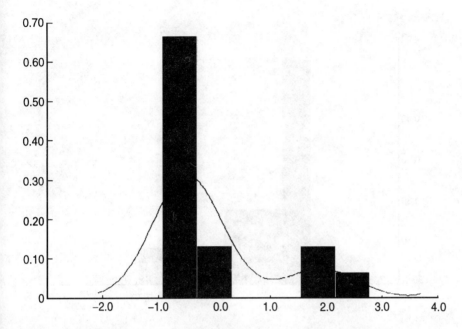

Figure A1.19   Dutch banks: frequency distribution of tier one capital, 1992

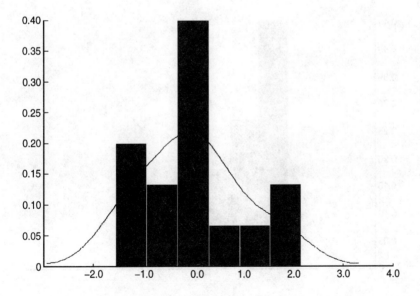

Figure A1.20   Dutch banks: frequency distribution of capital assets ratio, 1992

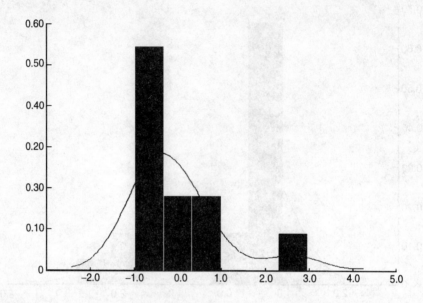

Figure A1.21   Portuguese banks: frequency distribution of total assets, 1992

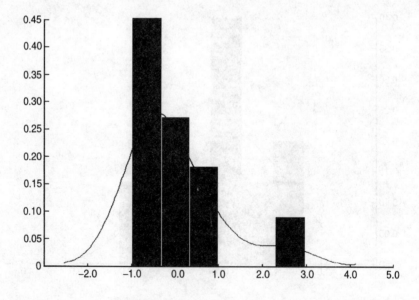

Figure A1.22   Portuguese banks: frequency distribution of tier one capital, 1992

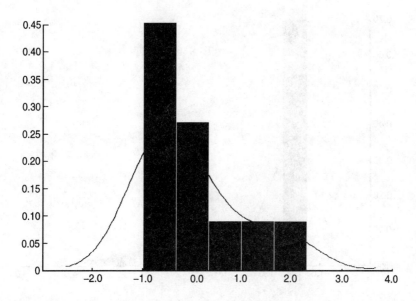

Figure A1.23   Portuguese banks: frequency distribution of capital assets ratio, 1992

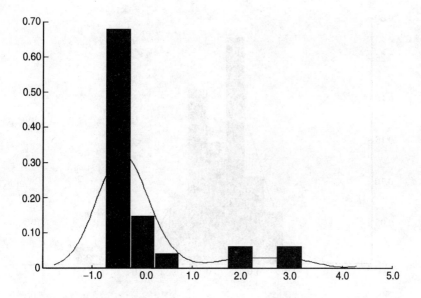

Figure A1.24   Spanish banks: frequency distribution of total assets, 1992

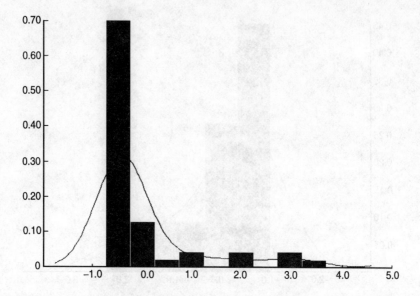

Figure A1.25   Spanish banks: frequency distribution of tier one capital, 1992

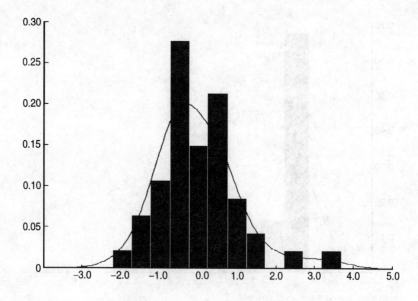

Figure A1.26   Spanish banks: frequency distribution of capital assets ratio, 1992

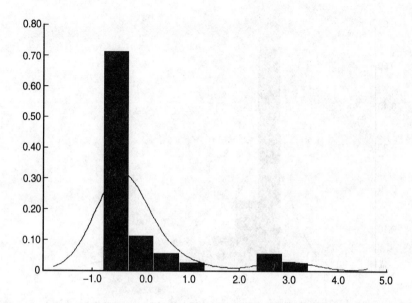

Figure A1.27   UK banks: frequency distribution of total assets, 1992

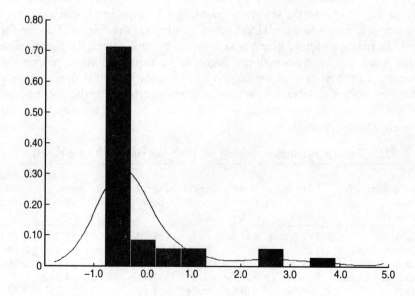

Figure A1.28   UK banks: frequency distribution of tier one capital, 1992

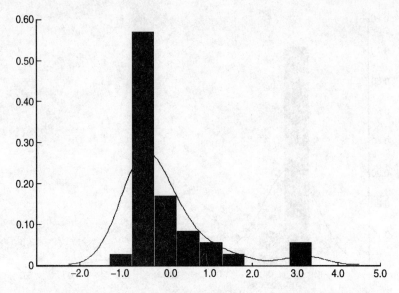

Figure A 1.29   UK banks: frequency distribution of capital assets ratio, 1992

mean than to the right. Following our previous example, this would imply that there are more smaller than average banks, and fewer larger than average banks. A high degree of positive skewness could then be associated with a banking industry structure with a few larger banks dominating the market. The reverse would be true if we found negative skewness. On similar lines, the significance of the mean also changes with the degree of kurtosis. The more peaked the distribution, the more representative of the population is the mean, since a greater number of observations lie close to the mean; the flatter the distribution, the less informative is the mean, since a wide range of sizes have a similar frequency to the mean.

Table A1.1   Banks in Belgium: analysis of the 1992 data (sample: 11 top banks)

Characteristics of the data distribution	Tier one capital ($m)	Total assets ($m)	Capital assets ratio (%)	Pre-tax profit ($m)	Real profits growth (%)	Average profits on capital (%)	Average return on assets (%)
Maximum	3 117.00	100 351.00	5.21	434.00	57.00	31.90	1.43
Minimum	116.00	2408.00	1.79	10.00	−44.40	5.50	0.13
Mean	1 128.70	40 587.70	3.14	138.40	16.02	13.06	0.40
Standard deviation	937.47	33 217.90	1.06	136.71	29.00	8.54	0.37
Skewness	0.84	0.41	0.84	1.12	−0.73	1.25	2.33
Kurtosis − 3	−0.25	−1.20	−0.31	0.13	0.34	0.57	4.08
Coefficient of variation	0.83	0.82	0.34	0.99	1.81	0.65	0.94

Table A1.2 Banks in Denmark: analysis of the 1992 data (sample: 11 top banks)

Characteristics of the data distribution	Tier one capital ($m)	Total assets ($m)	Capital assets ratio (%)	Pre-tax profit ($m)	Real profits growth (%)	Average profits on capital (%)	Average return on assets (%)
Maximum	2 911.00	53 828.00	8.46	12.00	−226.10	−5.80	1.71
Minimum	128.00	1 613.00	2.62	−727.00	−27 791.00	−70.90	−7.38
Mean	671.45	14 103.70	5.37	−151.36	−6 543.30	−26.32	−1.36
Standard deviation	871.35	16 775.60	1.76	207.78	11 914.00	20.54	2.31
Skewness	1.84	1.44	0.54	−2.11	−1.48	−1.01	−1.57
Kurtosis − 3	2.09	0.87	−0.64	3.58	0.22	0.16	2.42
Coefficient of variation	1.30	1.19	0.33	1.37	1.82	0.78	1.70

Table A1.3 Banks in France: analysis of the 1992 data (sample: 26 top banks)

Characteristics of the data distribution	Tier one capital ($m)	Total assets ($m)	Capital assets ratio (%)	Pre-tax profit ($m)	Real profits growth (%)	Average profits on capital (%)	Average return on assets (%)
Maximum	15 606.00	351 981.00	14.06	1 611.00	104.00	14.90	1.44
Minimum	104.00	741.00	2.72	−301.00	−224.90	−65.10	−2.04
Mean	3 077.60	78 405.60	5.55	205.54	−21.77	3.05	0.24
Standard deviation	4 202.20	109 111.90	2.78	394.02	70.60	16.44	0.65
Skewness	1.52	1.35	1.35	2.23	−0.91	−3.36	−1.71
Kurtosis − 3	1.38	0.38	1.47	5.18	1.62	11.25	4.96
Coefficient of variation	1.36	1.39	0.50	1.92	3.24	5.38	2.72

Table A1.4 Banks in Germany: analysis of the 1992 data (sample: 93 top banks)

Characteristics of the data distribution	Tier one capital ($m)	Total assets ($m)	Capital assets ratio (%)	Pre-tax profit ($m)	Real profits growth (%)	Average profits on capital (%)	Average return on assets (%)
Maximum	11 303.00	303 840.00	12.99	2 315.00	176.50	74.00	4.62
Minimum	103.00	1 771.00	1.34	7.00	−78.20	4.40	0.10
Mean	941.34	28 985.20	3.90	133.55	14.51	17.04	0.64
Standard deviation	1 706.20	50 465.70	1.56	293.00	43.48	10.92	0.59
Skewness	3.63	3.01	2.12	5.59	1.51	2.11	3.89
Kurtosis − 3	15.50	10.25	11.18	36.04	3.46	7.97	22.98
Coefficient of variation	1.81	1.74	0.40	2.19	3.00	0.64	0.92

Table A1.5   Banks in Greece: analysis of the 1992 data (sample: 8 top banks)

Characteristics of the data distribution	Tier one capital ($m)	Total assets ($m)	Capital assets ratio (%)	Pre-tax profit ($m)	Real profits growth (%)	Average profits on capital (%)	Average return on assets (%)
Maximum	1 234.00	30 230.00	17.85	144.00	1.10	69.60	4.21
Minimum	165.00	2 519.00	2.74	21.00	−55.20	12.40	0.17
Mean	536.75	9 507.10	6.87	90.12	−22.86	29.67	1.57
Standard deviation	381.78	8 832.80	4.72	52.33	23.31	23.25	1.40
Skewness	0.68	1.84	1.72	−0.32	−0.61	0.92	0.76
Kurtosis − 3	−0.78	2.05	1.95	−1.63	−1.24	−0.86	−0.55
Coefficient of variation	0.71	0.93	0.69	0.58	1.02	0.78	0.89

Table A1.6   Banks in Italy: analysis of the 1992 data (sample: 104 top banks)

Characteristics of the data distribution	Tier one capital ($m)	Total assets ($m)	Capital assets ratio (%)	Pre-tax profit ($m)	Real profits growth (%)	Average profits on capital (%)	Average return on assets (%)
Maximum	6 847.00	126 533.00	23.70	838.00	609.70	38.70	2.59
Minimum	100.00	776.00	2.17	6.00	−78.50	2.60	0.11
Mean	762.73	13 732.30	7.83	107.35	−0.73	15.82	1.05
Standard deviation	1 291.50	25 823.60	3.39	138.62	78.50	7.27	0.59
Skewness	3.07	2.86	1.24	2.76	6.40	0.57	0.51
Kurtosis − 3	9.57	7.42	3.25	9.42	47.26	0.52	−0.54
Coefficient of variation	1.69	1.88	0.43	1.29	106.25	0.46	0.56

Table A1.7   Banks in the Netherlands: analysis of the 1992 data (sample: 15 top banks)

Characteristics of the data distribution	Tier one capital ($m)	Total assets ($m)	Capital assets ratio (%)	Pre-tax profit ($m)	Real profits growth (%)	Average profits on capital (%)	Average return on assets (%)
Maximum	9 531.00	257 155.00	11.12	1 433.00	48.70	17.70	1.23
Minimum	99.00	1 066.00	3.24	9.00	0.90	6.20	0.32
Mean	2 054.50	43 864.30	6.71	354.91	15.49	11.78	0.62
Standard deviation	3 443.30	79 314.40	2.46	536.38	17.58	4.01	0.23
Skewness	1.49	1.78	0.33	1.17	0.92	0.11	1.53
Kurtosis − 3	0.34	1.79	−0.63	−0.37	−0.56	−1.39	2.52
Coefficient of variation	1.68	1.81	0.37	1.51	1.13	0.34	0.38

Table A1.8   Banks in Portugal: analysis of the 1992 data (sample: 11 top banks)

Characteristics of the data distribution	Tier one capital ($m)	Total assets ($m)	Capital assets ratio (%)	Pre-tax profit ($m)	Real profits growth (%)	Average profits on capital (%)	Average return on assets (%)
Maximum	1 940.00	33 118.00	11.90	370.00	56.20	39.80	3.09
Minimum	172.00	4 230.00	3.57	2.00	−87.10	1.40	0.05
Mean	647.00	11 050.60	6.13	119.64	−9.93	19.69	1.03
Standard deviation	514.39	8 401.10	2.81	111.37	42.93	14.39	0.90
Skewness	1.55	1.75	1.02	0.82	−0.11	−0.07	0.93
Kurtosis − 3	1.63	2.40	−0.24	0.28	−0.64	−1.46	0.54
Coefficient of variation	0.79	0.76	0.46	0.93	4.32	0.73	0.87

Table A1.9   Banks in Spain: analysis of the 1992 data (sample: 47 top banks)

Characteristics of the data distribution	Tier one capital ($m)	Total assets ($m)	Capital assets ratio (%)	Pre-tax profit ($m)	Real profits growth (%)	Average profits on capital (%)	Average return on assets (%)
Maximum	5 631.00	88 028.00	14.36	998.00	76.40	53.70	3.33
Minimum	117.00	1 161.00	2.46	0.00	−95.10	0.00	0.00
Mean	898.64	14 782.20	6.74	156.98	−5.20	19.52	1.16
Standard deviation	1 397.60	23 725.00	2.23	252.53	28.28	9.83	0.70
Skewness	2.25	2.19	1.09	2.22	0.002	1.19	1.23
Kurtosis − 3	3.92	3.37	1.99	3.62	2.61	2.94	2.04
Coefficient of variation	1.55	1.60	0.33	1.61	5.44	0.50	0.61

Table A1.10   Banks in the UK: analysis of the 1992 data (sample: 35 top banks)

Characteristics of the data distribution	Tier one capital ($m)	Total assets ($m)	Capital assets ratio (%)	Pre-tax profit ($m)	Real profits growth (%)	Average profits on capital (%)	Average return on assets (%)
Maximum	11 798.00	257 711.00	31.67	2 585.00	332.70	44.20	5.80
Minimum	128.00	468.00	1.84	−485.00	−143.80	−245.90	−36.40
Mean	1 610.80	34 823.10	8.85	181.09	27.76	3.73	−0.29
Standard deviation	2 817.20	66 764.8	7.10	523.90	97.12	46.55	6.62
Skewness	2.37	2.39	2.08	3.27	1.48	−4.85	−5.11
Kurtosis − 3	4.77	4.52	3.90	12.00	2.57	23.69	25.52
Coefficient of variation	1.75	1.92	0.80	2.89	3.50	12.48	22.76

The standard deviation is a measure of the dispersion of observations around the mean that takes into consideration the difference between each value in a data set and the mean of the same set. Thus, if all the observations were equal to the mean, the value of the standard deviation would be zero; the farther the observations are from the mean, the greater the value of the standard deviation. In terms of our example, a large standard deviation of the variable 'assets' would imply that there is a large dispersion of banks' sizes around the average-sized bank. However, the use of the standard deviation to compare the dispersion of distributions with very different means can be misleading. In fact, we would expect that, if the mean is numerically large, the squared deviations from the mean, and thus the standard deviation, will also be numerically large. Instead, in comparing distributions, what is interesting to know is the dimension of the standard deviation relative to the mean. This is exactly the information given by the coefficient of variation. An example of this can be given by comparing the total assets of French and German banks (Tables A1.3 and A1.4). Considering the standard deviation as the only measure of dispersion, the size of French banks appears to be much more dispersed, with a standard deviation of 109‡112, than the size of German banks, with a standard deviation of 50‡466. However, the average size of French banks ($78bn assets) is much greater than the average size of German banks ($29bn assets). When we take this into account by calculating the coefficient of variation, the size dispersion of French banks appears to be less than the size dispersion of German banks, with a coefficient of variation of 1.74 and 1.39 respectively.

2

The Internationalisation of EU Banking

2.1 Internationalisation and
globalisation
2.2 Internationalisation within the EU

The beginnings of international banking in Europe can be traced back to the thirteenth and fourteenth centuries, when merchant bankers started to operate in Italy financing trade by discounting bills and trading precious metals and foreign currencies. The Medici, Bardi and Peruzzi banks were all based in Florence and grew rapidly financing the international silk and wool cloth trade. They established branches, subsidiaries and representative offices across Europe (Gardener and Molyneux, 1990). These Italian banking houses experienced a decline in the fifteenth and sixteenth centuries, when German and French merchant banks started to expand abroad. Antwerp and Lyons then became international money centres.

In the seventeenth and eighteenth centuries, Europe experienced a period of political and economic turbulence, with the rise of nationalist and mercantilist movements. International banking declined and Amsterdam first, and London and Paris subsequently, became the major European money centres. During the nineteenth and early twentieth centuries, the emphasis in international banking shifted to raising loans for foreign governments, including the New World, and foreign investments. London became the main centre for this activity, with banks such as Baring Brothers, Rothschilds and Hambro arranging, underwriting, placing and holding issues of foreign bonds. This was also a tumultuous time, with international banks collapsing under the pressure of bond defaults, political turmoil, speculations and financial panics. Towards the end of the nineteenth century many consortium banks were established. Some merchant banks were also lending directly from their own resources, and British overseas banks, such as Hong Kong and Shanghai and Standard of South Africa, were created to lend funds to the Empire. Germany, with the establishment of Deutsche Bank, and France joined Britain in dominating international lending up to the First World War (Kindleberger, 1984).

The main influence on the development of international banking after the

First World War was the economic rise of the US and the corresponding decline of Europe. US banks expanded their business abroad and became the main source of capital to the world, with the US dollar acceptance credit displacing the UK sterling draft in international trade and New York displacing London as the most important financial world centre. However, with the Great Depression came a long period of quiescence in international banking, which only ended in the late 1950s when the major European currencies became once again convertible and world trade and foreign investment increased.

Modern international banking started in the early 1960s and it involved banks from all European countries. Banks developed international networks of branches and subsidiaries to expand their activities into overseas banking and financial markets. They expanded both geographically and in scope, aided by a number of factors, such as the growth of world trade and income; trade liberalisation and currency convertibility; regulation asymmetries, which particularly stimulated the development of the Euromarkets; technological advances and the associated financial innovation activity.

The fact that banks could operate in the Euromarkets without being subject to the relatively strict domestic banking regulations provided a strong incentive to the growth of Eurobanking activity. The phenomenal growth of the Eurocurrency market in particular stimulated in turn the growth of international banking activities, such as foreign-exchange trading, trade financing and international loans. Some specific developments in the United States also contributed to the development of the Euromarkets. Considerable US dollar outflows to Europe occurred as a consequence of the large US balance of payments deficits and Regulation Q interest rate ceilings on bank time deposits in the United States. The introduction by the US authorities of the Interest Equalization Tax in 1963 and the Voluntary Credit Foreign Restraint programme in 1965 increased the demand for Eurodollars by US corporations operating abroad. The Interest Equalization Tax also stimulated the development of the Eurobond market, where international banks acted as syndicate managers and underwriters and were active in secondary market trading. The Eurobond market became very active in the 1970s and was one of the least regulated capital markets in the world.

Another important development for international banks in the 1970s was the emergence of the syndicated loan market, or floating interest rate Eurocredit. Compared to the short-term Eurocurrency bank loan, the Eurocredit was issued through a syndicate agreement, with a medium-term maturity and a floating rate formula. The syndicated loan was one of the most popular international banking activities in the 1970s, when it became an instrument for recycling Arab oil money, or petrodollars (Gardener, 1990).

This success story was soon smeared by new crises in international banking. By the late 1970s it had become clear that floating exchange rates had created new risk management problems for international banks. Fears started to emerge about banks' international exposure and the solvency of some financial markets.

New initiatives in international banking supervision were called for. The country debt crisis, which emerged in August 1982 with Mexico's moratorium on the large repayments, profoundly affected the development of international banking. The need to improve quality became the main factor in the growth of securitisation in international markets and in the renewed demand for improved bank capital adequacy. Syndicated lending became more flexible for both borrowers and lenders through the introduction of multiple option facilities and a secondary market in loans and commitments. As a consequence of these developments, credit intermediation shifted away from the international banking system towards international capital markets, to become increasingly market-based intermediation. At the same time, international banks increased their activity in investment banking and technological advances facilitated the creation of new financial instruments, such as Euronotes or note issuance facilities. The income from these types of transactions was increasingly earned from fees and commissions, rather than the more traditional interest margin profits. The liquidity of the Euromarkets improved remarkably.

In 1987, the writing down of Third World debt losses and the stock market crash put an end to the bullish atmosphere of the 1980s in the international financial markets. After two years of exceptional growth, international bank activity settled down to a more moderate expansion pace. The events of 1987 emphasised the vulnerability of international banks and the liquidity limits of the Euromarket. Syndicated loans once again became popular and securitisation reallocated risk on terms more acceptable for both borrowers and lenders. In 1989, the growth of international banking aggregates accelerated again, without, however, reaching the growth levels of 1987.

2.1   Internationalisation and Globalisation

The rapid growth experienced by international banking since the middle of the 1960s is confirmed by the figures in Tables 2.1–2.5. In 1975 the foreign assets of deposit banks were 14 times larger than in 1965 (Tables 2.1 and 2.2). The quickest growth was registered in Asian and Central and South American countries; however, the activity of EC countries also accelerated at a fast pace, whereas US and Japanese banks did not experience the same fast growth of foreign assets. By 1975, EC banks were also responsible for more than half of the cross-border interbank activity (Table 2.3), although this share decreased in the following years with the expansion of US and Japanese banks' shares.

In recent years, Western Europe has recorded a growth in international banking activities. A high proportion of the world activity growth in 1989 occurred in the European markets, where the banks' international assets expanded by $314bn, more than twice as much as in 1988 (BIS, 1990). This expansion was mainly driven by the liberalisation of foreign exchange controls. French and British banks reported the largest increase in cross-border assets in

Table 2.1 Deposit banks' foreign assets and liabilities ($bn – year end).

Countries	1965 A	1965 L	1970 A	1970 L	1975 A	1975 L	1980 A	1980 L	1985 A	1985 L	1990 A	1990 L	1992 A	1992 L
EU	19.18	20.05	89.86	88.69	300.84	300.76	880.87	904.17	1275.97	1327.14	2866.86	3002.35	2918.25	3011.19
Belgium	1.00	1.52	4.92	5.73	17.78	20.15	60.68	72.95	92.63	112.92	192.03	239.79	188.62	226.06
Denmark	0.18	0.22	0.36	0.36	1.07	0.99	4.83	4.88	14.16	14.85	45.55	44.80	45.63	36.85
France	1.94	n.a.	10.14	10.83	41.17	41.92	160.21	146.68	184.38	197.18	458.72	519.67	513.27	523.98
Germany	3.45	2.25	14.27	9.14	38.32	21.91	85.17	72.09	112.93	75.77	394.78	226.37	386.80	264.48
Greece	0.05	0.04	0.10	0.14	0.28	0.98	1.19	5.15	1.98	6.98	3.46	16.46	18.61	21.10
Ireland	n.a.	n.a.	1.26	1.30	3.14	3.62	8.78	10.79	3.22	7.59	13.54	19.33	18.61	21.10
Italy	2.65	3.35	11.52	11.62	19.46	23.21	34.49	51.12	50.11	71.69	101.89	205.30	97.67	249.29
Luxembourg	0.40	0.20	3.68	3.24	30.15	28.39	104.83	98.45	130.95	117.20	355.12	308.09	376.50	320.64
Netherlands	1.56	1.23	5.28	5.06	20.14	17.51	62.63	64.35	72.88	65.68	185.92	153.43	189.49	164.70
Portugal	0.15	0.04	0.30	0.04	0.35	0.09	1.74	n.a.	1.93	8.92	5.49	n.a.	9.63	n.a.
Spain	0.23	0.35	1.00	1.28	3.24	6.37	n.a.	n.a.	20.73	22.62	41.40	68.37	72.28	86.32
UK	7.57	10.85	37.03	39.95	125.74	135.62	356.32	377.71	590.07	625.74	1068.96	1200.74	1019.75	1117.77
Other industrial countries[a] of which:	16.17	23.96	28.42	44.33	147.05	150.01	479.42	433.08	952.43	875.99	2254.07	2430.97	2070.70	2057.33
US	9.83	17.27	11.80	31.27	54.70	62.72	203.98	151.45	446.78	381.26	652.15	733.32	622.19	755.50
Japan	2.55	3.45	6.60	5.54	20.36	26.69	65.67	80.21	194.62	179.31	950.58	958.48	879.19	708.62
Other regions of which:	3.21	2.32	14.32	15.33	111.43	119.11	462.44	513.37	755.72	853.04	1668.14	1690.44	1717.27	1739.02
Asia[b]	0.92	0.54	2.69	2.02	23.04	21.87	103.02	111.40	257.13	267.19	866.64	837.34	890.31	868.55
Central and South America[c]	0.34	0.34	8.49	10.54	72.90	78.97	273.45	315.72	365.41	422.83	619.83	690.50	633.87	696.93
All countries	38.56	46.33	132.60	148.35	559.32	569.88	1822.73	1850.62	2984.12	3056.17	6789.07	7123.76	6706.22	6807.54

[a] US, Canada, Australia, Japan, New Zealand, Austria, Finland, Norway, Sweden and Switzerland. Austria, Finland and Sweden joined the EU on 1 January 1995.
[b] In 1990 and 1992 Hong Kong and Singapore accounted for more than 90% of the assets.
[c] In 1985 and 1990 the Bahamas and Cayman Islands accounted for 80-90% of the assets and 70-80% of the liabilities. In 1990 and 1992 the Cayman Islands alone accounted for more than 60% of the assets and 50% of the liabilities.
Source: IMF, International Financial Statistics, 1985 and 1993/own calculations.

Table 2.2 Deposit banks' foreign assets and liabilities (% of total)

Countries	1965 A	1965 L	1970 A	1970 L	1975 A	1975 L	1980 A	1980 L	1985 A	1985 L	1990 A	1990 L	1992 A	1992 L
EU	49.74	43.28	67.77	59.79	53.79	52.78	48.33	48.86	42.76	43.43	42.23	42.15	43.52	44.23
of which:														
Belgium	0.03	3.28	3.71	3.86	3.18	3.54	3.33	3.94	3.10	3.69	2.83	3.37	2.81	3.32
France	5.03	n.a.	7.65	7.30	7.36	7.36	8.79	7.93	6.18	6.45	6.76	7.29	7.65	7.70
Germany	8.95	4.86	10.76	6.16	6.85	3.84	4.67	3.89	3.78	2.48	5.81	3.18	5.77	3.88
Italy	6.87	7.23	8.69	7.83	3.48	4.07	1.89	2.76	1.68	2.35	1.50	2.88	1.46	3.66
Luxembourg	0.01	0.43	2.77	2.18	5.39	4.98	5.75	5.32	4.39	3.83	5.32	4.32	5.61	4.71
Netherlands	4.05	2.65	3.98	3.41	3.60	3.07	3.44	3.48	2.44	2.15	2.74	2.15	2.83	2.42
UK	19.63	23.42	27.93	26.93	22.48	23.80	19.55	20.41	19.77	20.47	15.74	16.85	15.21	16.42
Other industrial countries[a]	41.94	51.72	21.43	29.88	26.29	26.32	26.30	23.40	31.92	28.66	33.20	34.12	30.87	30.22
of which:														
US	25.49	37.28	8.90	21.08	9.78	11.01	111.91	8.18	14.97	12.48	9.61	10.29	9.28	11.10
Japan	6.61	7.45	4.98	3.73	3.64	4.68	3.60	4.33	6.52	5.87	14.00	13.45	13.11	10.41
Other regions[b]	8.32	5.00	10.80	10.33	19.92	20.90	25.37	27.74	25.32	27.91	24.57	23.73	25.61	25.55
of which:														
Asia[b]	2.39	1.17	2.03	1.36	4.12	3.84	5.65	6.02	8.62	8.74	12.76	11.75	13.28	12.76
Central and South America[c]	0.88	0.73	6.40	7.10	13.03	13.86	15.00	17.06	12.24	13.83	9.13	9.69	9.45	10.24
All countries	100.00	100.00	100.00	100.00	100.00	100.00	100.00	100.00	100.00	100.00	100.00	100.00	100.00	100.00

[a] US, Canada, Australia, Japan, New Zealand, Austria, Finland, Norway, Sweden and Switzerland. Austria, Finland and Sweden joined the EU on 1 January 1995.
[b] In 1990 and 1992 Hong Kong and Singapore accounted for more than 90% of the assets.
[c] In 1985 and 1990 the Bahamas and Cayman Islands accounted for 80–90% of the assets and 70–80% of the liabilities. In 1990 and 1992 the Cayman Islands alone accounted for more than 60% of the assets and 50% of the liabilities.
Source: IMF, *International Financial Statistics*, 1985 and 1993/own calculations.

Table 2.3 Cross-border interbank activity: claims by residence of lending bank and liabilities by residence of borrowing bank ($bn)

Countries	1975 C	1975 L	1980 C	1980 L	1985 C	1985 L	1990 C	1990 L	1992 C	1992 L
EU[a]	200.63	227.48	588.06	712.02	877.19	1008.99	1774.04	2144.83	1626.73	1864.31
Belgium–Luxembourg	26.95	39.74	95.68	142.60	134.16	185.44	n.a.	351.80	n.a.	319.02
Denmark	n.a.	n.a.	5.37	4.46	15.06	13.42	42.51	42.29	41.29	32.77
France	34.51	37.41	103.45	121.24	106.06	143.27	310.98	382.24	354.02	347.70
Germany	25.19	16.29	43.89	56.98	67.62	53.85	282.72	164.65	251.97	184.10
Greece	n.a.	n.a.	2.39	2.68	2.47	7.04	5.64	n.a.	n.a.	n.a.
Ireland	n.a.	n.a.	n.a.	n.a.	4.85	3.41	15.71	12.54	16.79	15.53
Italy	n.a.	n.a.	33.78	49.70	48.97	68.62	95.22	189.17	n.a.	n.a.
Netherlands	15.97	15.06	48.18	52.11	53.81	46.34	139.25	93.86	137.16	105.16
Portugal	n.a.	n.a.	2.49	n.a.	3.27	8.88	16.40	n.a.	24.93	n.a.
Spain	8.48	4.02	n.a.	n.a.	23.92	10.86	56.58	41.97	72.86	55.92
UK	89.53	114.96	252.83	282.25	417.00	467.86	809.03	866.31	727.71	804.11
Other industrial countries[b]	125.67	95.52	387.84	328.48	727.81	622.51	2239.96	2019.57	2181.47	1987.69
of which:										
US	33.84	18.51	146.63	129.92	336.08	307.42	562.19	640.49	536.88	663.38
Japan	n.a.	n.a.	47.62	78.10	136.09	173.10	769.44	945.13	678.64	690.91
Other regions	151.45	88.94	463.51	451.23	666.83	666.93	1373.87	1407.55	1390.45	1450.14
of which										
Major offshore banking centres	n.a.	n.a.	245.00	276.48	419.49	429.72	973.56	1088.29	933.89	1105.06
All countries	477.75	412.94	1439.41	1491.73	2271.83	2298.43	5387.87	5571.95	5198.65	5302.14

[a] This is the sum of the available individual countries' figures. Since for some countries data are missing in some years, this tends to be an underestimate of the true figure. In particular, no data are available for Belgium–Luxembourg in 1990 and 1992.

[b] US, Canada, Australia, Japan, New Zealand, Austria, Finland, Iceland, Norway, Sweden and Switzerland. Austria, Finland and Sweden joined the EU on 1 January 1995.

Source: IMF, International Financial Statistics, 1985 and 1993/own calculations.

Table 2.4 Cross-border bank credit to non-banks by residence of lending bank (LB) and by residence of borrower (B) ($bn)

Countries	1975 LB	1975 B	1980 LB	1980 B	1985 LB	1985 B	1990 LB	1990 B	1992 LB	1992 B
EU[a]	81.27	20.20	287.25	80.50	414.51	178.61	791.26	410.07	882.54	475.18
Belgium–Luxembourg	20.98	1.20	70.41	5.60	89.65	12.88	196.10	28.43	213.60	28.73
Denmark	n.a.	n.a.	0.12	10.10	0.16	15.62	6.37	33.46	8.00	22.85
France	6.67	1.80	56.75	7.80	78.32	19.71	147.75	29.23	159.25	36.51
Germany	13.13	8.90	41.28	30.40	45.31	43.26	112.05	83.89	134.83	121.81
Greece	n.a.	n.a.	0.02	n.a.	0.09	6.74	0.07	7.34	n.a.	7.08
Ireland	n.a.	n.a.	n.a.	3.10	0.59	7.39	2.06	15.95	4.50	22.57
Italy	n.a.	3.40	0.72	10.50	1.14	22.73	6.67	73.19	n.a.	84.10
Netherlands	4.16	1.80	14.45	4.50	19.06	9.39	46.67	55.43	52.33	56.02
Portugal	n.a.	n.a.	n.a.	n.a.	n.a.	10.00	n.a.	8.06	n.a.	9.02
Spain	0.12	n.a.	n.a.	n.a.	7.11	13.95	13.60	18.21	18.00	20.54
UK	36.21	3.10	103.50	8.50	173.08	16.94	259.92	56.88	292.03	65.95
Other industrial countries[b]	43.33	23.90	135.15	78.80	243.19	186.79	415.74	579.93	438.16	703.22
of which:										
US	20.87	6.10	57.35	15.80	110.69	94.08	89.96	270.25	86.02	309.41
Japan	n.a.	1.00	18.05	10.60	58.53	10.37	181.14	160.70	200.56	229.08
Other regions of which	42.60	n.a.	149.33	n.a.	238.80	368.47	548.82	399.24	646.34	447.66
Major offshore banking centres	n.a.	n.a.	135.77	n.a.	214.56	44.71	513.12	87.34	604.90	106.79
All countries	167.20	n.a.	571.73	n.a.	896.50	733.87	1755.82	1389.24	1967.04	1626.06

[a] This is the sum of the available individual countries' figures. Since data for some countries are missing in some years, this tends to be an underestimate of the true figure.
[b] US, Canada, Australia, Japan, New Zealand, Austria, Finland, Iceland, Norway, Sweden and Switzerland. Austria, Finland and Sweden joined the EU on 1 January 1995.
Source: IMF, International Financial Statistics, 1985 and 1993/own calculations.

Table 2.5 Cross-border bank deposits of non-banks by residence of borrowing bank (BB) and by residence of depositor (D) ($bn)

Countries	1975 BB	1975 D	1980 BB	1980 D	1985 BB	1985 D	1990 BB	1990 D	1992 BB	1992 D
EU[a]	44.46	8.40	183.28	34.00	324.10	109.46	855.87	405.20	900.36	453.88
Belgium–Luxembourg	8.80	1.50	28.80	6.20	44.69	14.68	196.07	38.46	227.68	38.83
Denmark	n.a.	n.a.	0.49	0.50	1.44	0.55	2.51	3.73	4.08	2.61
France	4.51	1.80	25.44	4.20	53.91	11.49	137.43	44.78	176.28	46.50
Germany	5.62	1.10	15.11	7.00	21.92	15.83	61.72	124.62	80.38	160.25
Greece	n.a.	n.a.	4.09	n.a.	6.36	5.87	14.21	11.45	n.a.	10.91
Ireland	n.a.	n.a.	n.a.	0.90	3.57	1.98	6.79	7.50	6.73	11.17
Italy	n.a.	1.60	1.42	2.60	3.07	10.90	16.14	31.18	n.a.	39.16
Netherlands	2.51	1.10	12.43	4.40	19.44	13.29	59.66	53.22	59.58	57.53
Portugal	n.a.	n.a.	0.04	n.a.	0.05	3.12	0.40	4.74	1.11	4.23
Spain	2.36	n.a.	n.a.	n.a.	11.78	5.93	26.50	13.73	30.86	17.91
UK	20.66	1.30	95.46	8.20	157.87	25.82	334.44	71.79	313.66	64.78
Other industrial countries[b]	81.24	20.70	134.72	104.70	254.10	239.24	449.53	434.50	448.34	386.62
of which:										
US	44.21	12.80	21.53	78.80	73.84	175.71	92.82	286.28	92.12	254.76
Japan	n.a.	0.20	2.11	0.80	6.20	4.22	13.34	22.11	17.71	18.19
Other regions	28.90	n.a.	129.07	n.a.	246.52	251.94	404.29	451.35	396.32	413.67
of which										
Major offshore banking centres	n.a.	n.a.	90.86	n.a.	174.36	70.72	336.41	142.88	317.61	135.00
All countries	154.60	n.a.	446.77	n.a.	824.72	816.70	1709.69	1694.40	1745.02	1727.40

[a] This is the sum of the available individual countries' figures. Since the data for some countries are missing in some years, this tends to be an underestimate of the true figure.

[b] US, Canada, Australia, Japan, New Zealand, Austria, Finland, Iceland, Norway, Sweden and Switzerland. Austria, Finland and Sweden joined the EU on 1 January 1995.

Source: IMF, *International Financial Statistics*, 1985 and 1993/own calculations.

foreign currency, with $50bn each, or 21.5% and 6.2% respectively. Swedish banks recorded an exceptional 50% rate of expansion in total foreign currency assets, while banks in Germany reported unusually rapid growth in their external claims in both domestic and foreign currency, which accelerated towards the end of the year due to the strong foreign demand for Euro-Deutsche Marks for the financing of purchases of German shares and bonds. British banks were large net importers of external funds, mainly used in the domestic takeover and merger activity.

In 1990, there was a worldwide decline in the share of interbank transactions, following the deterioration in credit standing of some banks, the need to comply with the capital adequacy standards, the wider use of derivative instruments and the further liberalisation of money markets in several countries. Japanese and US banks in particular contributed to this decline, whereas European banks, whose growth share had averaged about 35% in the preceding period, accounted for more than 75% of 1990's growth in international bank assets (BIS, 1991). If we exclude the claims on related offices and consider only the claims on non-related banks and non-banks, the share of German and French banks in total international claims, at 11.5% and 10.5% respectively, were higher of that of US banks at 8%. Although the overall growth of Japanese banks' international assets slowed down, they strengthened their presence in continental Europe, especially in France and Belgium.

The currency upheaval which dominated the second half of 1992 caused great turbulence on the European exchange markets and substantial net currency flows between national banking systems and the Euromarkets. However, once we allow for these exceptional flows, the 1990 and 1991 decline continued. Most of the 1992 and 1993 contraction in interbank business was still due to the rationalisation by Japanese banks of their international business and to the withdrawal of Nordic banks from the market caused by funding difficulties and problems with the repayments of foreign loans. On the contrary, international banking business expanded in Europe with most European banks increasing their international assets, apart of course from Nordic and Italian banks which were overburdened by the repayments of foreign currency loans in the wake of the 1992 currency upheaval, and for Swiss banks with a decline in their traditional trustee intermediation. The persisting ERM tension in the first half of 1993 caused major cross-border lending in domestic currencies by banks in France, Italy, Spain and Denmark, mainly to satisfy the hedging and speculative demand for their currencies. Large banking flows in the EC also originated from the growing securities business, dominated by the foreign acquisition of German bonds.

Although growth in international banking since the beginning of the 1980s has been particularly high in the United Kingdom, France, Switzerland and the Netherlands, most European countries had to respond to the worldwide movement towards globalisation of financial markets. The creation of a single European financial market must be seen in this broader context: whereas it is expected to have a direct impact on the organisation of domestic banking markets, it is unlikely to affect international developments which have been under way for at least a decade.

The two main international activities of European banks were Eurocurrency business and international loans, mostly carried out through branches and subsidiaries abroad. Throughout the 1970s and 1980s, European banks increasingly expanded in foreign markets by opening branches and offices in the major financial centres. At first, the internationalisation of banking was confined to the larger banks, with the exception of a few specialised institutions. They opened branches and offices abroad to operate in the Euromarkets and service multinational companies. In the early 1980s, commentators started to describe this process as 'globalisation', referring to a situation where the distinction between domestic and international operations was disappearing. Improvements in technology and the information revolution, structural deregulation, financial volatility and economic imbalances, financial innovations, such as the swaps market, all contributed to the increasing integration and interconnection of the world's financial markets. In particular, deregulation, such as the 1986 Big Bang in the London Stock Exchange, and the opening up of major financial markets, such as the Japanese and US financial markets, crucially contributed to both internationalisation and globalisation. The range of international banking activities expanded in the 1980s (Lewis and Davis, 1987) to include both more traditional financial intermediation functions, such as deposit-taking and credit facilities in a wide range of currencies to customers from a number of countries, foreign exchange transactions and trade credit; and newer activities, such as the swap market and specially designed project finance agreements.

In the wholesale financial markets, the division between domestic and international markets virtually disappeared. This was certainly an objective of the 1992 single market programme in the EC, with banks free to operate in all EC national markets under the same rules as apply to their domestic market. This type of internationalisation has provided incentives for the creation of diversified and sophisticated financial products and services (Baughn and Mandich, 1983; Williamson, 1988). It has also increased banks' funding opportunities and stimulated the interbank market. An important aspect of the process of globalisation has been the disintermediation of the credit market, with increasing securitisation. Negotiable CDs and Floating Rate Notes (FRNs) have become important sources of funds for international banks.

2.2   Internationalisation within the EU

The EU single market programme has very ambitious targets and in banking is trying to achieve in a few years what in the United States has yet to be accomplished: the complete integration of banking activities, with banks operating all over Europe through a network of branches and subsidiaries. This aim appears even more ambitious if we consider the disparity of the nature of banking in EU member states. Apart from the differences in industry concentration and banks' ownership, which are slowly becoming less accentuated, the existence of special credit institutions and the regional orientation of some banks may prove to sufficiently differentiate banking across European countries to create barriers to integration. German banking is a good example of a system fragmented by type of lending activity, with mortgage banks, instalment credit institutions, banks specialised in export finance, in servicing small and medium-sized companies, and more. France, too, has a number of specialised banks, such as the Crédit Foncier de France, which specialises in mortgage financing. In addition, the meaning of some categorisation of banking services varies from country to country. For example, Italian savings banks, the 'casse di risparmio', can perform many of the functions of commercial banks and the Istituto Mobiliare Italiano, created as a special industrial lending institution, can now offer a variety of financial services. It would therefore be misleading to conclude that the Italian banking system is fragmented just because it comprises a number of institutions which from their name appear to be specialised, when instead they can behave virtually as any other commercial bank.

Germany again offers a good example of regional banking with its 12 Landesbanken and five Zentralbanken. The Landesbanken are semi-public wholesale banks with dual activity: while they act as federal state banks and clearing houses for the regional savings banks, they can also offer most commercial banking services. Another determinant of the behaviour of German banks in their relationship to customers is the ownership of, and management participation in, non-financial companies (Cable, 1985). In addition, banks also participate in companies' decision-making through the use of proxy voting for their customers. It has been estimated that at the beginning of the 1990s the ten largest banks in Germany had majority control in 27 of the 32 largest industrial firms.[1] This type of relationship between bank/owner and firm/customer has been argued to decrease the risk deriving from potential asymmetries in information and thus reduces the cost of services and the likelihood of credit rationing. In fact, German banks are not only the dominant source of finance for non-financial firms, but they also underwrite and place with their customers marketable securities. This close relationship has been thought to potentially lead to conflicts of interest and thus has been considered undesirable (Krummel, 1980). However, even if it were to come to an end, the effects of it will probably last well beyond its abolition and it will remain difficult for foreign banks to break into the German industrial financing market. Although banks in France and Spain are also allowed to hold sizeable shares in the ownership of non-financial firms, in other EU countries there are significant limitations

---

[1] For more information on banking power over non-financial companies in Germany, see 'German banks facing curbs', *International Herald Tribune*, 8 November 1989; and 'The Deutsche bank juggernaut will keep on rolling', *Euromoney*, January 1990.

Table 2.6   Market share absorbed by foreign
institutions (end 1987 – % of total assets)

Country	
Belgium	46
Denmark	1
France	16
Germany	4
Ireland	11
Italy	3
Luxembourg	91
Netherlands	10
Portugal	3
Spain	11
UK	60

Source: Steinherr, A. and Gilbert, P. (1988), 'The impact
of freeing trade in financial services and capital movements on the European banking industry', mimeo.

on such participations. A different, but related, issue is the ownership of banks
by non-financial companies. Although some participation is allowed, there are
quite strict limitations in most EU countries. An exception in this respect is
Italy, where there is no legislation to stop non-financial firms purchasing banks,
even if the Banca d'Italia has strongly opposed any attempt by industrial groups
to take over banks.

Because of all these differences, it is likely that the expected rationalisation
of the banking industry in Europe will be limited to the national systems, at
least until more homogeneity is achieved. Although this situation may impede
major cross-border bank mergers, it has not stopped banks from operating in
foreign markets, at least for some services. In most European countries, foreign

Table 2.7   Profitability of banks in EU countries, 1984

Country	Rate of return on assets	Rate of return on deposits (excluding interbank)
Belgium	0.34	1.29
Germany	0.76	1.34
Denmark	1.00	N.A.
Spain	0.80	1.03
France	0.30	0.85
Greece	0.45	0.45
Italy	0.77	1.33
Luxembourg	0.30	1.29
Netherlands	0.51	1.02
Portugal	0.34	0.40
UK	0.85	0.87

Source: OECD/own calculations.

Table 2.8 Profitability of major banks in 1989 and 1992.[a]

Countries	Number of banks	Return on assets[b]		Loan loss provisions		Net interest margin		Operating costs	
		1989	1992	1989	1992	1989	1992	1991	1992
				as a percentage of total assets					
EU									
Denmark	2	n.a.	-1.03	n.a.	1.56	n.a.	2.78	2.30	2.34
France	6	0.55	0.29	0.53	0.73	2.42	2.20	2.15	2.07
Germany[e]	3	0.89	0.67	n.a.	n.a.	1.97	2.11	2.30	2.30
Netherlands	3	0.61	0.61	n.a.	n.a.	2.11	2.20	2.08	2.11
Spain[g]	6	1.73	0.94	0.47	0.60	4.33	3.00	2.98[j]	2.88[k]
United Kingdom	4	0.04	0.29	1.81	1.50	3.25	2.99	3.60	3.49
Other European									
Finland[k]	3	0.44[i]	-1.67	0.33	2.23	1.58	1.47	2.32	2.12
Norway	4	0.26[i]	-1.22	1.41	2.34	2.97	2.69	3.63	3.00
Sweden[h,k]	6	0.95[i]	-1.99	0.16	3.20	1.90	2.28	1.85	2.05
Switzerland	3	0.71	0.73	n.a.	0.57	0.94	1.40	2.07	2.18
Non-European									
Australia[d]	4	1.67	-0.25	0.70	1.88	3.77	3.43	3.61	3.71
Canada[d]	6	0.83	0.60	1.20	1.11	3.40	3.12	2.80	2.80
Japan[c,d]	21[f]	0.82	0.22	0.07	0.14	0.96	0.97	0.65	0.69
US	15	0.90	1.12	1.35	0.97	3.08	3.45	3.93	3.89[a]

[a] The data are not fully comparable across countries.
[b] Pre-tax profit.
[c] Half-year results at an annual rate.
[d] Fiscal year.
[e] Partial net operating profit, which excludes loan loss provisions, gain/losses on own trading and extraordinary items.
[f] Only 12 banks for 1989.
[g] For 1989, 7 banks.
[h] For 1989, 4 banks.
[i] Net increase before appropriations.
[j] Only 5 banks.
[k] Finland and Sweden joined the EU on 1 January 1995.
Source: BIS Annual Report, June 1991 and 1993.

Table 2.9 Non-EU banks in the EU, 1992.

EU countries		EFTA[a]	Eastern Europe	North America	Latin America	Australia & New Zealand	Asian NIEs	Other Asia	Middle East	Africa	Japan	Total
Belgium	B			3	1			2		2	5	13
	S			1			1	1			13	16
Denmark	B			1								1
	S											–
France	B	1	1	3	3	2	3	6	9	2	8	38
	S	5	1	12			2		3		2	25
Germany	B			6	3	1	3	5	6			24
	S	10	5	10			3	1	3		22	54
Greece	B		1	4		1			3			9
	S											–
Irish Republic	B			3							1	4
	S			2								2
Italy	B	1		7	1				2		7	18
	S											–
Luxembourg	B	3		1								4
	S	23	1	9	1		5	1	1		9	50
Netherlands	B	1		3			1	1			11	17
	S	2					1					3
Portugal	B			1	1						1	3
	S											–
Spain	B	1		5	4						8	18
	S			2							1	3
UK	B	23	2	33	15	9	16	21	25	8	28	180
	S	3	1	7	3	1	2		6	1	9	33

B = Branch; S = Subsidiary.
[a] Austria, Finland and Sweden joined the EU on 1 January 1995.
Source: The Banker, December 1992/own calculations.

Table 2.10   Top 20 US banks: interest margins.[a]

	1988	1989	1990	% 1991	1992	1993
Bank America	4.32	4.58	4.29	4.36	4.75	4.81
Citicorp	4.05	3.77	3.51	3.72	3.76	3.82
Chemical Banking	3.36	2.90	2.81	3.33	3.82	3.82
Nations Bank	4.30	4.02	3.75	3.82	4.10	4.17
JP Morgan	2.46	1.53	1.46	1.77	1.78	1.64
Chase Manhattan	4.06	3.40	3.46	3.85	4.09	4.94
Banc One	5.37	5.15	5.27	6.01	6.22	6.54
PNC Bank Corp	3.76	3.64	3.40	3.73	4.03	4.18
Bankers Trust	1.98	1.74	1.48	1.46	1.81	1.79
First Union	4.72	4.23	4.06	4.27	4.77	5.06
Bank of New York	3.67	3.09	3.29	3.43	3.55	3.69
Wachovia Corp	4.80	4.46	4.38	4.46	4.75	4.79
Fleet Financial	5.11	4.96	3.92	4.05	4.81	5.07
NBD Bancorp	4.02	4.17	4.10	4.22	4.39	4.51
Wells Fargo	4.96	5.11	5.12	5.18	5.70	5.97
First Chicago	2.99	3.07	2.77	2.51	2.61	2.58
Norwest Corp	4.76	4.68	4.71	5.08	5.58	5.83
Sun Trust Banks	5.10	5.02	4.84	4.79	5.07	4.94
First Interstate	5.00	5.00	5.06	5.04	4.89	4.91
National City Corp	4.86	4.80	4.59	4.60	4.65	4.89
Average	4.18	3.97	3.81	3.98	4.26	4.40

[a]Net interest income/average-earnings assets.
Source: Keefe, Bruyette and Woods, and *The Banker*, July, various years/own calculations.

banks' presence has grown rapidly since the 1960s. This growth has not been homogeneous across countries, mainly due to the differences in policies towards the entry of foreign banks and the comparative development and openness of different countries' financial systems. The degree of penetration by foreign banks at the end of the 1980s varied substantially across the EU (Table 2.6), the market share absorbed by foreign institutions ranging from 1% in Denmark to 91% in Luxembourg. Comparing countries of similar size, large differences appeared between Belgium (46%) and Holland (10%), or the UK (60%) and West Germany (4%) and Italy (3%). This is somewhat puzzling, given that there was no overt discrimination against foreign establishments in any of the

Table 2.11   Four largest UK banks[a]: interest margins.[b]

	1986	1987	1988	% 1989	1990	1991	1992
Domestic	5.6	5.5	5.0	4.7	4.3	4.0	3.8
International	2.0	1.8	1.8	1.8	1.9	2.1	2.3
Overall	3.6	3.6	3.6	3.4	3.3	3.3	3.3

[a]Barclays, Lloyds, Midland, NatWest.
[b]Net interest income/average interest-earning assets.
Source: Bank of England Banking Act Report 1992/93.

Table 2.12   Concentration of banking industry in EU countries: 1983.

Country	Market share absorbed by five largest firms (%)	Herfindahl Index [a]
Belgium	70	0.119
Denmark	78	n.a.
France	50	0.086
Germany	44	0.046
Greece	83	n.a.
Italy	55	0.050
Luxembourg	30	0.086
The Netherlands	84	0.177
Portugal	78	n.a.
Spain	46	0.086
UK	36	0.036

[a]$H = (V^2 + 1)/n$; where V is the coefficient of variation of the variable chosen to measure concentration (in this case total assets) and n is the number of banks.
Source: Baltensberger, .E and Dermine, J. (1988),' European banking, prudential and regulatory issues', mimeo

cited countries, apart from Italy. Also, as Revell (1987) has pointed out, there is no evidence that these differences could be explained by different profit levels or different degrees of concentration in different markets.

The profitability of banks in EC member countries in 1984 is shown in Table 2.7, while Table 2.8 provides more recent data and compares European with

Table 2.13   Relative size of the banking industry in selected countries: % of banks' assets over GDP[a] – 1992.

Countries	
EU	
Belgium	259.8
Denmark	170.2
France	198.4
Germany	200.4
Greece	97.8
Irish Republic	139.0
Italy	147.5
Luxembourg	920.8
Netherlands	263.6
Portugal	139.2
Spain	142.5
U.K.	133.1
Japan	316.5
U.S.A.	46.3

[a]The data refer to the world's Top 1000 Banks and the European Top 500 Banks, published by *The Banker.*
Source: The Banker, July and September 1993 and OECD, Annual Accounts/own calculations.

Table 2.14   Foreign banks in London.

Region of origin	1990		1993	
	B	S	B	S
EU countries	70	14	73	8
Belgium	5	1	6	-
Denmark	2	1	2	1
France	16	3	13	3
Germany	15	3	15	1
Greece	1	-	2	-
Irish Republic	1	-	2	-
Italy	12	4	15	1
Luxembourg	2	-	1	1
Netherlands	7	-	6	-
Portugal	3	-	4	-
Spain	6	2	7	1
EFTA countries[a]	23	7	23	2
Eastern Europe	3	1	2	1
North America	39	8	32	7
Latin America	10	1	9	2
Australasia	10	2	7	-
Asia	58	11	65	13
Japan	22	10	28	9
NIEs countries	15	1	16	3
Middle East	29	6	23	10
Africa	9	-	8	3
Total	251	50	242	46

B = Branch; S = Subsidiary
[a]This catagory includes Austria, Finland, Liechtenstein, Norway, Sweden and Switzerland. Austria, Finland and Sweden joined the EU on 1 January 1995.
Source: The Banker, November 1990 and November 1992/own calculations.

major non-European countries. Although Denmark was the country with the highest rate of return on assets, penetration by foreign banks was at the lowest level. Italy and Germany also show a pattern similar to Denmark, while in Belgium, which had one of the lowest rate of return on assets, foreign banks accounted for 46% of the market. If we refer to the presence of non-EU banks in EU member states (Table 2.9), North American and Japanese banks form the majority of EU foreign banks and they have tended to be situated in the UK. However, once again, the profitability of banks in the UK has recently been low relative both to other European countries and to other geographical areas (Table 2.8). In particular, if we compare the largest US and UK banks in the last few years (Tables 2.10 and 2.11), the average interest margins of US banks have been consistently above the UK figure.

The degree of concentration has also been suggested as possible explanation for foreign penetration. This would be due to the fact that foreign banks would prefer to penetrate less concentrated markets, given that the potential for retaliation from a very concentrated industry would be more severe. However, the figures presented in Table 1.6 and 2.12 do not appear to substantiate this

Table 2.15   Cost of living in the most important financial centres relative to London.

	1st April 1991	1st April 1992	1st Sept. 1992	Housing differential % + /-
	- excluding housing costs -			
EU cities				
London	100	100	100	0
Paris	100	102	104	-31
Milan	105	102	104	+12
Barcelona	99	103	103	-43
Brussels	99	100	103	-47
Frankfurt	97	93	95	-43
Other European cities				
Oslo	120	127	129	-46
Zurich	112	107	111	0
Budapest	63	65	61	-13
Non-European cities				
Tokyo	140	142	135	+49
New York	96	96	84	+26
Washington	87	84	73	-66
Toronto	90	84	73	-65

Source: P-E International and *The Banker*, 24 November 1992

view. The UK, Luxembourg and Belgium, where foreign penetration is high, have rather concentrated banking sectors, whereas Germany has low concentration and low foreign bank penetration.

Other motives thus need to be identified. Perhaps the importance of banking in the whole economy of a country might matter. Overseas banks may feel that if banking is a major activity within a country, it will be given priority over other activities by the country's authorities. If we consider the percentage of banks' assets over GDP (Table 2.13), this explanation appears plausible for Luxembourg. However, comparing Germany to the UK and France, the relative size of the banking industry does not explain foreign banks' penetration. Then perhaps the cost of living in different financial centres may be related to the choice of foreign banks to locate in certain cities. If we compare the figures in Tables 2.14 and 2.15, the evidence for this explanation appears rather weak. London is more expensive, especially in terms of housing costs, then Frankfurt or Washington, and yet many German and US banks locate in the City of London.

Whereas it is difficult to identify explanatory factors which apply generally to all countries, the significant presence of foreign banks in the UK must be due to London's special position as one of the leading international financial centres, and its liberal attitude towards the establishment of banks from abroad. Foreign banks have traditionally been particularly active in the UK and their presence in London grew at a relatively quick pace during the 1970s and 1980s. In more recent years the number of foreign banks has been declining slightly, but this could well be due to the general rationalisation of the industry (Table 2.14). Western Europe and Asia are the two main areas of origin, followed by North America, the EFTA countries and the Middle East. Other European countries, such as Switzerland, the Netherlands, France and Belgium have also attracted foreign banks. The penetration of foreign banks into these countries appears to be associated with the penetration of multinational corporations, which would imply that the foreign banks may have followed their corporate customers abroad to service their financial needs. Traditionally these countries have also had comparatively liberal policies towards foreign banks and their financial systems have been relatively advanced. For example, Paris and Brussels are Eurocurrency centres.

3

The Development of Banking in the United States

3.1 Regulatory Environment

Prior to the early 1900s, the financial environment in the United States was typified by fragmentation and a lack of adequate regulatory oversight. By the beginning of the 1900s the system was in such a state of disarray that Congress finally saw the need for some type of regulatory banking agency. Toward this goal, one of the most important and revolutionary banking Acts ever was enacted, the Federal Reserve Act, passed in 1913. Among other things, this Act created the Federal Reserve Organization. This entity, 'the Fed', would have the ability to juggle and control the nation's money supply, thereby establishing an efficient tool for supervision of the banks and, in turn, the US economy.

Although the establishment of the Fed is the most widely known provision of the Federal Reserve Act, the following provisions were also included in the Act:

1. Banks in the Federal Reserve system were required to keep specific balances in reserve. By increasing or decreasing these balances the Fed could increase or decrease the amount of money in circulation.
2. The Fed took on the role of 'lender of last resort' and introduced what is known as the discount window. The discount window is the interest rate the Fed charges to extend credit to other financial institutions. This interest rate, otherwise known as the discount rate, would later become the base rate for determining the interest rates banks charge their customers.
3. A total of 12 Federal Reserve districts were formed. Each district would have its own regulatory centre, or bank, which would control the reserve policies for that particular district.

4. Finally, and perhaps most importantly, the Federal Open Market Committee was created. This committee controlled the sales and purchases of all US government obligations. These transactions directly affect the country's economy.

Nonetheless, even with these added regulations, not all the inefficiencies in the system were purged. As with any legislation put through Congress, compromises were imposed upon the Bill. In order to ensure its passage, Congress made membership into the Fed optional, in order to secure the support of the opposition. Many banks took advantage of this, opting not to join the Federal Reserve system. This created an entire entity of banks outside of the boundaries of the Fed's control. Non-member banks were governed by individual states, and therefore were subject to their respective reserve and branching laws. On the average, the Fed's regulations were stricter than the states' regulations. Member banks felt that they were at a disadvantage; while state banks prospered, the Federal Reserve banks were forced to operate at a competitive disadvantage. In spite of these shortcomings, the Federal Reserve Act accomplished many of its aims. It established an effective cheque-clearing system and created the Federal Reserve note.

The 1920s were a golden age for the US economy, a time of seemingly unlimited wealth and opportunity. The nation thrived and banks helped finance the prosperity. Within this environment of capitalism run wild, Congress passed the 1927 McFadden Bank Branching Act. The intention of this Act was to encourage membership in the Fed, by putting the Federal Reserve banks on the same footing as state chartered banks. The Act achieved this aim by liberalising the branching and investment powers of national banks. Additional provisions allowed national banks to make real estate loans and invest in securities, and increased the maximum loan amount that could be advanced to an individual borrower. Although the McFadden Act extended the branching privileges, it also in turn placed limits on the types and number of inter- and intra-state branches allowed. National banks would be guided by the laws of their resident states. Further restrictions were enacted to prevent the creation of nationwide banking empires.

The banks' slow, tenuous climb toward respectability and public confidence was ended abruptly in the early 1930s by the Depression. Between 1929 and 1933 more than 10 000 banks failed (Federal Reserve statistics). There was widespread panic, and depositors withdrew their money from otherwise healthy banks, thereby resulting in additional bank failures. The severe economic climate forced the US government to take action. In 1933 the Glass-Steagall Act was passed, establishing the Federal Deposit Insurance Corporation (FDIC). The FDIC guaranteed, or 'insured', deposits of up to $2500. The effect on the economy was swift and life-saving. People took their savings out from under their mattresses and once again put their trust in the banks. This effectively stemmed the flood of bank failures. While in 1933 alone, 4004 banks failed, in 1934 only 61 banks failed. Although bank failures rose slightly in 1937 and 1938, to 84 and 81 failures respectively, they never again approached the rate of failure experienced prior to the establishment of the FDIC. By 1943, bank failures per annum decreased to single digits, where they remained there until the late 1970s, averaging less than five failures per year (Cooper and Fraser, 1986).

Whereas the most famous part of the Glass-Steagall Act was the creation of the FDIC, the Act did contain other provisions. Congress felt that the banks had been taking huge risks, at their clients' expense. The time had come to cut short the free banking of the 1920s, and return the bankers to their traditional conservative paths. The Glass-Steagall Act eliminated interest payments on demand deposits. Furthermore, commercial banks were prohibited from dealing in securities, and thereby separated commercial banking activities from those of investment banks.

The separation of commercial from investment banking as a means of reducing the incidence of speculation was circumvented by the establishment of entities known as Holding Companies (HCs). The HCs purchased both commercial and investment banks. These HCs were not banks, and hence were not subject to the conditions under which they now have to operate. In this way companies such as J.P. Morgan amassed vast fortunes and built extensive empires. In response to the growth of HCs, the 1956 Bank Holding Company Act was 'enacted as a restrictive measure aimed at regulating and contracting the growing numbers and powers of bank holding companies . . . . [it] provided a definition of a bank holding company as a corporation able to vote 25% of the voting share of two or more banks' (Pollard *et al.*, 1988).

Thus, the aim of the 1956 Act was to restrict the proliferation of holding companies. However, the results were rather different to the intent. Before 1956 many companies were reluctant to form mergers, knowing that when legislation was passed, they might be required to disperse their network of businesses. The Bank Holding Act of 1956 defined what was legal, and therefore cleared up the grey area that existed before the Bill's passage. Plans that had originally been put on hold due to the previously murky definition of the law, could now be defined and acted upon. Since the 1956 regulation prohibited the holding of two or more companies, One-Bank Holding Companies (OBHCs) prospered. By 1970 more than 1000 OBHCs were in existence. This loophole in the Bill was not addressed until the passage of the 1970 Bank Holding Amendment.

During the 1950s many of the banking industry's largest mergers took place. This of course raised fears about centralisation of power and money. To ease these fears, in 1960 Congress passed the Bank Mergers Act, which gave the Comptroller of the Currency advisory authority over all mergers. By the 1960s the profusion of legislation and federal interest rate ceilings had made it almost impossible for banks to offer high interest paying accounts. They were rapidly losing large deposit customers to competitive non-bank institutions. In 1961,

First National City Bank of New York (now Citibank), issued to 'bearers' a negotiable certificate of deposit (CD) for $1,000,000. This issue, radical for the times, created the first banking deposit unfettered by the Fed's rate caps. Citibank seized this concept and went on to market $100,000 minimum deposit CDs. The idea flourished, and by 1962 American banks had issued about $5.8bn worth of CDs.

Many would label 1980 as the year when deregulation began, and would consider the Depository Institutions Deregulation and Monetary Control Act (DIDMCA) as the first deregulation directive. Others would argue that deregulation began in 1970, with the amendment that allowed banks to venture in to 'closely related' fields. A third opinion is that the environment for deregulation began in 1961 when the first CD was issued. Regardless of which view is favoured, in the years preceding 1982 many global changes took place which led to the desire for deregulation of banking. Jeremy Taylor (1989) makes a point for four major external factors that influenced the direction and need for change in the early 1980s. Firstly, during the early 1970s, interest rates began to rise. No longer could a family borrow money to buy a house at a low mortgage rate of only 4%. The Fed felt that Americans were spending too much, and initiated deflationary measures. The reserve level was increased and a tight monetary policy went into effect. As planned, interest rates climbed. By 1976 they were over 12%. In 1978 interest rates briefly dipped, only to return to the upward spiral, finally reaching an all-time prime rate high of 21.50% between 19 December 1980 and 2 January 1981. In 1983 interest rates started to drop; however, they never again got down to their pre-1970 levels.

Secondly, in 1973, the OPEC nations put the entire world at their mercy by charging exorbitant prices for crude oil. This in turn spelled exorbitant profits for the OPEC member nations. Billions of 'petrodollars' were then invested in banks around the world. All these funds were now available for the banks to loan. Bankers, especially North Americans, felt it was time to assist the developing countries (LDCs). Petrodollars were loaned to the LDCs with almost no regard to payback ability. By the early 1980s the developing countries were not only still in the process of economic development but they were now also very deeply in debt. At the same time the American banks realised that they might never receive any payback for their earlier generosity.

The third factor was the issue of the first CD in 1961. This caused a revolution in the money markets and since then there have been major innovations in all aspects of the capital and money market. In November 1972 a New York investment firm started a money market plan which combined many small investments together to equal the price of one $100,000 CD. This opened up the elite market to the smaller investor, offering CD interest rates for even the smallest deposit. In 1975 the New York Stock Exchange eliminated the fixed commission schedule. Also in 1975 Merrill Lynch offered Cash Management Accounts (CMAs) to any client with over $20,000. This idea was so radical that Merrill Lynch patented it.

By the early 1970s the country began to experience localised recessions – first the real estate slump in Texas and other oil-producing states, then the agricultural market collapse in the 'Bible belt'. Finally, there were the failed energy loans which forced the closure of banks such as Penn Square Bank in Oklahoma City. Congress felt that something had to be done to enhance the opportunities available to banks. With the aim of bringing market share back to the banks, and making banking profitable once again, Congress passed the Depository Institutions Deregulation and Monetary Control Act (DIDMCA) in 1980. As stated in the Act itself, the DIDMCA had two goals: (i) to improve the effectiveness of monetary policy by making the fulcrum on which that policy operates more stable; and (ii) to provide competitive equity among financial institutions, which, given uniform reserve requirements, would be placed on a more equal footing and, given new authorities, would be able to offer more equivalent services to their customers.

The provisions of the Act pointed banks in the direction that they wanted to go. However there were other ramifications that the banks did not foresee. One of the main grievances of the Fed member banks was the reserve requirement. They felt that the requirement gave non-member banks an unfair advantage, since the Act established uniform reserve requirements for all banks, member and non-member alike. Furthermore, before 1980 services such as cheque-clearing and electronic funds transfer were free for Fed members. The services would now be provided for a fee, competitive with fees in the private sector. This led to further reductions in the already small interest spread.

On the other hand, the Monetary Control Act also called for the gradual elimination of Regulation Q, which set interest ceilings on all time-deposits and which had been a constant hindrance to the banks. Moreover, the Act also made available nationwide NOW accounts, before then only available in some states. The options used by, and the services offered by the savings and loans institutions were further expanded. The Act allowed them to invest up to 20% of their assets in commercial paper, consumer loans, and corporate debt issues. Federally chartered associations were authorised to grant mortgage loans in unlimited amounts without geographic restrictions, and to offer credit cards and exercise trust powers.

As the 1970s passed into the 1980s, the distance lessened between the interest rates stated in the old usury laws and the new interest rates. The DIDMCA pre-empted state usuary laws with regard to mortgages, businesses and agricultural loans. It also created new ceilings on interest rates for these types of loans.

With the passage of the DIDMCA, the US banking industry was on its way to complete a full circle from 1933 to 1980. The vast powers that had been afforded to banks before the Depression, and which were then taken away by the Glass-Steagall and McFadden acts, were almost all reinstated. However, the environment of 1980s was not the same environment as 1933. In 1933 banks enjoyed a solitary domain in the world of investment and lending. By

1980 they had to share ground with such groups as credit unions, savings and loans, brokerage houses and mutual savings banks. In fact, the DIDMCA not only improved opportunities for the banks, it also improved conditions for their competitors. Credit cards (affinity cards) were offered by almost every organisation, from Greenpeace to the National Rifle Association. Car loans no longer had to be financed by banks, but could be negotiated by Ford or Chrysler right at the car dealership. Sears could not only sell houses but could also provide a mortgage. The American Automobile Association could draw up a travel trip-tik, and then issue the traveller's cheques. IBM took care of their employees and established a credit union that could offer most of the services that were formerly provided by banks. Essentially, commercial banks were increasingly having their power and uniqueness usurped by non-banks.

The year 1981 was significant due to the increased level of activity in the field of mergers and acquisition and new ways of raising capital. Prudential Insurance acquired Bache Securities, American Express merged with Shearson Loeb Rhoades, and Sears bought Dean Witter Reynolds and Coldwell Banker. BankAmerica Corp. bought Charles Schwab & Co., the nation's largest discount broker. Chase Manhattan Bank, in an attempt to strategically position itself for interstate banking, claimed Equibank of Pittsburgh. Chemical New York also acquired First National Banks of Florida. The Federal Home Loan Bank Board authorised a merger of three thrifts from three different states, California, New York and Florida, thereby creating the first interstate savings and loan institution.

What was originally viewed as a problem of too many competitors, and therefore too few customers, became the case of the diminishing margin. Banks tried to offer the same lending rate as non-banks without the same in-house investment opportunities. Senator Jake Garn (Utah; Republican) believed that although the 1980 Act was going in the right direction, the non-bank system still had a major advantage, and that even wider restructuring was necessary. He therefore petitioned for the 1982 Garn-St. Germain Act, which was passed just two years after the Depository Institutions Deregulation and Monetary Control Act. One of the main intentions of the Act was to stem the flow of funds from the banks and savings and loans to the mutual funds of the brokerage houses and other institutions that afforded a higher rate of return (Taylor, 1989).

The provisions of the 1982 Act allowed the FDIC/FSLIC to give assistance to failing banks. It also approved certain types of acquisitions when it was felt that the combination could save either one or both of the institutions from failing. The allowable categories according to priority were: (i) same type institution, same state; (ii) same type institution, different state; (iii) different type institution, same state; and (iv) different type institution, different state.

In addition banks were also given the capacity to issue net worth certificates, a debt swap instrument. The activities of the savings and loans institutions were further expanded, giving them the power to operate deposit/lending services. They were also granted the ability to offer demand deposit services to qualified commercial, corporate, and agricultural customers, as well as to expand their consumer lending and to engage in a limited amount of commercial lending (Cooper and Fraser, 1986).

Furthermore the Depository Institutions Deregulation Committee authorised the establishment of a new banking product offering, known as the Money Market Deposit Accounts (MMDA). This instrument was to be competitive with the money market mutual funds offered by investment brokerage houses.

In 1982, for the first time since the Depression, the number of bank failures was higher than the usual 17 per annum. The 1982 failure of Penn Square was of such an enormous proportion that it created problems for such banks as Chase Manhattan Bank, Continental Illinois National Bank and Trust Co. Seattle-First National Bank and Michigan National Bank. Eventually Seattle-First was taken over by Bank of America, which was in turn taken over by First Interstate. The Penn Square failure caused such significant financial distress for Continental Illinois that eventually the FDIC was required to give a blanket guarantee on all loans. In 1982 a total of 42 banks failed.

In 1983 banks established the Super-NOW account, another attempt to compete with non-bank facilities. This account had variable interest rates ranging from 6% to 9%. The interest rate ceiling was eliminated, as were monthly transaction fees. The minimum deposit for an MMDA was dropped to $2 500. In spite of the various innovations, 48 banks failed in 1983.

American banking, although in trouble on the home front, still held a respectable place worldwide. In 1984, of the ten largest banks in the world, six were American. A total of 14 500 American banks were in existence, the highest number since the Depression. From 1984 to 1989, new charters grew at an annual rate of 1.6%. However, the total number of banks declined, due to a combination of bank failures and consolidations (Boyd and Graham, 1991). The number of bank failures increased to 79 in 1984. Banks realised that in order to continue to exist they must be able to compete with non-banks on their own ground. In 1985 the banks requested exemption from section 20 of the Glass-Steagall Act, which states: 'No member bank shall be affiliated in any manner ... with any corporation, association, business trust, or other similar organization engaged principally in the issue, flotation, underwriting, public sale, or distribution at wholesale or retail ... of stocks, bonds, debentures, notes or other securities.'

Between 1980 and 1984, almost to a rule, all the banks that had failed were considered small banks, those with assets of less than $30m. However, by 1985, 10% of the failed banks had assets exceeding $150m. What was once considered a safe option, a medium to large bank, had become a risky venture. Between 1985 and 1986, 62% of the failed banks were banks with at least 25% of their portfolio dedicated to agricultural loans. In 1985 a total of 116 banks failed.

In 1986 the FDIC ruled that banks that were not in the Fed system would not be required to abide by section 20. In a letter to Sovran Financial Corp, the

Federal Reserve Bank stated that they would allow bank holding companies, through their subsidiaries, to sell mutual funds and unit investment trusts. The year 1986 was also significant due to the global oil price collapse. Banks with a substantial amount of their portfolio in the energy sector started to feel the effect of the price collapse. Recovery for these banks did not begin to take place until the end of 1988. Another 138 banks failed in 1986.

Similar to the airline industry's experience after deregulation, the banking industry likewise experienced an upsurge of mergers and acquisitions. The weaker banks failed, or were bought out by larger, stronger banks. Holding companies such as J.P. Morgan and Bankers Trust New York Corp engaged in commercial and investment banking. In 1987 alone, 133 banks were purchased. Congress felt it had to curb some of this merger and acquisition activity, and as such the Competitive Equality Banking Act was enacted.

But 1987 was primarily the year of the stock market crash. In one day, the Dow Jones Industrials lost more than 600 points, the largest fall since the Depression. In that same year, what many large banks (defined as those with assets of more than $10bn) dreaded even to contemplate, became a reality. The loans extended to the developing countries in the 1970s became essentially non-performing assets. More than $7bn in losses were reported by the larger banks as bad debt from these non-performing loans. Even more damaging to some banks, 70% of the exposure risk was absorbed by the ten largest banks.

The trend toward bigger banks was accelerating. The Federal Reserve Bank reported that by the beginning of 1987, 37 states permitted some form of interstate banking. Simple calculations showed that it was less expensive to merge an insolvent bank with a strong bank, than it was to reimburse depositors at a failed bank. The number of banks with total assets of over $5bn had grown from 0.2% of the market in 1976 to 0.9% of the market in 1987. At the opposite end of the spectrum, banks with assets of less than $50m had shrunk from 85% of the market to 62% (Boyd and Graham, 1991). If one of the ultimate goals of deregulation had been to 'weed out' the smaller, inefficient institutions, then deregulation was certainly on the road to achieving their objectives. A total of 184 banks failed in 1987.

By 1988, banks that catered to the farmers started to experience a slow recovery. Non-performing agricultural loans were down from a high of 8.6% in 1986, to a new low of 3.1%. Another positive note was Brazil's resumption of interest payments on previously non-producing loans. However, banks were still leery of international loans, and foreign loans were down for the fifth consecutive year.

Although the banking industry was aware in the early 1980s of the impending savings and loans crisis, the impact and severity of the problem did not become apparent until 1988. For the first time the public realised the genuine magnitude of the S & L problem. That was the first year since the establishment of the FDIC that it did not operate in the black. The number of bank failures increased to 200.

In 1989, as a response to the S & L crisis, Congress passed the Financial Institution Reform, Recovery and Enforcement Act (FIRREA). Although it was apparent that banks were also heading down the same path of destruction, bank issues were not even addressed in the Act. By January 1989, 43 states had relaxed their interstate banking restrictions and allowed various forms of statewide branching. Two of the remaining seven states had already legislated for branching to take place at some later date. Insider trading continued to be in the news, and in October of that year the junk bond market crashed. In 1989, 206 banks failed. President Bush and the Treasury, separately, started to plan a draft for a broad-based bank bill. Although the President was not to announce his intentions until the State of the Union message in 1991, rumours abounded about the contents. Another 168 banks failed in 1990.

The failure of the Bank of New England in January 1991 generated shock waves throughout the banking industry. Because of the sheer size of the bank's portfolio, the FDIC felt that they could not let the bank fail, and therefore redeemed insured as well as uninsured depositors for their holdings. The rescue of the Bank of New England by the FDIC, while other banks failed without similar resuscitation, started a debate within the financial community. The Bank of New England's rescue was the quintessence of the Too-Big-To-Fail phenomenon. Large uninsured banks would be saved, while small uninsured ones would fall by the wayside. Directors of large banks could depend on the FDIC to cover for any mistakes in risky investments, while small bank directors had no such coverage. In 1991, of the ten largest banks in the world, seven were Japanese. Of the 100 largest banks in the world, the largest American bank, Citicorp, was ranked number 22. The next largest bank, BankAmerica, was 49th.

The early 1990s was a true test of the Too-Big-To-Fail assertion. There is no empirical evidence to suggest that very large banks ($1bn assets or larger), experience better economies than mid-size ($30–$100m assets) banks. Indeed, the reverse is true. In the last decade many studies have been done researching economies of scale, profitability and return on assets, among other measures of performance, of various size banks. Boyd and Graham (1991) concluded that: 'Contrary to popular belief, large banks are not more profitable than middle-size ones or less likely to impose cost on the Federal Deposit Insurance Corporation. In fact, according to the data, middle-sized banks, have had the advantage on both counts for roughly the past two decades.' Further evidence is provided by Clark (1988), as well as Berger and Humphrey (1991).

This is not to suggest that consolidation will not continue to take place. The trend will continue for a variety of reasons, and indeed at an ever-increasing pace. First, government policy supports mergers and consolidation. Second, there is a direct relationship between the salary of top management and the size of the bank. Third, although there is no cost advantage from mid-size to large banks, there are cost benefits from small to medium. A number of studies did find significant scale economies in the industry; however, they are exhausted below the relatively modest size of $100m in deposits. Equally, banks with assets of less than $10m have shown greater signs of deterioration in their assets, equity and core deposit growth than any other size banks (Damanpour, 1988).

3.2   Foreign Banking Activities in the US

To look at the origins of foreign banking, it would be necessary to go back to the thirteenth century in Europe. Since we are here discussing foreign banking in the United States, we must travel back only to the nineteenth century. It is widely disputed exactly where, when, and who was the first foreign banking institution to reach American soil. Some sources state that in 1818, the Bank of Montreal had an agency in New York City (Damanpour, 1990). Another source states that the Darmstadler Bank of Germany took an interest in a New York City bank in 1854. Finally, many commentators state that Japanese and Canadian banking institutions had already set up shop on the West Coast by the 1870s (Damanpour, 1990). The Directory of Foreign Banks clarifies that in 1859, the Bank of Montreal set up a representative office in New York City (Lees, 1976). The first British banking interest reached the US in 1875 with the Hong Kong & Shanghai Banking Corp., operating in San Francisco. Other banks from the United Kingdom, which was the leading foreign banking nation at that time, included Lloyds, Barclays, and National Westminster Bank.

There are many reasons which explain the move of foreign banks to the United States. First, banks followed their national citizens to the US. With an increasing number of people doing business in the growing US market, foreign banks made it easier to finance trade and transfer funds from their home country. Also, these banks were better positioned to take part in the New York bond and stock markets.

Soon, however, foreign banks began to see the advantages of offering their services to US citizens. Namely, US deposits were a cheap source of funds – less expensive than transferring currencies from their home countries. Also, foreign banks began to make investments in the then industrialising US. For example, British bankers made profits with their investments in the railroad system, as well as in land and cattle in the South. French bankers also found it lucrative to invest in the railroads of the North East, primarily New York and Pennsylvania, which enabled their small operations in St Louis and San Francisco to grow. Lastly, the Germans acquired funds through securities in both the railroads and the US government (Damanpour, 1990).

The turn of the century marked an important realisation by the United States as to the role that foreign banks would play. In 1906 Massachusetts became the first state to pass a law officially allowing foreign banks to operate within their borders. Other states were soon to follow, including Oregon (1907), California (1909) and New York (1911). Banking during the early twentieth century was basically limited to either the East Coast or West Coast areas.

The 1911 New York State Banking Law was the most important legislation to come out of the early government efforts to regulate foreign banking. The law allowed for the chartering of investment companies in the United States, giving foreign institutions more flexibility in their operations. This was important, due to New York's importance in the foreign banking world. New York City was the financial centre of the nation and the chief port of call for Europe, making it the prime location for most foreign banks. One prime example of the power of these newly licensed investment companies is supported by the fact that in 1913, one-third of all British investment outside of the United Kingdom was held in New York City. In fact, of the 25 foreign institutions that operated prior to 1930, 21 were located in New York City (Damanpour, 1990).

The First World War brought about a surge of investment banking into the United States, as the US became established as a world leader (Lees, 1976). Banks from 11 different nations – the UK, Italy, Japan, Hong Kong, Philippines, Greece, Mexico, Spain, Palestine and the leading foreign banking nation in the 1920s, Canada – operated in the US in the post-WWI era. However, the Great Depression brought the expansion of foreign banking in the US to a halt. Between 1930 and 1945, no institutions entered the US market. Ironically, however, even in the unstable financial condition of the US, no foreign bank left the market.

After the Second World War the growth of foreign banks in the US started again and the dollar became the medium of world exchange (Kim and Miller, 1983). The 1940s and 1950s were marked by moderate growth, mainly attributed to the increase in resources in the US, linked to post-war affluence. New countries were also entering the market as the US widened the number of countries allowed for reciprocal banking. This gave countries in which US banks already operated the opportunity to open institutions in the US.

The final boost to foreign banking growth occurred in 1961. New York, still the centre of banking in the US, became the first state to pass a law allowing foreign banking institutions to open branches. This was the first time foreign banks were allowed to operate in this form in the US. To show the impact of allowing branches, it is important to recall the distinction between forms of foreign banking. There are seven forms of foreign banking in the US: representative offices, branch banks, banking subsidiaries, affiliates, agencies, international banking facilities, and Edge Act corporations. A representative office is not a 'banking office', but it is merely a consulting office between a parent bank and its customers in a foreign country. It cannot accept deposits, make loans, commit the parent bank to a loan, or deal in drafts, letters of credit or currency markets. Its basic function is to provide information, advice and local contacts for the parent bank's business clients and to provide a location where business people from either country can enquire about the parent's services (Eiteman *et al.*, 1992).

A foreign branch bank is a legal and operational extension of the parent bank. Unlike a representative office, it carries out all normal commercial banking activities. Because it is a part of the parent bank, it shares its assets, liabilities, and loan limit with the parent. This provides the client with a full range of banking services, including international services. However, a possible disadvantage of a branch bank arrangement is that they are subject to the banking regulations of both the home country and the host country. A banking subsidiary also provides normal commercial banking services, but is a separately incorporated bank. As a separate corporation, it is subject to only the host country's regulations and is more likely to engage in domestic retail business. Its loan limit is also limited to its own equity capital, rather than that of the parent bank. On the hand, an affiliate is simply a locally incorporated bank owned in part, but not necessarily controlled by, a foreign bank. The remainder of the ownership may be local or it may be held by another foreign bank. This is beneficial to the affiliate because of the exchange of expertise it receives from its international owners.

International banking facilities (IBFs) were first allowed in New York State in 1981. An IBF is not a separate institution from its parent, but it does maintain separate accounts of assets and liabilities. This makes it an accounting entity rather than a legal one. The IBF works primarily on a wholesale banking level and can only lend and accept deposits from foreign residents. The main beneficiaries of IBFs appear to have been foreign banks, particularly Japanese ones wishing to maintain a presence in the United States market to gain easy access to US dollars. In fact, almost all the growth in IBFs since 1981 has been in foreign-owned IBFs, which now hold about three times as many assets as US-owned IBFs.

The last form of foreign banking in the United States is an Edge Act corporation, also known as an agreement corporation. An Edge Act corporation is a banking subsidiary physically located in the US that only engages in international banking and financing operations. The International Banking Act of 1978 extended this banking privilege to foreign banks operating in the US. This enabled foreign banks to participate in financing commercial, industrial, or financial projects in other foreign countries from their US Edge Act subsidiary.

During the 1970s, the United States witnessed the greatest growth period in foreign banking ever: banking assets owned by foreign institutions increased by over 650%. The number of banking branches and agencies tripled, increasing from 105 in 1972 to 339 in 1980. By 1980, 10% of all banking assets in the United States were controlled by foreign banks (Damanpour, 1990). One of the surprising factors that explained this sudden growth was the fact that foreign institutions were no longer starting from scratch in the US market. Unlike their pattern in the 1950s and 1960s of starting new banks, foreign institutions began to acquire existing US banking agencies. One example was the 1972–73 acquisition of the Frankling National Bank by the European-American Bank and Trust. This major takeover triggered a series of moves by foreign institutions that totalled 100 between the years 1970 and 1980 (Kim and Miller, 1983).

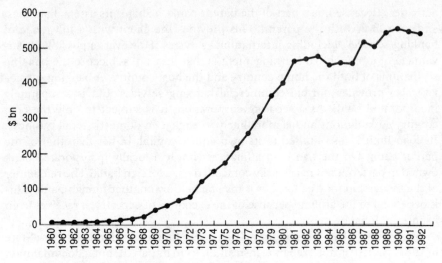

Source: Federal Reserve Bulletin: Balance sheet data.

Figure 3.1   Foreign branches of US banks: asset size

Many factors contributed to the tremendous growth of foreign banking in the US. One factor was the fluctuating exchange rates, as a result of the US abandoning the gold standard. This caused an increase in international finance and banking activities, taking advantage of the opportunities created by the floating exchange rates regime. Secondly, the United States had a very open national policy toward foreign banking. Little regulation was in place to monitor the activities of foreign banks. As far as existing US institutions were concerned, foreign banks were helpful in fostering competition in the banking industry. Finally, the appreciation of Japanese and European currencies gave those two markets a competitive advantage in the US (Kim and Miller, 1983).

Before the 1970s, Canada had held on to its position as the number one foreign banking country in North America. This quickly changed, as reciprocal laws introduced in the US in the 1950s hindered Canada's position. Due to the fact that they placed severe restrictions specifically on New York banks, Canada had many problems entering the important New York City market in the 1970s. This allowed the European and Japanese banks to gain control of much of the foreign banking assets in the US. In fact, throughout the decade, Japanese and European banks combined controlled an average of 75% of all foreign banking assets.

Despite the fact that during the 1970s there was a significant increase in the number of foreign-owned banks in the US, it was not until 1978 that any legitimate legislation was passed regarding foreign banks in the US. It became clear at this point that foreign banks had several advantages over domestically owned banks and that something had to be done to change this. These factors led to the passage of the International Banking Act of 1978. The aim of the IBA was simply to establish parity between foreign and domestic banks operating in the US. All restrictions placed on foreign banks in this Act had already been placed on domestically owned banks, yet there were still certain areas where foreign banks maintained their advantage. One requirement that foreign banks would have to follow regarded minimum reserves: these were to be set at 10%, which rate would then vary in line with changes in requirements on domestic banks. Another restriction placed on foreign banks dealt with the limitation of geographic expansion comparable to regulations already placed on US banking organisations (*Federal Reserve Bulletin*, 1993). FDIC requirements were placed on certain branches of foreign banks, namely all federal branches, and in state branches where the law of the state required it. In the way of supervision, a somewhat vague yet important facet of the legislation mentioned a coordination between states and the federal government in the regulation of foreign banks. This section would be expanded upon greatly in the Foreign Bank Supervision Enhancement Act of 1991. One final important aspect of the legislation was an attempt to adapt the dual banking system. This concerns the discretion of banks to be chartered by either state or federal authorities.

After its passage, the IBA was said to be the finest-ever legislation regarding foreign-owned banks in the US, on the basis of two characteristics. First of all, it evened the playing field somewhat by creating greater equality between foreign and domestically owned banks, although, essentially, foreign banks were still free of certain federal requirements placed on US banks (*Federal Reserve Bulletin*, 1993). These included not requiring prior federal review of foreign banks trying to enter the US market, which caused problems and was dealt with later. Another aspect which was later rectified was the absence of a federal role in the termination of a state licensed branch or agency of a foreign bank.

US banking has traditionally differed from banking in most OECD countries, US legislation maintaining a separation between commercial banking and some securities businesses, especially underwriting of corporate equities. In particular, the Glass-Steagall Act of 1933 prevents US banks from developing into the universal type of bank found in Switzerland or Germany. US banks, both domestic and foreign-owned, are also prevented from investing significantly in commerce and industry and from forging links with the non-bank corporate sector through holding companies, as happens in Germany and Japan (Mullineux, 1987). Another significant difference in the US banking system is the use of long-term lending. In France, Germany and Japan, long-term lending is common. In the United States such lending is rare, partly due to the highly developed capital markets in the US. However, unlike most of the OECD countries, Japan's banking system resembles the US system, perhaps due to the US presence in Japan following the Second World War. The Japanese have privatised state banks and have given more independence to their central bank, practise similar US short-term interest rate control and most importantly have been guided by Article 65, which is similar to the Glass-Steagall Act.

In the 1990s, the development of US banks' activities seems to be getting farther away from, rather than closer to, the type of development of European and Japanese banks. For the first time in US banking history, in 1992 large US corporations reported using more foreign banks on average than domestic banks. In 1992, the Japanese banks increased their US loan participation by 30% while, from the UK, Barclays Bank and National Westminster Bank increased their participation by roughly 50%. Additionally, German and Dutch banks are entering the US market with their large international service capabilities and are attracting US businesses that the US banks used to serve when they had large networks across Europe. The large Dutch bank, ABN AMRO, created from a merger in 1991, has worldwide total assets of $250bn, dwarfing even the world giant Citicorp, which at year end had $214bn in total assets. ABN AMRO Bank alone has $36bn in US assets, and over 8000 employees in the US.

The acquisitions of US banks by foreign banks can be seen as another way in which US banks are losing to foreign competition. Many foreign banks are particularly interested in acquiring domestic US banks, because they often do not have established positions in domestic banking markets. Marine Midland is a prime example of this strategy. Up till 1980, Marine Midland was a Buffalo-based regional bank. It had 315 branches and was New York State's third largest consumer lender. At about this time Hong Kong & Shanghai Banking Corp. was looking to acquire Marine Midland to help its growth outside of Asia. The New York State Bank Superintendent at that time refused to approve a takeover bid, fearing that international concerns would eclipse domestic concerns. However, the merger was still carried out by converting Marine Midland from a state chartered to a federal chartered bank. In March 1980, Hong Kong bank owned 41% of Marine's stock, and 51% by year end. Marine remained an affiliate of Hong Kong Bank until 1988 when Hong Kong Bank acquired the remainder of Marine's shares.

The Bank of Credit and Commerce International (BCCI) scandal, which shook the banking industry, has several implications regarding the future of foreign bank regulations. A little background on the scandal is in order here so that we may understand some of the problems involving foreign banks in the US and why we need stronger regulation. The BCCI, through a network of subsidiaries, affiliates, and branches operated in 73 countries. Most of its banking offices were located in Europe, the Middle East, the Caribbean, and South America. The holding company for these entities was chartered in Luxembourg. BCCI had operated agencies in the US located in California, New York, and Florida. The organisation was primarily owned by investors in the Middle East, with control of most of its shares concentrated in the hands of the ruling family and government of Abu Dhabi. Due to the fact that BCCI managed most of its global business out of offices in London, the Luxembourg authorities did not provide consolidated supervision of BCCI. As a result of this incident, Luxembourg has indicated that it will no longer license holding companies that do not conduct a banking business in their country. The disjointed, peripheral structure of BCCI discouraged and impeded the periodic reporting of crucial financial information; supervision was very difficult to accomplish. This 'disjointed' structure of BCCI and lack of supervision facilitated unethical and illegal financial activities involving the organisation. In October of 1988, the BCCI was indicted for money laundering out of its Tampa, Florida, office. The BCCI also encountered other legal problems in addition to money laundering. Examinations of the Miami and San Francisco offices revealed problems in asset quality and internal controls. Furthermore, the BCCI ran into problems with Financial General Bankshares, a holding company. In 1977 and 1978 four clients of the organisation, acting on the recommendation of the CEO of the BCCI, Mr Abedi, began purchasing shares of Financial General, eventually acquiring 20% of its voting shares. The BCCI claimed that it acted only as an investment adviser to these persons in connection with their purchases of the shares, and did not itself own, control, or vote with, any of the shares. The reality was that the BCCI, quite clearly, did control more than 5% of Financial General's shares, and this was in violation of the Williams Act. This acquisition was illegal because it undermined the integrity of BCCI's financial assets. The stock was a risky acquisition and it unfairly exposed those people who had money with BCCI to this risk.

Due to these numerous illegal dealings, the organisation had to close all of its US offices. The reason why the BCCI multibillion-dollar fraud went undetected for years was because of bank secrecy and offshore branches. Information was therefore hard to come by and foreign cooperation was lacking. Based on the Federal Reserve's experience with BCCI and other foreign organisations, it was decided that new supervisory regulations regarding foreign banks were in order and that this new legislation should include issues involving access to information and cooperation with foreign supervisors, among other items.

Besides the BCCI case prompting new regulatory legislation, unfair cost advantages enjoyed by foreign banks has also encouraged new legislation. These unfair cost advantages allow foreign banks to provide higher interest rates to lenders and to charge lower interest rates to borrowers. Some of these cost advantages stem from certain laws and regulations that domestic banks have to adhere to, but which foreign banks are exempt from. For example, certain foreign banks in the past did not have to pay FDIC insurance premiums.

In the 1980s and early 1990s the growth of foreign-owned banks in the US was explosive. By 1991, there were about 280 foreign bank agencies, with US assets of over $630bn, accounting for nearly 20% of the total banking assets in the US. Between 1980 and 1992, the number of branches had nearly doubled from 300 to just under 600. As a result of this large expansion, coupled with cases of fraud and other criminal activity by foreign banks such as BCCI, along with the IBA's deficiencies, many were convinced that new legislation was necessary.

The Foreign Bank Supervision Enhancement Act (FBSEA) of 1991 is perhaps the most important and prominent piece of legislation that has been enacted to correct some of the unfair advantages that foreign banks hold over domestic banks. It has also been created to provide clearer and more concrete guidelines for bank supervision, in order to ensure that another BCCI scandal does not take place in the future. This Act was proposed to 'ensure that foreign bank operations in the US are regulated, supervised, and examined in the same manner as US banks'. This Act deals with many of the problems with the IBA and aims at correcting them, as well as dealing with problems that foreign banking as a whole faced during the 1980s.

Clearly, a major hole left by the IBA that has been covered by the new Act is the requirement for federal review and approval for foreign banks wishing to have state and federally licensed branches and agencies in the US. Originally the Office of the Comptroller of the Currency was to deal with the federally licensed branches, but this power has been extended to the Federal Reserve as well. A set of standards has also been determined in deciding whether a bank would be approved. These standards include comprehensive consolidated supervision by the home country (*Federal Reserve Bulletin*, 1993). Again, the BCCI scandal was a major driving force behind this action.

Comprehensive consolidated supervision is a crucial aspect of the FBSEA. Basically it is used to determine 'whether the foreign bank is supervised or regulated in such a manner that its home country supervisor received sufficient information on the worldwide operations of the foreign bank (including the relationship of the bank to any affiliate) to assess the foreign bank's overall financial condition and compliance with law and regulation' (*Federal Reserve Bulletin*, 1993). The Federal Reserve Board was adamant in this view and rejected the suggestion that applicants from a home country that was making significant progress towards comprehensive consolidated supervision, but had not yet reached it, should be allowed to qualify. Only in the case of representative offices was this type of flexibility allowed. Although in this way the Act was thus more relaxed towards representative offices, it was also somewhat more stringent towards them in other ways. The FBSEA included a requirement of prior federal approval for foreign banks to establish representative offices in the US, as well as the power to regularly examine these offices to make sure that they did not take part in any unlicensed banking activity.

Another flaw of the 1978 IBA that was resolved concerned the Federal Reserve's authority in the termination of foreign-owned banks. The FBSEA gave the Fed the ability to terminate activities of foreign-owned state licensed branches, agencies, commercial lending companies, or representative offices for violations of law or for unsound banking practices. This was a complement to the Fed's authority to allow the establishment of such offices. The Act also set forth a section maintaining that foreign-owned banks with branches or agencies in the US must obtain approval from the Federal Reserve before acquiring more than 5% of the voting shares of a bank or bank holding company. This was to ensure that standards set in the Bank Holding Company Act of 1956 would also be applied to foreign-owned banks as well. (Basically, a holding company is a business that has stock in other organisations and uses its leverage to dominate over management.) This law, which was already applied to US-owned banks, was put into effect to prevent foreign-owned banks from becoming too powerful.

Members of the Federal Reserve Board realised that they were asking a great deal of their foreign counterparts in the way of information to determine whether to accept a bank's application or not. They also realised that these associates might request similar information in regard to US banks as well. The board decided that federal banking authorities should be allowed to share supervisory information with their foreign counterparts, subject to a high level of confidentiality, and when the information would not prejudice the best interests of the US.

The aforementioned sections of the FBSEA were passed and became effective on 19 December 1991. However, there were some important additions that were discussed and dealt with soon after this as well. One of the new restrictions concerned deposit-taking by foreign banks. Basically, it stated that no foreign bank was allowed to have deposit accounts of less than $100 000, except through an insured banking subsidiary (*Federal Reserve Bulletin*, 1993). This was a somewhat stricter rule than under the IBA, because it covered all foreign-owned banks instead of just all federal banks and some state branches.

The final statute of major importance referred to the capital standards established by the Basle Accord of 1988 to provide a common basis in the evaluation of the general equivalency of capital from banks of various countries. Basically, countries adhering to the accord, among them the Group of Ten countries that proposed it, have to meet the minimum requirements set by the accord and administered by home country supervisors. If a country does not subscribe to the Basle standards, all information regarding capital standards must be provided from the home country, as well as any other information deemed necessary for determining an applicant's capital position. If possible, this data must be appropriately adjusted, due to accounting and structural differences, and must be presented in a format as close as possible to the Basle framework (*Federal Reserve Bulletin*, 1993). Of 22 foreign-owned banks, accounting for 97% of total US banking assets held by foreign-owned banks, 20 either followed the Basle Accord or had policies that were very similar.

The FBSEA of 1991 has basically remained unaltered to this date. There have been some minor alterations, and some facets of the Act were made more specific, but generally the main points have remained the same. For the most part, most members of the Federal Reserve Board have declared themselves satisfied with it. One area, though, that has been debated by various authorities is the application process followed by foreign banks. This process has proved more inefficient than it was expected to be. The main problem is the length of time taken to process applications, lengthy delays being encountered while conducting background checks of applicants. Although the Board is making its decisions on consolidated supervision on individual banks, instead of on a country-by-country basis, applicants from the same country will be allowed to use previously submitted information in regard to consolidated supervision. They will only have to describe how this information pertains to them, and how if at all the system has changed since the last time the information was brought before the board.

Another problem is the fact that the Board, the OCC and state supervisors all request separate applications that are often quite redundant to the applicants. However, at the time of writing they were working on a common application format, which was expected to be agreed in the near future. Until this happens, the Board has decided that it will accept a copy of either the state or OCC application (*Federal Reserve Bulletin*, 1993).

With regards to the examination of the banks, the rule provides for annual on-site examinations of branches, agencies, and commercial lending companies by a US banking supervisor. Representative banks will be taken care of by the Reserve bank. In order to minimise the time taken and burden falling on the banks, the Board has taken a flexible approach towards examinations. They have also tried, whenever possible, to coordinate these check-ups with state regulators, to lessen the amount of repetitive work in reviewing banks. At the time of writing, these changes in procedures seem to have been appropriate and effective.

Overall, the FBSEA seems to have significantly improved the regulation of foreign-owned banks. It has eliminated many of the seemingly unfair advantages enjoyed by foreign banks, and has attempted to alleviate problems that became relevant during the 1980s. These improvements have been seen as very important by the domestic banking community, since it is widely believed that foreign banks are (and will be even more in the near future) challenging domestic banks for local and community market share, as well as for national and international business. In a recent congressional testimony, Thomas Labrecque, Chase Manhattan Bank's president, warned that because of outdated regulations, US banks are threatened with losing even more market share to foreign banks and this applies to both community banks across the US and money centre banks in New York.

This type of local and community-level competition from foreign banks is relatively new. Most foreign banks, in the interest of big profits, have traditionally limited their business to the largest US cities, concentrating on large corporate finance projects. Foreign institutions are just beginning to view the local and community-level markets, regarding small-scale lending as potentially as lucrative and profitable as the 'big' business. Those foreign banks that currently have US consumer holdings are expected to expand them considerably in the future. Currently, for example, Japanese banks are a major force in California, owning one quarter of the state's banking assets. The Bank of Tokyo's $15bn Union Bank is the largest bank. Japanese banks are moving fast and aggressively, charging competitive prices and increasing their holdings by diversifying from corporate finance to middle market lending, homeowner loans and retail banking. They are providing more smaller-sized loans than before in response to the growing recognition that the corporate lending market is becoming saturated and that there is a need to capitalise at the level of local markets. As mentioned earlier, due to certain cost advantages, foreign banks are able to provide higher interest rates to lenders and charge lower interest rates to borrowers. Many domestic bankers view the radical pricing regimes of Japanese banks as extremely aggressive and they have accused them of selling below fair market value, providing practically unbeatable pricing; domestic banks feel that they cannot compete effectively with Japanese banks. Much to the dismay of domestic bankers, Japanese banks are expected to expand east into the California desert, Nevada, Arizona, Oregon, and Washington, as the market in southern California becomes saturated.

Not all foreign banks, however, are interested in competing on the local to middle market level. Deutsche Bank, for example, seems to have little interest in domestic loans and short-term CDs, having committed itself to the highest levels of world finance and bankrolling the transforming markets of Eastern and Central Europe. However, banks from Canada, Spain, Ireland, Mexico, Greece, and Scotland have some consumers' holdings which they are looking to expand. It is interesting to note that many Irish and Scottish banks are located in the North East, in order to take advantage of that region's predominant ethnic make-up and strong cultural identification with Ireland and the United Kingdom. In particular, Canadian banks have had great success in increasing their market share by expanding their lending to small and medium-sized corporations. They have regained some of their market share lost to both European and Japanese banking interests in the 1970s. An example of this success is seen in the Bank of Montreal, which is planning to double earnings in the US through increased middle market lending. Part of this success can be attributed to the fact that Canadian banks have been operating in the US for over 100 years. Also, they have experience with nationwide branch networks, they are geographically close, and with the US/Canada Free Trade pact, profits are easier to come by.

In spite of these successes, some bankers and executives still believe that foreign banks are at a disadvantage at the community level. Local people perceive that money is going abroad rather than staying in the community, and they also feel that foreign banks would rather make big loans than small loans. Thus, at the community level, people feel that they have more power, influence, better service, and greater flexibility with the local banker. Many banking executives believe that foreign banks cannot be as quick or as flexible in making loans as smaller independent banks. However, many foreign banks are beginning to limit their bank bureaucracies, in order to add more flexibility and speed in making small loans. The battle certainly seems open in many local markets.

Foreign banks possess several important and unique advantages over US banks. The primary advantage of foreign banks is the ease of arranging export financing and a global network of business assistance. Foreign institutions have a broader scope of power and operations. They are permitted to engage in a broader range of activities, investments, and affiliations – in 'non-banking' areas, too – than domestic banks. Foreign banks, for example, have developed close ties with non-bank enterprises, such as many foreign companies. Many US businesses are going abroad and they are seeking the expertise of foreign banks to help them. With few exceptions, US banks lack the international capabilities to help US companies expand globally.

There is some evidence that, as major US corporations are consolidating their banking relationships, they are looking at foreign banks as a more attractive alternative to US banks. A company may have come to rely on several different US banks to satisfy all of its various banking needs, when in fact they can conveniently depend on one foreign bank to take care of all their requirements. This encourages many corporations to go one-stop shopping with foreign banks.

In general, due to the lack of growth, and size restrictions that are imposed on domestic banks, foreign banks can provide more services than US banks, especially global services. Therefore, in spite of the improvements in foreign banking regulation, there remain concerns about the competitive disadvantage faced by US banks when compared with foreign banks.

One idea is that consolidating US banks would help them to become more competitive, and would lessen their disadvantage, since it would create 'universal' banking institutions where more services could be provided. US corporations could then take care of all their banking needs in one place. Many foreign countries, especially in Europe, have already consolidated their banks to give them a competitive edge. In addition to allowing domestic banks to provide more services, consolidation would also make bank supervision by government agencies easier, as there would be a smaller number of banks to monitor.

The only problem with consolidation is that it is currently illegal, as there are a number of antitrust, pro-competitive, and merger laws which prohibit consolidation. However, recently, the enforcement of these laws has been relaxed and consolidation is starting to take place. Legalising consolidation has been proposed within the past two years and will most likely take place in the near future. Congress was ready to legalise consolidation just a short time ago, but that time ironically the banks pulled out and lost their desire to consolidate, when they realised that they would be regulated more closely if consolidation was allowed to take place. A consolidation law will most likely be passed that requires only a slightly higher degree of bank supervision than at present, and banks will most likely approve of this.

When consolidation takes place, the ludicrous former situation in which US institutions were not allowed to consolidate and take over domestic banks, except in the case of a failing bank, but foreign banks were allowed to take over domestic banks, will be history. Basically, foreign banks will then only be allowed to acquire failing domestic institutions, and healthy US banks will not be allowed to be taken over by foreign institutions, as was the case in the past. The Bank Holding Company Act, mentioned earlier, is a good example of this trend of closer foreign acquisition regulation. The Act requires foreign banks to obtain approval from the Federal Reserve before acquiring 5% of the voting shares of a bank or holding company. The future trend is towards consolidation and the retainment of domestic ownership of banking institutions, and this will make it increasingly hard for foreign banks to take over US banks. Consolidation appears to be one of the solutions to the problem of making domestic banks more competitive and solving the current banking crisis.

3.3   Structural Adjustments

The US banking industry is currently very concentrated. Although there are more than 12 000 operating institutions, most of the assets are concentrated in a few banks. US international banking is also concentrated. As few as 12 banks have conducted some 75% of all US-originated international banking activities in recent years (Spindler, 1984: p. 185).

The players

The top ten banks in the world in 1992 are listed in Table 3.1. Seven of the top ten banks are Japanese, which is partially due to the current strength of the yen versus the dollar. This is true for both asset size and tier one capital (the amount of shareholders' equity available to cover actual or potential losses).

The top US banks are listed in Table 3.2. The top US bank, ranked by tier one capital, is BankAmerica Corporation, followed by Citicorp, which is number one measured by asset size.

Merger activity

The first wave of mergers in the US banking industry started in the early 1950s. The activity was centred mostly on New York City, where six of the ten biggest banks entered into mergers primarily intended to allow access into complementary product/service offerings. The alarm raised by these changes initially led Congress to pass the Bank Merger Act of 1960. The Act created specific authorities that were charged with the responsibility of evaluating the underlying factors in any proposed merger and also the power to grant or disapprove proposals. The designated authorities included the Comptroller of the

Table 3.1 Top 10 world banks for strength, soundness and performance (1992).

	Strength Tier one capital ($bn.)	Soundness Capital assets ratio %	Performance	
			Profits on capital (%)	Return on assets (%)
1.	Sumitomo Bank (Japan) 19.5	1. United Gulf Bank (Bahrain) 85.58	1. Bank Handlowy w Warszawie (Poland) 158.7	1. Chinatrust Commercial Bank (Taiwan) 14.32
2.	Dai-Ichi Kangyo Bank (Japan) 17.4	2. Chinatrust Commercial Bank (Taiwan) 77.54	2. TC Ziraat Bankasi (Turkey) 127.2	2. Pomorski Bank Kredytowy (Poland) 11.90
3.	Sanwa Bank (Japan) 17.2	3. Bahrain International Bank 56.37	3. Bank Tejarat (Iran) 116.2	3. Bank Handlowy w Warszawie (Poland) 9.66
4.	Fuji Bank (Japan) 17.0	4. Banque de Depots (CH) 46.28	4. Pomorski Bank Kredytowy (Poland) 113.6	4. Beogradska Banka (Siberia) 9.61
5.	Mitsubishi Bank (Japan) 16.0	5. Cosmos Bank Taipei (Taiwan) 36.02	5. Banomex (Mexico) 98.1	5. United Gulf Bank (Bahrain) 8.36
6.	Sakura Bank (Japan) 15.6	6. Bank SinoPac (Taiwan) 34.44	6. Ceska Sporitelna (Czech & Sloviac Fed) 97.6	6. Wielkopolski Bank Kredytowy (Poland) 6.98
7.	Credit Agricole (F) 15.6	7. E. Sun Bank (Taiwan) 33.55	7. Bancomer (Mexico) 94.8	7. Jugobanka DD Beograd (Serbia) 6.87
8.	Union Bank of Switzerland (CH) 12.8	8. Whiteaway Laidlaw Bank (UK) 31.67	8. Banco Mercantile de Norte (Mexico) 91.3	8. Turkiye Garanti Bankasi (Turkey) 5.99
9.	Industrial Bank of Japan (Japan) 12.0	9. Asia Pacific Bank (Taiwan) 30.14	9. Ceskosolvenska obcdodni banka (Czech & Sloviac Fed) 84.3	9. Whiteaway Laidlaw Bank (UK) 5.80
10.	HSBC Holdings (UK) 11.8	10. Banco Mercantil de Sao Paul (Brazil) 28.76	10. Jugobanka DD Beograd (Serbia) 80.7	10. TC Ziraat Bankasi (Turkey) 5.88

Source: The Banker, Top 1000 Banks, July 1993

Table 3.2 Top 10 US banks for strength, soundness and performance (1992).

Strength Tier one capital ($bn)		Soundness Capital/assets ration (%)		Performance Profits on capital (%)		Return on assets (%)	
1. BankAmerica Corp	8.6	1. National Bankcorp of Alaska	12.64	1. MBNA Corp	43.9	1. MBNA Corp	4.21
2. Citicorp	7.7	2. Mercantile Bankshares Corp	10.58	2. First National Bank of Nebraska	42.0	2. Wilmington Trust Corp	2.53
3. Chemical Banking Corp	7.4	3. MBNA Corp	10.11	3. Provident Bankcorp	37.8	3. International Bancshares Corp	2.47
4. NationsBank	7.2	4. Bankers Corp	10.10	4. First Commerce Corp	36.2	4. National Bancorp of Alaska	2.41
5. JP Morgan & Co	6.8	5. Susquehanna Bancshares	9.93	5. BankAmerica Corp	35.4	5. Fifth Thrid Bancorp	2.35
6. Chase Manhattan Corp	4.8	6. Fifth Third Bancorp	9.52	6. Zions Bancorporation	32.9	6. First National Bank of Nebraska	2.30
7. Banc One Corp	4.7	7. Jefferson Bancshares	9.48	7. Society Corp	32.5	7. Bankers Corp	2.29
8. PNC Financial Corp	3.6	8. Dauphin Deposit Corp	9.29	8. Mellon Bank Corp	31.7	8. Mercantile Bankshares Corp	2.25
9. Bankers Trust of New York Corp	3.6	9. Marshall & Isley Corp	9.24	9. KeyCorp	31.7	9. Marshall & Isley Corp	2.22
10. First Union Corp	2.9	10. United Bancshares	9.23	10. Us Trust Corp	31.3	10. National Commerce Bancorporation	2.21

Source: The Banker, Top 1000 Banks, July 1993.

Table 3.3 Number of mergers by US banks, 1982–1992

1982	1983	1984	1985	1986	1987	1988	1989	1990	1991	1992
283	352	329	330	339	545	597	411	392	448	429

Source: FDIC, *Statistics on Banking*, various issues.

Table 3.4 Number of mergers due to failure by US banks, 1984–1992

1984	1985	1986	1987	1988	1989	1990	1991	1992
62	96	120	172	202	197	151	101	72

Source: FDIC, *Statistics on Banking*, various issues.

Currency, the Federal Reserve, the FDIC, or the appropriate state banking department, based on the charter of the entities involved. These regulatory authorities were instructed to conduct a micro and macro cost-benefit analysis; i.e. to disapprove a merger proposal unless it could be demonstrated that the potential gains to the depositors and the community surpassed any anti-competitive ramifications.

The realities of the new competitive climate in which banks have to operate has altered the regulatory environment relating to merger activity by banking institutions. An important factor that is responsible for the increasing number of bank mergers, as shown in Table 3.3, is the relaxation of the rules whereby stronger banks are allowed to take over failing banks. This reduces the number of insured banks that must be bailed out by the FDIC due to insolvency.

It is unlikely that the US banking structure will evolve into the oligopolistic European structure. However, it is clear that the fragmented nature of the industry will slowly evolve into a more concentrated structure. Tables 3.3 and 3.4 provide data on the number of bank mergers and mergers due to failures respectively.

Over-capacity and the need to cut costs has reduced the number of banks in the last several years. There has been a large number of recent mergers. Recently merged North Carolina-based NationsBank and BancOne of Columbus, Ohio are now listed in the top ten banks. Many of the top ten US banks have increased their ranking by recent mergers.[1]

Mergers are attractive for their cost savings and ability to strengthen operations. The merger of Chemical Banking and Manufacturers Hanover, for example, has resulted in surprisingly little overlap internationally. According to Mark Solow, senior executive vice-president: '. . . the two banks went about solving the problem of their capital ratios in different ways. Chemical had cut back internationally, while Manny Hanny preferred to build capital by selling off marginal businesses. But, it is not our strategy to be a worldwide retail bank.'[2]

While the large money centre banks located in New York, Chicago and on

---

[1] See *The Banker*, June 1993: p. 38.
[2] See *The Banker*, June 1993: p. 39.

the West Coast have been recovering from bad loans to LDCs and poor real estate loans, the regional and super-regional banks have been increasing in asset size and capital strength. They are beginning to take away market share from the money centre banks. The super-regionals have been able to build up interstate cross-border business as a result of agreements between individual states which often formally excluded the money centre banks because of their size. The regional and super-regional banks may become the first effective nationwide retail banking operations as the barriers to interstate banking break down.

Recent trends and the future

US money centre banks have recently begun to fight back against the problems of the last two years, when they have had to reduce their international ambitions in order to focus on problems domestically. Currently, lower interest rates and the start of an economic recovery are helping profits and US money centre banks are rebounding.

An exception to the general trend is Citibank, which is trying to become a global consumer bank, not just a wholesale bank. While others were pulling back, it has fought hard to hold on to its international retail banking franchise. The group covers over 90 countries, with about 40 of them designated as consumer, rather than purely global wholesale operations. Tom Jones, executive vice-president, argues that the group's coverage gives it advantages on both fronts:[3] 'In Europe, for example, a company would not use Citibank in its own country because of our expertise there, but perhaps because of our presence in Latin American.' On the retail side, he maintains, an international franchise brings a number of advantages – sharing overhead costs, the ability to market new products internationally and to export those developed for the domestic market and the capacity to spot problems in one market-place and take precautions elsewhere. He admits that the policy has not been universally successful; in particular the UK and Japan, with strong local banks, have proved difficult. Jones emphasises that 'we don't want to be a US bank in these countries; we want to be a local bank in every country, part of the local fabric ... In a sense, we don't really regard the US as home; it is just another country.'

The Basle Committee of Bank Supervisors has issued guidelines for virtually all countries with international banks. The guidelines prescribe that total capital be a minimum of 8 % of risk-weighted assets (Kapstein, 1992: p. 31). US banks were affected by the 1991 Federal Deposit Insurance Corporation Improvement Act, which applied the basic Basle minimum capital requirements to US bank holding companies, and ranked individual banks in five categories from 'well-capitalized' down to 'critically under-capitalized'. This ranking affects both the business that the banks are allowed to do and the premiums that they

[3] See *The Banker*, June 1993: pp. 37–38.

have to pay under the deposit insurance scheme. To reach the top category, banks have to meet three separate criteria: (i) tier one capital of 8% of risk-adjusted assets; (ii) total capital of at least 10%; and (iii) leverage ratio (tier one capital to quarterly average assets) of at least 5%. The capital requirements are stricter than the Basle requirements if a bank is to qualify as 'well-capitalised'.

The trend toward consolidation and rationalisation is expected to continue. Analyst Jim McDermott of Keefe, Bruyett & Woods says: '. . . There has been a sea-change in the condition of US banks generally. Two years ago they were on a precipice. Now they have acquired over $20 billion of new capital. The future is very encouraging for the near-term outlook for commercial banks.'[4] The question is which banks? Keefe was expecting more than 100 significant mergers and takeovers during the course of the year.

US money centre banks are becoming increasingly differentiated from each other as they attempt to meet capital requirements. They have developed various strategies to meet the stricter rules. Many have pulled back from international banking, as capital resources have become scare. BankAmerica, the number one bank in the US ranked by capital, after its reportedly difficult merger with Security Pacific, has decreased its international activity. Observers say it is now starting to emerge again, but with more of a Pacific Basin focus.[5]

Competitive posture of US banks

The role of US commercial banks expanded greatly in the 1970s and 1980s, which reflected the growth of international trade, the emergence of newly industrialised countries requiring foreign capital and the need to recycle petro-dollars. The growing internationalisation increased both opportunities and risk. The 1990s saw a withdrawal from international business in response to the debt crisis, domestic problems and disintermediation.

There has been a recent decline in global bank lending by banks in many countries, including the US. The trend of disintermediation is accelerating and banks are changing their strategies away from traditional lending. US banks have been leading the world in this trend and are switching out of lending and are using their cash to buy low risk-weighted government securities. 'It is in the ferment and upheaval among US banks, particularly the money centre banks, that the first glimpses of the future of banking can be seen. Already, you can get an idea of how successful banks in the 1990s will appear by looking at the way US banks are developing' (Evans, 1993: p. 47).

In order to be successful, US banks need to place a greater emphasis on profitability and capital adequacy. In order to be competitive in the world market, US banks must decide on a niche. They must differentiate themselves

---

[4] See *The Banker*, June 1993: p. 40.
[5] See *The Banker*, June 1993: p. 36.

and decide whether to serve the world on the basis of volume in conventional services, or to specialise in clients, either geographically or functionally. One opportunity which US investment banks have is in the privatisation of French businesses. US investment banks have traditionally done well in international flotations, since the US does not permit commercial banks to engage in investment banking, which most European countries allow. The result is international issuers have to go through American investment banks in order to gain access to US investors (Lanchner, 1993: pp. 52–3). Another opportunity exists in Hong Kong, which is becoming the base for investing in China. US and other global investment banks such as Salomon Brothers and Merrill Lynch are vying for Hong Kong or overseas offerings for Chinese companies. Citibank is working on global and US depository receipt issuance (Evans, 1993: pp. 62–3). Although Japanese banks rank in the top ten and have higher ratios of assets per employee by a factor of 10, compared to US banks, they have recently experienced bad loans (not reflected in the data in Table 3.1). Their boom years could be ending.

The US money centre banks face increased competition from the regional and super-regional US banks, who are becoming more powerful and are increasing their international presence. The pressure to meet the new rules has brought a diversity of methods of raising new funds. The need to maintain or improve profitability as well as finding new sources of fee and commission revenue has meant cost-cutting. It has forced many banks to cut back on their international ambitions, and to put more emphasis on building strength, rather than simply asset growth.

US banks must work to rebuild their profitability, both as a direct source of new capital and in order to restore access to the equity markets. Each bank must decide if the potential profits justify the risks of each international relationship; they must understand the business and banking systems in every country. The US banks are actually at an advantage, already having stricter capital guidelines than the rest of the world, and having experienced problems before other nations' banks.

US banks will increasingly have to look abroad for more investors and lenders. Opportunities abound in the new European Union. The United States' GNP is shrinking relative to the global GNP, which continues to increase. The world has indeed become a global market, and if US industries want to participate overseas, then US banks should be there to serve them. Unfortunately US banks are too cost inefficient to operate overseas. Too much of their costs are tied up in items such as multiple headquarters, due to their having facilities in multiple states. BankAmerica's Richard Rosenberg has stated that: 'the high cost structure dictated by the excess number of banking institutions has hobbled the US banking industry in international markets'.[6]

Along with the new expanded options, banks' capital levels must be raised.

[6] *The Banker*, 1991.

This process has already started to occur. In order to operate abroad, international regulators require banks to meet new higher capital ratios as well as risk-based capital standards. The standards started to be phased-in during 1990, and many banks indeed meet the standards. However, to assure the public, both in the US and abroad, it has been suggested that the minimum capital level should be raised even higher.

US banks will eventually have a network of branches extending from coast to coast. Although Congress is still hesitant to allow the insurance business to become part of the banking business, some feel that it is only a matter of time. As mentioned earlier in this chapter, the Depository Institutions Deregulation Committee has supported the option of commercial banking being involved in investments. Commercial banks in the US are indeed on the way to providing some notion of universal banking. Even if Congress wanted to return banks to their mould of 30 years ago, it would not be feasible. The issue of the 'vanishing spread' is very real as is the issue of the vanishing customer. Unless banks offer services that are equal to, if not better than, their competitors, they will not be able to attract clients. Banks should be allowed to diversify their portfolio in the light of the activities of non-bank banks. Almost to a rule, the banks that failed had high concentrations in one or two types of businesses or locales. Diversification should lead to lower risk due to the possible spread in banks' investment portfolios.

It is of course realised that the relaxation of the regulatory environment for banks in terms of scale and scope could lead to too much power concentration. Furthermore, this power concentration may lead to greed and increased moral hazard. However, along with the transformation of the banking industry, the regulatory agencies must also be transformed, according to prevailing market realities.

Appendix: Foreign Banking in the US

Alan Greenspan, Chairman of the Board of Governors of the Federal Reserve System, made the following remarks before the Committee on Banking Finance and Urban Affairs, at the US House of Representatives, on 11 June 1991:

> The liquidity and depth of the US banking environment have, to a great extent, been made possible by the participation of foreign banks. The active presence of foreign banks in this country has helped to assure the continued importance of the United States in international financial markets and has contributed to the growth of banking, including international banking.

Experts argue the pros and cons of the effect of foreign banks on the US economy. Henry C. Wallace of the Federal Reserve Board believes that foreign banks have had a good effect, domestically, where:

- they have introduced innovations and have increased competition;
- they have introduced new pricing techniques, such as LIBOR;
- they have contributed to the capitalisation of US banks by providing for the flow of home-office capital into bank deposits in the US and the US balance of payment capital account;
- they have tried to create a stronger dollar base for their own international operations, and have helped to solidify the international role of the dollar as well as enhancing the American banking market as the world financial centre, thus contributing to the general betterment of the US economy;
- with respect to acquisition of problem banks, foreign banks have helped to resolve problems created by the US law which prohibits interstate mergers and acquisitions within individual states (Damanpour, 1986).

On the other side of the issue, there are those who are concerned that foreign banking is harmful to the American economy and specifically American banking. Their concerns are as follows:

- 'grandfathering'[7] gives some foreign banks an unfair advantage with respect to American banks and other foreign banks that entered the US after the IBA;
- foreign banks operating in the US benefit by more liberal bank legislation;
- foreign banks may be less responsive to the community needs;
- foreign banks have bought large US banks (Damanpour, 1986).

The first two concerns are real and undeniable. Nevertheless, foreign banks have proven to be very concerned about the local community. Also, almost every time a foreign bank has bought a large US bank, they have infused cash into that facility.

Advantages of banking in the United States

Banking has evolved into a global business. Barry F. Sullivan, Chairman of the Board of the First National Bank of Chicago, states three interrelated, overriding, factors for the sudden surge of international banking, and specifically the barrage of foreign banks in the United States (Sullivan, 1991):

- industrial companies are increasingly moving overseas, and the banks are following their customers (competitive alliances);
- technology and innovation have created highly efficient financial markets – communications and information processing can be accessed globally;
- because of the effectiveness of technology and financial markets, banks can now utilise international differences to create a profit.

---

[7] The term 'grandfathering' is used to describe a situation in which entities are allowed to be exempt from current or impending legislation as a result of prior regulatory environment. This is one of the mechanisms sometimes used by banks to change the 'rules of the game'.

In the US market, due to the combination of technology, communication, and bank innovation, there is a significant capital cost advantage for most foreign banks:[8]

- call-money rates in Japan average 5.2%, in Germany 5.4% and in the US 8.1%;
- government long-term bond yields in Japan are 5.6%, in Germany 7.1% and in the US 8.1%;
- the price–earnings ratio of Japanese equity markets is 44.2, while the US equity market price–earning ratio is 14.6.

There are also significant cost disadvantages in the US financial market:

- the cost of equity averages for US banks 11.9%, for German banks 6.9% and for Japanese banks 3.1%;
- the net spread on corporate loans needed to cover the cost of equity, as measured by the New York Federal Reserve Bank, is 15 basis points for a Japanese bank, 70 points for a German bank, and 80 points for an American bank.

Time line[9]

1818

A Montreal bank is reported to have set up shop in New York, thereby becoming the first foreign bank in the US.

1854

The Darmstadler Bank of Germany acquires an interest in a New York City bank. Some sources count this acquisition as the first foreign bank in America.

1870s

Sensing an opportunity in the gold rush, Japanese and Canadian banks set up operations in California, Oregon and Washington State.

1913

One-third of all foreign bank investments of the British Empire are located in the United States. This is the peak year for British investment in America.

---

[8] The following figures refer to early 1991.
[9] For more details on the following time line, see Damanpour (1986, 1990).

1919

Senator Walter E. Edge of New Jersey proposes the creation of federally chartered Edge Corporations with the ability to engage in activities related to international banking, trade and financing.

1961

On January 1, New York adopts legislation allowing foreign banks to open branches. This attracts more foreign banks to America and acts as an impetus to other states to allow similar rights to foreign banks.

Early 1960s

Eight states – Illinois, Massachusetts, California, Washington, Oregon, Utah, Georgia, and Hawaii – vote in legislation explicitly allowing foreign banks to operate within the state borders.

1970s

The main factors behind the increased activity in foreign banks in the US during the 1970s are as follows:

- foreign corporations expand internationally, and foreign banks follow their customers;
- the dollar enjoys a domestic surplus and a dominant position in international finance;
- the US banking regulations at the time favour foreign competition;
- the US market is larger, more diverse, and wealthier than most other markets;
- the US economy is sound and stable;
- the accessible location of the US international money market makes it easy for foreign banks to compete for wholesale multinational corporate business.

1972

There are no official documented statistics of foreign banking presence in the US before 1972. In 1972 assets of foreign-owned US banks represent about 3.3% of total domestic assets. There are 105 banking facilities under foreign ownership.

1977

Due to fears of further restrictions to entry in the US banking markets, there is a surge of foreign offices being settled in the US. There is a 26% increase in the number of foreign offices located in the US. During 1977 and 1978 there is a 23.8% and 37.6% rise, respectively, in the dollar amount of foreign bank assets in the US.

1978

American bankers feel that foreign banks operating stateside are governed under laxer restrictions and therefore enjoy unfair advantages. To that end, the International Banking Act (IBA) of 1978 was enacted to put foreign banks on an equal footing with their American counterparts with regard to limitations imposed by the McFadden Act and the Douglas Amendment to the Bank Holding Company Act. The IBA requires foreign banks to comply to the same reserve requirements, geographic limitations, and banking activities as those governing US banks. Highlights of the Act are as follows. The Act:

*   restricts foreign bank expansion of interstate deposits;
*   requires foreign branches and agencies to abide by Federal Reserve requirements and interest rate regulations;
*   requires branches which engage in retail banking to have deposit insurance;
*   expands the restriction imposed by the Bank Holding Company Act on foreign banks involved in non-bank activities to include foreign branches and agencies;
*   makes the Federal Reserve Banks payment services and discount window available to agencies and branches;
*   permits foreign banks to own Edge corporations.

The IBA, along with the Bank Holding Act, gives the Federal Reserve the authority and responsibility to supervise foreign banking activity. The IBA 'established an overall framework for regulating the full range of activities of foreign banks in the United States and provided for a federal role in the supervision of branches and agencies of foreign banks.[10]

Under the IBA, foreign banks which wish to establish a banking facility in the United States are given the option of applying for either a federal licence through the Office of the Comptroller of the Currency (OCC) or through one of the states. Federally licensed offices are patrolled by the OCC, while state offices are supervised by the states. The Act further determines that the Federal Reserve should have overall supervisory authority over both the OCC and the states.

[10] Statement by William Taylor, Staff Director, Division of Banking Supervision and Regulation, Board of Governors of the Federal Reserve System, before the Committee on Banking, Finance and Urban Affairs, US House of Representatives, 16 October 1990, *Federal Reserve Bulletin*, December 1990: pp. 1032–5.

The responsibilities of the Federal Reserve are as follows:

- the Fed has established uniform examination practices and reporting systems. They work in coordination with the states and other federal bank regulatory agencies;
- the Fed reviews and follows up any examination performed by another agency. They also monitor any corrective action needed by a foreign office resulting from an examination performed by another source;
- the Fed directly supervises the non-banking financial operation of foreign banks. They also review foreign banks to ensure that they are in satisfactory condition;
- the Federal Reserve staff meet on a regular basis with personnel from foreign banks.

While the IBA went far to create a more equal environment between foreign and domestic banks, three problems remained:

- non-banking activities such as securities activities that existed before 23 May 1977 are permanently grandfathered;
- foreign banks are granted a one-time only right to 'redesignate' or expand home offices further into the US market;
- foreign banks' Edge corporations are given broader market participation rights, allowing them to engage in activities other than loans related to international transactions.

1979

Assets of foreign-owned US offices (banks, agencies and branches) equals 12% of total US domestic assets. Powers of the Edge Act corporations expand to include a 'home' state and interstate banking privileges. Edge corporations are also permitted to hold stock in non-banking companies and may underwrite, distribute and deal in debt and equity securities outside the United States. Both activities are forbidden to domestic banks under section 25 of the Federal Reserve Act (Kim and Miller, 1983).

1980

The Monetary Act of 1980 makes Federal Reserve services such as cheque-clearing, coin and paper currency ordering, and direct transferral of funds by wire through the central bank available for foreign bank branches and agencies which have maintained basic reserve balances at the central bank. Foreign banks hold 20% of all corporate loans made in the US.[11] Marine Midland Bank of upstate New York, with assets of $10.514m, is acquired by a Far Eastern bank.

[11] See B. Sullivan, Chairman of the Board of the First National Bank of Chicago, 'A Perspective on Banking and Global Markets', *The World of Banking*, September–October 1991: pp. 5–7.

The number of Edge Act corporations expands from six in 1955 to 85 (Kim and Miller, 1983: pp. 13–18).

1982

Foreign banking assets account for 15.5% of total US bank assets. US branches of foreign banks hold 11.2% of total bank deposits (Dugger, 1990).

1985

There are 610 foreign banking offices in the US and foreign banking assets account for 16.7% of total US bank assets. On 24 October, the Regulation K revision of the Edge Act defined an Edge Act corporation as

> a U.S. corporation engaged directly or indirectly in activities in the United States that are permitted by the sixth paragraph of Section 25(a) of the Federal Reserve Act and are incidental to international or foreign business. These activities include receiving deposits from foreign governments or person . . . if such . . . funds [are] to be used for payment of obligations abroad . . . The deposit account may consist of transaction account, savings and time deposit accounts, and issuance of negotiable certificates of deposit.
>
> (Damanpour, 1990: p. 39)

1988

No paper on foreign banking in the US would be complete without a mention of the Bank of Credit and Commerce International (BCCI) scandal. This incident is mentioned time and again in support for more restrictive banking measures. BCCI is indicted for money laundering and soon afterwards the Federal Reserve starts an inquiry into the accusation that BCCI acquired First American in violation of the Bank Holding Company Act. In 1990 evidence comes to light that BCCI owns several shares in First American's holding company, Credit and Commerce American Holdings NV (CCAH). In January of 1991, the board authorises a full investigation, issues a cease and desist order, makes criminal referrals, and requires BCCI to divest its shares in CCAH and terminate its activities in the US.[12]

1989

Foreign banking is not restricted to traditional banking activities. Foreign banks participate in the purchase and sale of securities and bonds. 'Foreign

---

[12] See the Statement by J. Virgil Mattingly, Jr., General Counsel, Board of Governors of the Federal Reserve System, before the Subcommittee on Consumer and Regulatory Affairs of the Committee on Banking, Finance and Urban Affairs, US House of Representatives, 23 May 1991, *Federal Reserve Bulletin*, July 1991: pp. 572–82.

purchases and sales of U.S. Treasury securities surpassed $4 trillion on a gross basis in 1989, up from $100 billion to $200 billion earlier in the decade.'[13] US branches of foreign banks hold 17.3% of total bank deposits in the US. Foreign-owned banks account for 28.5% of US commercial and industrial loan markets (Dugger, 1990).

1990

'At the end of 1990, there were 290 foreign banks with operations in the United States having aggregate assets of $800 billion [approximately 21% of US banking assets]. The bulk of these operations were conducted in branches and agencies, which alone had aggregate assets of $626 billion, or 18% of total banking assets in this country, as of the end of 1990.'[14]

1991

Foreign banks hold 12% of all domestic, commercial and industrial loans, and 33% of all corporate loans made in the US (Sullivan, 1991). They also hold 23% of total banking assets in the US (Kraus, 1991). The composition of the foreign banking community is changing. Due to the fall in the Japanese stock market, many of the Japanese banks are experiencing financial difficulties, and therefore scaling back activities. In contrast, the European banks are looking forward to expanding further into the US market. The percentage of assets held by European banks in the US had increased by 7.6% in 1990, and it now increases again by 12.3%. Conversely, the percentages of assets held by Japanese banks had increased by 12.1% in 1990; it increased now by only 9.1%. Although the Japanese banks are still the largest foreign presence in the US, the Europeans are gaining ground. In a survey performed by *American Banker*, 18 of the 22 banks questioned replied that they were planning on expanding in 1992, even though they realised that the US was suffering one of the severest recessions since the Depression (Orr, 1990).

Japanese banks

It was only recently that Japan was a small player in the world banking scene. In 1972 Japanese banks did not even appear on the list of the top 15 global banks by asset size. By 1982 they had captured five of the top 15 (Coxe, 1991), and as of winter 1990, eight of the world's largest ten banks were Japanese, as were nine of the ten largest financial services companies (Dugger, 1990).

[13] See the Statement by Alan Greenspan, Chairman, Board of Governors of the Federal Reserve System in Chicago, before the Subcommittee on Financial Institutions Supervision, Regulation and Insurance of the Committee on Banking, Finance and Urban Affairs, US House of Representatives, 14 May 1990, *Federal Reserve Bulletin*, July 1990: pp. 507–12.
[14] See the statements by Alan Greenspan, Chairman, Board of Governors of the Federal Reserve System, before the Committee on Banking Finance and Urban Affairs, US House of Representatives, 11 June 1991, *Federal Reserve Bulletin*, August 1991: pp. 644–50.

Japanese automobile manufacturers first entered the US automobile market by offering budget cars, and then expanding upmarket. Japanese bankers are following the same marketing strategy. Initially Japanese banks engaged in only the most basic transactions. Recently they have expanded into loans to small and mid-size businesses. They are also launching into the primary markets, rather than buying prepackaged from the secondary markets. Similar to the growth of the Japanese car market in the US, Japanese banks are capturing larger and larger shares of the banking market. Also similar to the auto industry, the banks have come in with better rates than any US firm can offer. There is the accusation that Japanese banks are breaking even, or even losing money on the loans in an attempt to capture market share.

The rate of expansion of Japanese banks from 1983 to 1989 exceeds even the growth rate of the Japanese car industry over that same period. From 1984 to 1989, 15 stateside Japanese banks accounted for 50.5% of total growth of loans in the federal reserve system (Coxe, 1991). The original supposition is that Japanese banks follow Japanese industries to the US market, with the goal of servicing those customers, and as the Japanese industries expand, the Japanese banks expand to meet their demand. Research completed by the Federal Reserve Bank of New York disproves this theory (Seth and Quijano, 1991).

It may be true that Japanese banks did initially follow their clientele to America. However, Japanese banking portfolios changed in the mid-1980s. In the period from 1984 to 1988, the lending activities of Japanese branches and agencies increased sixfold. In the same period, borrowing by US-based non-financial Japanese firms increased by less than fourfold. The end result of this is that while 77% of the 1984 portfolio of Japanese banks were loans to US-based Japanese affiliates, only 41% of the 1989 portfolio was of this type. The remainder, 59%, were loans made to US residents. At the same time, the share of Japanese assets to total assets in the US banks went from 23% in 1984 to 38.2% in 1988. The share of US assets went from 26.4% in 1984 to 14.6% in 1988.

> Assets of all foreign branches of Japanese banks, of which those in the United States and the United Kingdom account for nearly three-fourths of the total, increased about 380% between December 1981 and year-end 1988 . . . International assets of Japanese banks were estimated to be more than two and one-half times as large as international assets of U.S. banks, the second largest national group.
>
> (Terrell et al., 1990)

The percentage of foreign-held banking assets from the state of California did not vary for the majority of the 1980s; yet the Japanese banks' share of the assets grew from 10% to 25%. Over this same period, the British share of the market shrank from 15% to practically nothing. Gary C. Zimmerman, an economist at the San Francisco Federal Reserve, summarised the situation as follows: 'Over the last five years [dating from 1988], foreign banks' market share increased only modestly, from 30.8% to 32.3%. Rather than wresting market share from domestic banks, Japanese banks have essentially replaced the British banks as the dominant foreign banking power in the California market' (Orr, 1990). As of December 1988, Japanese banks accounted for approximately 50% of all foreign banking activity in the United States. In 1980 the assets of American-based Japanese offices totalled $60.8bn, by year end 1988, those assets equalled $306.7bn. The fastest-growing segments of Japanese activities were commercial and industrial loans to US residents and real estate.

American proposals for the future

Alan Greenspan, Chairman of the Board of Governors of the Federal Reserve System, believes that the current method of patrolling foreign banks is too lax and should be changed. He proposes the enactment of the Foreign Bank Supervision Enhancement Act:

> The legislative proposal would establish uniform federal standards for entry and expansion of foreign banks in the United States, including, importantly, a requirement of consolidated home country supervision a prerequisite for entry into the United States and the application of the comparable financial, managerial, and operational standards that govern US banks. The proposal would also grant regulators the power to terminate the activities of a foreign bank that is engaging in illegal, unsafe, or unsound practices and provide regulators with the information-gathering tools necessary to carry out their supervisory responsibilities. The proposal would clarify the Board's examination authority over foreign banks by providing that it may coordinate examinations of all U.S. offices of a foreign bank.[15]

In addition to the Foreign Bank Supervision Enhancement Act, Greenspan also recommended adding section 231 to the Financial Institutions Safety and Consumer Choice Act of 1991 (H.R. 15015). The International Banking Act of 1978 does not require foreign banks to submit to a federal review before entry into the US market. Section 231 is designed to compensate for that oversight:

> Section 231 of H.R. 15015, the Treasury's banking reform legislation, would require a foreign bank that desires to engage in newly authorized financial activities, such as securities, establish a financial services holding company in the United States through which such activities would have to be conducted by subsidiaries. The provision would also require any foreign bank that chooses to engage in the new financial activities to conduct all of its US banking business

---

[15] See the Statement by Alan Greenspan, Chairman, Board of Governors of the Federal Reserve System, before the Committee on Banking Finance and Urban Affairs, US House of Representatives, 11 June 1991, *Federal Reserve Bulletin*, August 1991: pp. 644–50.

through a US subsidiary bank and to close and 'roll up' its US branches and agencies into that bank. Finally, under the provision, foreign banks would lose their grandfather rights for US securities affiliates after three years and would be required to obtain approval for appropriate authorities to engage in underwriting and dealing in securities activities in the US in the same way that a US banking organization would.

Lester Thurow, Dean of MIT's Sloan School of Management and professor of international economics, has dire predictions for the future of US banking. He feels that the core problem is that American society is a society based on credit, not on saving. This extends into the banking market; Americans do not save as much as others and therefore the US has to pay more for domestic savings. In addition to that, Thurow believes that the current system of banking laws is archaic and hinders US banking's ability to function. 'We have to get rid of our interstate banking restrictions and also we would have to get rid of the Glass-Steagall Act, which prohibits banks from holding shares in industrial companies' (Deutsch, 1991).

Foreign proposals for the future

As could be foreseen, foreign bankers are alarmed at the prospect of tighter regulations. On 23 March 1990, during his address to the American Enterprise Institute, Sir Leon Brittan, Vice-President of the Commission of the European Communities, noted that applying US banking restrictions to foreign banks so as to require 'non-US banks and insurance companies that establish controlling relationships with each other outside the United States' to divest either existing US banking or insurance operations 'would be a cause for concern to us.' He went on to say that regulations should be loosened, not tightened. If stricter regulations were imposed on foreign banks, these would be reluctant to pursue markets in the US. The imposition of strict regulations would be considered isolationist by the countries of the world and would result in an exodus of foreign banks from the American banking scene. This in turn would harm the US economy. Other countries might feel the need to retaliate by restricting US access to foreign financial markets (Bellanger, 1990).

Foreign reaction to Regulation K

Regulation K of the Federal Reserve Board stipulates that in order for a foreign bank to be exempt from certain US restrictions, they must comply by the following two provisions:

1. In order to insure that a foreign bank is truly foreign, the bank must perform the majority of its business abroad.

2. The institution must perform more banking activities than non-banking activities.

A major point of contention among foreign counterparts is the US restriction on combining banking activities with security dealing or insurance activities. American law considers the first activity banking and subsequent activities as non-banking. For many of the foreign institutions the US definition of banking, combined with Regulation K, inhibits them from operating stateside.

Increasingly the restrictive nature of US banking is creating barriers to entry from foreign banks. It has become a trend in Europe to combine banks with insurance companies. Compagnie Financière de Suez, parent of Banque Indosuez, merged with France's largest private insurance company, Victoire-Colonia, in 1989. Germany's largest bank, Deutsche Bank, has formed their own insurance company. Lloyds Bank PLC has a controlling interest in Abbey Life Group, while Standard Life Assurance Co. owns over 30% of the Bank of Scotland. Due to Regulation K requiring a majority of the facilities to be banking, some of these banks may choose not to do business in America. At a time when capital is in short supply in America, an exodus of banks could cause dire consequences to the American economy (Bellanger, 1990).

Definitions[16]

Agency
According to the International Banking Act of 1978, an agency is 'any office or any place of business of a foreign bank located in any state of the United States or District of Columbia at which credit balances are maintained, checks are paid, or money is lent, but at which deposits may not be accepted from a citizen or resident of the United States.'

Branch
A branch is defined as 'any office or any place of business of a foreign bank located in any state of the United States or District of Columbia that may accept domestic deposits that are incidental to, or for the purpose of, carrying out transactions in foreign countries.' In New York State many foreign banks are allowed to issue large-denomination deposits to both domestic and foreign residents. According to the Federal Reserve Board's policy, these banks are also classified as branches.

Commercial bank
Traditionally a commercial bank is a financial institution whose goal is to provide financial assistance to businesses. Funds are provided by demand deposits, time and savings deposits, and short-term loans made to businesses.

---

[16] The definitions in this section are based on the *American Banker*'s special edition on Foreign Banks in the US, 27 February 1990, p. 39A; and on Cooper and Fraser (1986: pp. 8–16 and 63–6).

Although not originally part of their function, commercial banks are increasingly participating in the mortgage markets. The Federal Deposit Insurance Corporation (FDIC) was created by the Banking Act of 1933. Its purpose was to supervise, regulate and insure commercial banks.

Credit unions (CU)

Designed to fill the gap between the S&L and the commercial bank, the CUs were originally associated with a specific organisation, such as IBM Credit Union, and all customers at the CU had to be employees or connected to that specified company. CUs specialised in personalised credit and small personal loans such as car loans. CUs now offer savings certificate accounts, transaction accounts, and can make loans for residential homes and home improvements. Ties between the specified firm are no longer as well defined as they were in the early 1980s. The National Credit Union Act of 1970 created the National Credit Union Administration (NCUA), whose purpose is to insure, regulate and supervise credit unions.

Edge Act corporation

An Edge Act corporation is a 'nationally chartered organization set up to engage in international banking and investment, under the rules established in the 1919 Edge Act', as listed in the International Banking Act of 1978. An Edge Act corporation can 'make loans, accept deposits, and provide a wide range of banking services, but all of these must be directly related to foreign or international transactions.'

International Banking Facilities (IBF)

IBFs are involved in money market transactions and may offer daily time deposits to non-bank residents (Damanpour, 1986).

Investment Company

An investment company, as established under Article XII of the New York State banking law, is similar to a state chartered bank, except for the three following major differences: '(i) An investment company is not subject to the 10% lending limitation, while a commercial bank cannot lend any one person an amount greater than 10% of its capital stock, surplus, and undivided profits; (ii) an investment company has no restriction on investing in stocks of corporations, while banks cannot acquire the stock of any corporation; and (iii) an investment company cannot accept deposits, but can only maintain credit balances incidental to the conduct of its lawful business.'

Savings and loan associations (S&L)

Originally, these financial institutions served non-business customers. S&Ls specialised in home mortgages, and were not allowed to have demand deposit accounts. As of 1980, as allowed under the Depository Institutions Deregulations and Monetary Control Act, S&Ls can now offer Negotiable Order of Withdrawal (NOW) accounts, which are comparable to the commercial banks' cheque accounts. In 1982, S&Ls powers were expanded by the Barn-St Germain Deposit Institutions Act to permit money market deposit accounts, comparable to money market funds. Savings and loans are regulated and insured by the Federal Savings and Loan Insurance Corporation (FSLIC).

Subsidiary

'A subsidiary bank is legally separate from the parent bank. It has a full range of banking powers and is subject to the same restrictions as U.S. domestic banks' (Kim and Miller, 1983: p. 41).

4

International Activities of US Banks

4.1   US Banking in the LDCs
4.2   US Banking in Europe
4.3   US Banking in Asia
Appendix: US banks overseas

Many consider the development of US international banking

> recent vintage in comparison to the history of the United States banking system. Its brief history is largely due to heavy state restrictions and regulations toward the banking sector, especially international banking. During the earliest stage of US multinational banking, US national banks were prohibited from foreign branch ownership. Overseas banking was limited to state-chartered banks and to private unincorporated institutions. In addition, not all states permitted foreign branching.
>
> (Khoury, 1980)

Thus, few US banks were able to venture abroad. Most US banks outside of the United States were owned by J. P. Morgan, the International Banking Corporation, Lazard Frères, Seligman and Morton, Bliss and Co. and Jarvis-Conklin Trust Company (Khoury, 1980). These firms set up branch banks in Europe and concentrated in London, which at the beginning of the twentieth century was the financial capital of the world during that period.

The regulatory restrictions did not prevent US banks from establishing the needed infrastructure in preparation for banking overseas. Some US banks tried to secure foreign markets for sale of banking services prior to the Federal Reserve Act of 1913. Most of these initial efforts consisted of foreign lending of US dollars by major US banks from their domestic offices (Hultman, 1990).

Prior to 1914, US participation in the global banking market was negligible. There were approximately 25 US foreign branches in a world market which consisted of 2000 branch banks (Khoury, 1980). After the turn of the century, international trade and US foreign investment continued to grow between the United States, Europe and other parts of the world. Due to the strong interdependence between international trade and investment and finance, the Federal Reserve Board deemed it necessary to eliminate some of the previous banking restrictions in order to help 'the furtherance of the foreign commerce of the United States' (Khoury, 1980). In 1913, the Board passed the Federal Reserve Act, which allowed US national banks with assets over $1 million to establish overseas branches.

The US national banks reacted vigorously to the new global market. In a period of seven years, US foreign bank branches appeared in Europe, Latin America, and the Far East. Citibank was the first and most vigorous in the pursuit of these new markets, establishing its first foreign branch in Buenos Aires in 1914. Furthermore, it bought a controlling interest in the International Banking Corporation, which enabled Citibank to gain access to 13 countries and territories with a network of 21 branches (Bogen and Nadler, 1993).

In 1919, the growth of US international banking was aided by the enactment of the Edge Act, which further deregulated the international market for US banks. Under the Edge Act, special corporations known as Edge Act corporations (EACs or Edges) could be established as subsidiaries of US banks to assist commercial activities with foreign firms. In addition, Edge Act corporations were free to engage in international transactions (Hultman, 1990). US foreign bank branches increased from 24 in 1914 to 181 in 1920. As a result of its early efforts, Citibank alone had 100 overseas branches, or 75% of the total US overseas branches (Khoury, 1980).

This growth persisted into the early 1920s. However, from the mid-1920s to 1945, it stalled and reversed its direction. This reversal was caused by a combination of complex issues, some external to, that is beyond the control of, the banking industry and some internal, that is generated by the banking industry. The external problems were primarily the result of the global political and economic instability which existed during the period 1925–45. The Great

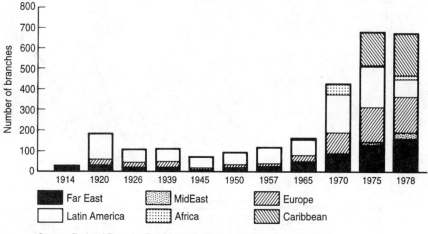

Source: Federal Reserve Board, 1914–75 Pecchioli Book, p. 59, 1976.

Figure 4.1 US overseas branches by region.

Depression of the 1930s was a worldwide phenomenon which had a disastrous impact on international banking. Because of the decline in world trade, international banking fell sharply. Failures to make repayments on international debts were as widespread as the general hostility against banking. With the outbreak of the Second World War, trade in goods and services became controlled by the state. Large shares of international finance were not undertaken by the banking industry, but rather were carried out on a 'government-to-government' basis (Bogen and Nadler, 1993). The internal problems that banks faced were the result of various mistakes made within the financial sector. The factors which contributed to these problems included inexperience of the US bankers, rapid expansion of the financial sector, excessive speculation on loans, high overhead costs, and Europe's financial problems as a result of its political instability. These factors led to a high number of both domestic and overseas banking failures. In order to alleviate this problem, various reforms were introduced to the banking industry. One of these reforms, the Glass-Steagall Act, was passed on 27 February 1932 to prohibit US banks, US agencies, and US foreign bank branches from conducting commercial banking activities along with investment banking and underwriting of securities (Bogen and Nadler, 1993).

Despite the introduction of new banking policies, the efforts failed to offset or prevent the enormous effects of the aforementioned forces. As a result, many overseas US branches ceased operations and their number shrunk from a total of 181 branches, to 72 in 1945. Of the remaining branches, 54 were located in Latin America, 12 in Europe and six in Asia. With the exception of Citibank's

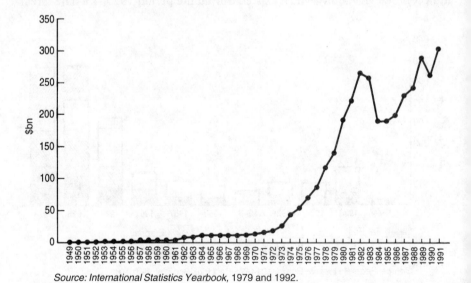

Source: International Statistics Yearbook, 1979 and 1992.

Figure 4.2   Foreign assets of US commercial banks, 1949–1992.

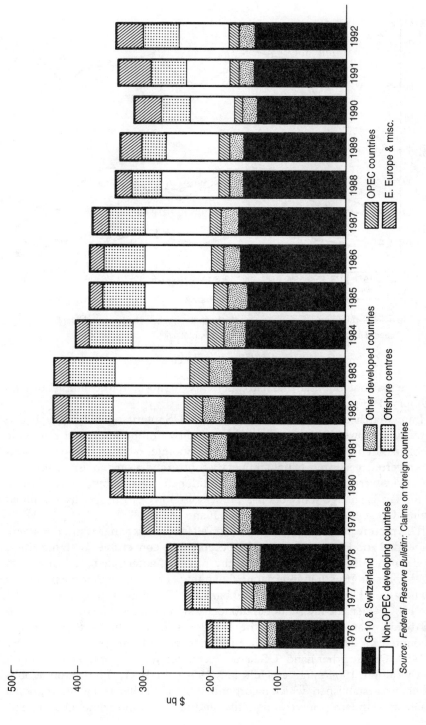

Figure 4.3 Claims on foreign countries, US commercial banks, 1976–1992.

Source: Federal Reserve Bulletin: Claims on foreign countries

Legend:
- G-10 & Switzerland
- Non-OPEC developing countries
- Other developed countries
- Offshore centres
- OPEC countries
- E. Europe & misc.

Axis: $ bn (100, 200, 300, 400, 500)

Years: 1976, 1977, 1978, 1979, 1980, 1981, 1982, 1983, 1984, 1985, 1986, 1987, 1988, 1989, 1990, 1991, 1992

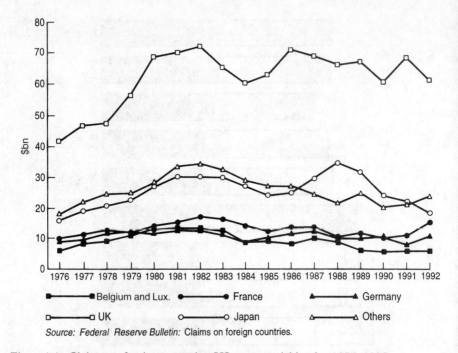

Source: Federal Reserve Bulletin: Claims on foreign countries.

Figure 4.4   Claims on foreign countries, US commercial banks, 1976–1992.

branches, all but four branches had experienced a substantial decline in business (Khoury, 1980).

Immediately after the Second World War, US international banking began to recover. However, the pace was hampered by Europe's post-war economic problems. In order to help their shattered economies recover, European countries reverted to a system of tight monetary control and protectionism. European currencies were no longer convertible. Additionally, restrictions were placed on all foreign exchange transactions. Trade was slow, as Europe discriminated against US goods, despite the Marshall Plan.

This picture persisted until 1958, when all foreign exchange restrictions were suspended and European currencies became fully convertible. With the emergence of the Eurocurrency market, the recovery accelerated, bringing forth another major growth in international banking. The United States emerged as the new world leader in international banking. The shift of status began in the late 1960s when the international monetary system became favourable toward US banks that operated from the US dollar source. In 1968, UK banks accounted for 27% of foreign office facilities, down from approximately 40% in 1954. On the other hand, US banks accounted for 18% of foreign facilities, nearly double 1954's figure (Hultman, 1990). In 1971, the Bretton Woods system was established, which incorporated the US dollar as the 'international monetary standard, source of liquidity, and means of international exchange'

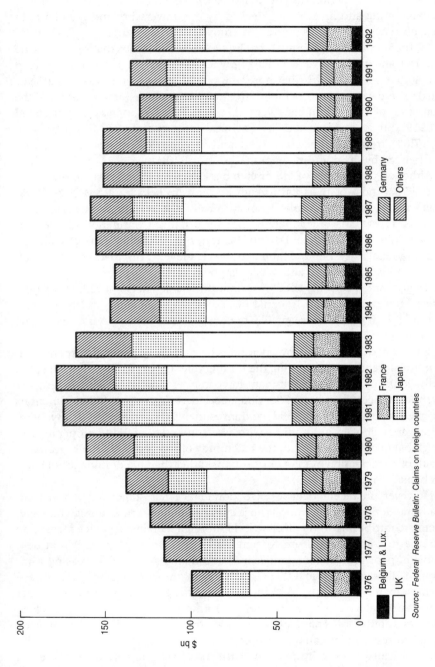

Figure 4.5 Claims on foreign countries, US commercial banks, 1976–1992.

Source: *Federal Reserve Bulletin:* Claims on foreign countries

Belgium & Lux.
UK
France
Japan
Germany
Others

(Hultman, 1990). As a result, the dollar became the most widely-used currency in global trade and investment. Backed by the universality and popularity of their currency, US banks started to enjoy an unprecedented expansion. By 1975, the number of US branch banks was nearly six times that of 1958. One hundred and twenty-five US banks owned 732 foreign branches scattered throughout the world. Furthermore, the rate of increase in assets was at least equal to, and was sometimes four or five times, that of the domestic offices. The total assets of foreign branches were $176.5bn. By 1976, total assets amounted to $219.2bn, an increase of 24%. The total at the end of 1977 was $258.9bn, up 17.8% from the preceding year, and in contrast with the 7% increase experienced by the domestic banks (Khoury, 1980).

Although the number of US branch banks grew tremendously in the 1960s and 1970s, most of the total foreign assets were held by a few New York, Californian, and Illinois banks. Khoury's (1980) list includes Bank of America, Bankers Trust, Chase Manhattan, Chemical Bank, Continental Illinois National Banks, First National Bank of Boston, First National Bank of Chicago, First National City Bank, Manufacturers Hanover Trust, Marine Midland, Morgan Guaranty Trust, and Wells Fargo Bank. In 1974, for example, these banks accounted for only 22.2% of domestic bank assets and 29.6% of total assets. However, the same 12 banks owned 76.8% of the total foreign branches and held 74.8% of all foreign US branch assets. The top four banks alone accounted for 58%.

The United States' banking operations overseas have generally expanded in an upward trend since assuming the leading role. Up until the early 1980s, US banks continued to be the dominant force in international banking in terms of 'overseas offices, volume of lending, and performance of other functions designed to facilitate world trade and investment' (Hultman, 1990). By 1986, there were still over 2000 offices with assets in excess of $500bn operating in the global market. In addition, the magnitude of US banks gradually grew as a 'result of participation of many institutions rather than the dominance of a few US banks' (Hultman, 1990).

However, in recent decades, US dominance has somewhat diminished. Many major financial institutions have curtailed their efforts in foreign banking. Factors contributing to the decline in US foreign banking presence include an increase in competition from foreign banks, the growing Third World debt problem, poor profit opportunities in domestic markets, and increasing comparative disadvantages in US products. With the strong emergence of the Japanese banking industry, US international banking will face even tougher competition ahead. There are various forms and degrees of US banking overseas. International banking activities are usually conducted in the following forms: correspondent banking, representative office, agency, subsidiary, affiliate, syndicate, joint venture, and consortia. Each vary in their degree of involvement in the host market.

There are several reasons why US banks decided to branch abroad. Between

1967 and 1972, there was an increase from 14 to 115 US banks with branches overseas. Directions were given to the overseas branches from the parent bank regarding authorised lending limits and other matters. Overseas branches also facilitated the growth and development of international banking activities. One reason why US banks established branches overseas was the expansion of US foreign business investment. Banks wanted to follow US clients doing business abroad, because it simplified the provision of services for them in the foreign country. Branches have the advantage of an already familiar name and the credit standing of the parent bank. It also gives many branches the opportunity to participate in the local banking market. In many overseas areas local banking facilities are inadequate, and cannot provide the range of banking services that US branches can. US banks have more financial resources to back up their branches and are able to send their skilled workers abroad. In addition, it is easier for banks to transfer funds, collect bills, and to reduce any collection time.

In 1965, the Foreign Credit Restraint Program limited US lending to foreigners. Consequently, American branches began establishing overseas branches in order to continue serving customers in foreign countries. In addition, they were able to loan money throughout their subsidiaries. Another factor has been the US Treasury's need for depository institutions for funds held abroad. However, some countries do not allow the establishment of foreign banks. Others have restrictions that make branching impractical. Banks sometimes feel that the risk of branching may not justify the expected profits. That is why it is essential that a bank should make a country risk assessment.

Before banks decide to branch out into another country, they must first make a country risk assessment. That is, they measure the risk of losing the bank's assets or investments, by evaluating the country's economic and political situation, and the regulations on foreign-owned businesses. Extreme types of risk include wars, revolutions, or a coup. However, less dramatic events such as a change in government can also affect banks abroad. There have been cases where a new government has been very hostile to foreign interests; such a government can expropriate the foreign-owned banks, seizing their assets with or without compensation.

Economic risks include high inflation and/or large balance of payments deficits. Banks fear making any loans to such countries, or investing in them. The bank must also study the regulations of the country towards foreign-owned branches, what are the tax rates, or the country's currency convertibility. These are questions that a US bank asks before deciding whether to branch overseas. It also depends on what kind of relationship there is between the US and the host country. Generally, US banks and their branches in other countries prefer to give short-term rather than long-term loans, because their assessments are less likely to be accurate in the long run.

Finally, when discussing US banking abroad, it is important to consider more closely the five major US banks involved in global banking: Citicorp, Bank of America, Chemical Bank, Chase Manhattan, and Morgan Stanley Group. It is

Table 4.1   Problems with rating banks

Rating by:
Total assets:
- do not include off-balance sheet assets (sometimes larger than assets on the books)
- tell little about bank's strengths, profitability, and ability to grow

Market capitalisation:
- too volatile
- subject to prejudices of immediate stock market fluctuations
- JP Morgan is no. 1 in this category

Assets under control:
(bank assets, off-balance sheet assets, and funds from trusts and other areas)
- difficult to obtain

Profitability:
- high degree of volatability

Tangible total equity:
(includes past profitability, present stability, and the bank's ability to grow)
- best measure
- Citicorp is no. 1 in this category

Source: 'Measuring banks: still hope for Citicorp', *The Banker*, vol. 102, January 1992: p. 6.

very difficult to say which of these banks is the best, because of the difficulties of rating banks; as Table 4.1 shows, each measure has its own strengths and weaknesses. However, if we consider tangible total equity as being the best measure because it takes into account the bank's past, present, and future performance, then Citicorp is the leader of this category. Despite the ratings given to the five banks, each has its own area of expertise which allows them to lead in that area of international banking.

Citicorp is the leader in global consumer banking. It is the only major US bank to offer its overseas customers all of the same services offered in the US market. These services include: 24-hour banking (ATMs), Citibank Visa, telephone banking services, as well as the standard banking services provided in the US. Also, while other banks have been retrenching, pulling out of certain markets in order to focus on one or two particular countries/areas, Citicorp has remained committed to becoming a global giant by expanding into new markets whenever and wherever it is permitted to do so.

Bank of America is one of the leaders in electronic funds transfers and corporate lending, as is Chemical Bank, which has merged with Manufacturers Hanover. In addition, however, Chemical Bank's strong international corporate finance capabilities enable it to raise money to fund corporate projects in most of the world's major financial markets.

Chase Manhattan is the leader in global custody. When a pension fund or investment company wants to invest in overseas markets, they are confronted with the problems of dealing with multiple brokers and trying to keep their records organised. Chase Manhattan Bank deals with the brokers in each individual country for them and holds the stocks or bonds abroad. This facilitates the quick buying and selling of these securities, avoiding the delays associated with sending the stocks home to the US. In addition, since all of the securities worldwide are held by Chase and its subsidiaries, records can be accessed within a matter of hours. Therefore, global custody helps pension funds and investment companies to manage their overseas funds. Finally, the Morgan Stanley Group is the leader in investment banking. Since the main component of the group, J. P. Morgan, is an investment bank on Wall Street, it is not too hard to see their advantage in this area.

Clearly, US banks are a major force in the international banking arena. Despite tough regulations and the competition that they face from foreign-owned banks, they are able to service their markets in all parts of the world. As world trade continues to increase and the world economies become more interdependent, US banks are poised to take their place in the new banking era.

4.1   US banking in the LDCs

The debt crisis for the LDCs began in the 1970s when oil prices increased; then between 1979 and 1980 prices again went up. This led to higher interest rates which affected all non-oil producing countries. It increased inflation and caused a worldwide recession. Interest rates on money borrowed by LDCs from US banks all increased as well. Furthermore, the dollar strengthened against most other currencies, but particularly against LDCs' currencies. This led to a situation in which the LDCs could not even pay the interest on their loans. US banks and branches rescheduled loans and reduced some of the debt in order to help these countries to get back on track. However, money gained from exports or loans was used by these countries to repay debts, rather than being reinvested. This situation does of course limit, or even halt, growth. The US thus lost business because these countries could not afford to import goods, especially when paid in dollars. The 'debt overhang', whereby the burden of debt servicing displaces productive investment, continues to have repercussions on the lender countries. International financial institutions such as the IMF and the World Bank have developed numerous plans to help debtor countries, particularly from Latin America, to control inflation and solve their debt problems. These international financial institutions have also assumed the role of lenders of last resort to the Western banking institutions in respect of their 'bad debts' portfolios. Murshed (1992) points out that, as the exposure of private, mainly US, banks declined, the exposure of international financial institutions increased accordingly. From a historical perspective, it is interesting to note that the lending activities of US banks in Latin America were far from being based on altruistic motives. Instead, the lending was primarily motivated by factors such as declining profitability and investment opportunities in the OECD countries, coupled with the need to recycle petrodollars.

One programme still in its early stages is the extension of the US and Canada's Free Trade Agreement to include Mexico. NAFTA (North American

Free Trade Agreement) is designed to benefit all three countries and should help Mexico to become a stronger growing nation. The boost in trade and investment due to NAFTA should give Mexico the means to repay its debts to US banks both in the US and in Mexico. In addition, it allows US banks free access to the Mexican market. Thus, US banks stand to benefit as well, with the increasing business and services that US companies will require of US banks' branches in Mexico. As it stands at present, NAFTA will allow US and Canadian banks to enter the market immediately; however, restrictions will be placed on their activities for up to ten years; thereafter these restrictions will cease. Some foreign banks will enter partnerships with local banks, and contribute their expertise, technology and special skills. Citibank, in particular, is set to benefit from the new NAFTA, since it has been in Mexico since 1929 and it is the only US bank with a fully fledged local operation. It was one of the few foreign banks to commit new money to Mexico under the country's 1990 debt-restructuring arrangement. The bank has helped in raising about $10bn from Mexican borrowers, although it is not trying to build a consumer banking business.

As for restrictions placed on US and Canadian banks, they may enter the market immediately through separately capitalised subsidiaries. As a group, they cannot have more than 8% of the total capital of the Mexican banking system at the start. They may increase it up to 15% over six years and to 25% over ten years. Individual subsidiaries, however are limited to 1.5%.

Panama, the Bahamas, Geneva and the Cayman Islands are some of the other areas where foreign banks have branched out because they are safe havens. These areas attracts large deposit amounts by individuals and corporations, because they are politically stable areas, free from exchange controls and free of corporate income taxes. Since 1973, the stability of tax rates in the Bahamas compared to increasing rates in other international financial centres led many US banks to abandon London, which until then had been an essential area in their operations. In the mid-1970s there was a growth of international financial operations in the Cayman Islands.

Individual US banks seem to have had different policies towards expansion abroad. Chase Manhattan, for example, was interested in South America despite the region's high inflation because the US had strong ties with South America and it was a fast-growing area. Chase contemplated whether to establish branches or to acquire local banks. Branches were preferable because their earnings would be counted on the US bank's balance sheet. However, Chase did not have a large number of specially trained personnel to send to foreign banks, and many South American governments disliked the establishment of new facilities by foreign banks. They therefore decided to seek interest in local banks. Chase acquired interests in five countries: Brazil, Venezuela, Peru, Colombia and Argentina. The most successful bank through the years was Banco Lar, in Brazil. In the 1970s Banco Lar made Chase the leading foreign bank serving Brazilians, Americans and customers from all nations. By that time, Chase had increased its ownership to 99%. In 1986, the name was changed to Banco Chase Manhattan. Chase later realised that having not branched out more in foreign countries had been an error.

There are over 1000 overseas branches of US banks, with assets of about $460bn. From a parent company's perspective, having a subsidiary branch abroad is beneficial. They can provide larger loans, as well as other activities that the US does not allow the parent bank to do. For example, the branch can invest in securities of government agencies of the host country. Other functions of US branches are to solicit foreign deposits, and to buy and sell foreign exchange. Moreover, US firms abroad tend to seek out the services of US branches.

The return on capital invested by the parent bank is influenced by matters such as the degree of flexibility given to the foreign operation, the dividend policy of the host country, and the tax system. US branches have the responsibility of justifying the need for conducting operations which are regarded as beyond the normal banking activities in this country. Foreign affiliate Edge Act corporations are given more flexibility, and may carry extensive investment banking and underwriting activities overseas. All net income of a foreign branch, after local taxes, is available to the parent bank as earnings. For foreign affiliates, only the share of declared dividends is available to the parent bank. US branches abroad are subject to the same federal tax on profits as the US bank. However, the US branch may reinvest the income net of taxes where it chooses to do so.

4.2 US banking in Europe

Although US banks have suffered a crisis and are hesitant to invest in South America, the opposite is true for US banks investing in Europe. US banks have been very eager to invest in Europe, but they have had to deal with regulations restricting their presence in Europe. As mentioned earlier, US banks were allowed to establish foreign branches under the Federal Reserve Act. Restrictions were then imposed upon them in Europe, following the Second World War, because Europe was devastated by the war and felt their banks needed protection from foreign banks. Abrogation of these measures in the mid-1960s was followed by a tremendous amount of investment by US banks in Europe. Initially, US banking in Europe began in the form of foreign lending of US dollars by major US banks from their home offices. As trade and investment expanded to this area, so did the presence of US banks. The advantage to US banks of being present in European countries was their ability to service the needs of US companies much more quickly and efficiently than the local European banks. However, US banks also became interested in expanding their operations to include services to the local customers of the countries in which they were located. There were several reasons behind this market strategy. One obvious reason was that they wanted to expand their market share. Another reason was because many countries in Europe have fewer regulations imposed upon their banking systems and thus, once the US banks were established in the European countries, they were also able to enjoy less restrictions on their banking activities as well.

Europe is an area in which, throughout the years, US banks have invested substantial amounts. However, a distinction must be made between Eastern and Western Europe. In Eastern Europe, US private investment would be very welcome; however, US financiers are hesitant to invest in this area until the risk represented by these countries is reduced. Eastern European countries are still too politically and economically unstable to have a significant amount of investment made by US banks. There are banking services offered to the Eastern European countries by US banks, but they are fee-based services rather than loans. Citicorp, for example, supports local currency joint ventures. Other banks such as Security Pacific and First Chicago offer short-term trade finance, correspondent banking, capital market transaction and advisory services.

Western Europe, on the other hand, is a very desirable part of the world to establish US banks. Not only are there, for the most part, countries that are stable economically and politically but, in addition, Western European countries offer US banks, as well as other foreign banks, the ability to expand their banking services into areas in which they are prohibited in their own country. One of these areas includes the combination of commercial and investment banking services. Investment banking includes areas such as the stock market, securities, insurance and real estate. Commercial banking includes retail, wholesale, and service banking. As mentioned earlier the combination of commercial and investment banking is prohibited in the US by the Glass-Steagall Act. Western European countries in which the US has a high degree of investment include Switzerland, Germany, France and the UK. One aspect of banking which these countries have in common is that they all have universal-type banking systems, where one bank can offer all types of services, both commercial and investment banking. Due perhaps to the ability to combine services, each of these four countries has only three or four dominant banks, whereas the US has over 10 000 banks.

In addition to universal banking, there are specific features which attract US banks to Switzerland in particular. One such feature is the safety and stability found within the country; another is the secrecy and confidentiality of the Swiss banking system in regard to deposits made in their banks. Since the banking system in Switzerland is relatively free of regulations, it has become a popular country in which foreign banks invest. This in turn has made Switzerland a major international financial centre. The only restriction imposed upon foreign banks when entering the country is to provide proof that reciprocity is granted to Swiss banks in their respective home countries (Barry et al., 1992).

Another country that is attractive for US banks is Germany. Germany has a universal banking system and there are very few restrictions imposed on banks' product/service offerings. As a result, their banking system has been able to operate with high efficiency and has been credited with making a substantial contribution to the stability and success of the German economy. Germany's stable economy is an attraction to US banks seeking investment opportunities. There are few restrictions and no special conditions imposed on branches of foreign banks – these are considered domestic banks for all supervisory purposes. In spite of this, the scale of foreign banks' operations in Germany is relatively small. This is due to the fact that German banks are well established in the universal market, whereas US banks tend to be more specialised in wholesale banking, short and medium-term lending to corporate customers, and export industry services. Other areas in which US banks participate in the German financial market are Euroloans, foreign exchange market, international payments services and the securities market. US banks in Germany generally take the form of either full branches, representative offices, or subsidiaries (Barry *et al.*, 1992).

Apart from France's universal banking system, US banks are attracted by the opportunities found in the Paris financial market. A popular feature of the Paris financial market to US banks is that it facilitates their participation in the Euromarket, especially in the Eurocurrency and Eurobond markets. In addition to this, US banks can service domestic clients' overseas needs and finance foreign trade in a country where foreign-owned banks are essentially treated the same as domestic banks. This means there are no official discriminatory policies or rules in existence to discourage foreign banks from entering the French financial market. The most common ways in which US banks have established themselves in France is through foreign branches or consortia.

The fourth European country that is particularly attractive to US banks is the United Kingdom. Again there are several reasons for this. Firstly, London is the largest financial market in the world. Foreign banks are allowed to operate here with minimal restrictions and they can deal in the securities markets and the Euromarket. In addition to the securities markets, US banks in London are active in corporate, wholesale and international banking. The most common ways of establishing in the UK are through branches, subsidiaries, representative offices and consortia (Barry *et al.*, 1992).

US banks have a considerable amount of investment in Europe and an issue that is frequently raised concerns the ramifications of the European Union. The initial impact of the formation of the EU so far has been minimal. US banks have found it difficult to establish universal banks due to lack of experience, hence they have concentrated in more specific areas such as wholesale banking, which is already relatively unrestricted and efficient in the European market. Consequently, any further deregulation arising from the formation of the EU will not have a great impact on the US banks. Moreover, they have emphasised cross-border, product-based and 'niche' services, which include foreign exchange and interest risk management. Since the US banks are already specialised in these areas, they will not have to try to establish themselves in what will be a competitive market. An area in which they may see an increase in demand for their services is in mergers and acquisitions advice and financing services. This is due to the expected growth of corporate structuring in Europe. Because of the experience, skills and relative objectivity that US banks possess, they could be a major provider of such services.

There are some long-term effects that US banks may experience. One significant effect may be the structural change seen in the US banking system rather than in Europe. There have been geographical and product restrictions in the US, based on the MacFadden and the Glass-Steagall Acts. These regulations are likely to come under increasing pressure by the EU, whose banks may want to penetrate the US market in order to expand their banking services. Another effect related to the structural change is the EU's application of the reciprocity doctrine. If US banks can participate in all areas of banking in Europe, then Europe expects the same treatment for its banks in the US. This means that the very regulated and diversified system in the US would have to expand the range of permissible activities and bring its regulatory policy in line with that of the EU. The convergence of banking systems worldwide was also alluded to in a study of the US banking industry (Lewis, 1992). The case of Japan was specifically referred to, due to the similarity between the Japanese and the US banking systems.

The Euromarkets

US banks choose to operate in Paris and London because these cities are the hosts of international financial markets. The Eurocurrency market is one specific feature of these markets in which US foreign branch banks are interested and participate. The Eurocurrency market is essentially a short-term capital market of money deposited in banks outside the country of denomination. Eurodollars make up the largest portion of this market. Other currencies are widely used, such as the German mark, the Swiss and French francs, and the Japanese yen, but they account for smaller proportions of the market. Other areas of the Euromarket in which US banks participate are the Eurobond, Eurocommercial paper and Euronotes market. Euromarkets are much less regulated in terms of reserve requirements and deposit insurance premiums than domestic markets. Therefore, banks operating in Euromarkets can offer higher interest rates on deposits and can extend loans at a lower rate than banks operating from a national base.

4.3 US Banking in Asia

US banks have made investments and attained tremendous benefits from establishing themselves in Europe. However, global competition has been increasing and the US banks must find new markets in which to sell their products and services. One area of the world that has seen substantial growth is Asia.

The reasons why US banks have chosen to establish operations in Asia are similar to those for entering the European market. At the outset, US banks chose to enter Asia to follow their customers overseas and serve their needs in the host country. However, banks quickly realised that serving only this segment of the market was not profitable; therefore, they began servicing the local market. The banking climates of countries in Asia sometimes provide a favourable environment in which to operate. This prompts US banks to expand overseas in order to take advantage of these conditions and escape home regulations, such as the McFadden and Glass-Steagall Acts discussed earlier.

Besides these reasons for US banks entering Asia, there are other factors that have contributed to stimulate their interest in Asia. The biggest factor is the population growth rate of these countries. Most of the countries that are considered growth areas have a population growth rate of 1% or higher. The only exceptions are Hong Kong and South Korea, both of which are slightly under 1%. Other contributing factors are specific to individual countries, such as China and Vietnam.

China, with its population of over one billion people, has the potential to become one of the world's largest markets. In addition to its size, China has been attracting investors with its newly created stock markets in Shenzhen and Shanghai, and its successes with economic reform. The stability and support of the Chinese government has led to China's economic reforms being more profitable to outside capital than those of Eastern Europe. Furthermore, the personal savings accumulated by Chinese citizens are quite remarkable. Ordinary citizens in Shanghai hold an estimated $600m in foreign exchange. Personal savings in banks are about $280bn, with the average person's deposits being equal to ten years' salary. Because of the tremendous amount of savings, Chinese citizens are eager to invest in markets, banks, and local and foreign companies. Finally, with many infrastructure projects under construction, financing opportunities for US banks are available.

Vietnam also represents growth opportunities. As in China, the government has provided the support and stability to facilitate economic reform. The Vietnamese are highly educated and hard working, and are eager to take advantage of capitalist reforms. In addition to the untapped consumer market, Vietnam has great potential in the area of trade finance because of its vast oil reserves and rice production. However, one major obstacle to US banks entering this market is the US embargo of Vietnam, set up in 1963. The first part of the embargo forbids US companies from trading with or investing in Vietnam. In 1979, after the Vietnamese invasion of Cambodia, the second part of the embargo was established. The US, with Japan's reluctant support, has been vetoing International Monetary Fund, World Bank, and Asian Development Bank loans. Nevertheless, Vietnam is reserving space for US banks in anticipation of the embargo being lifted. Likewise, US banks are eagerly awaiting the opportunity to invest in Vietnam. Finally, any discussion of growth countries would be incomplete without mentioning the emergence of Singapore as a major financial centre. Because of the uncertainty surrounding China's eventual takeover of Hong Kong, some investors have started doing business in Singapore.

Along with increased investment in Asia comes the responsibility for following the regulations of the host country. Although regulations vary from country to country, there are certain rules that can be generalised. These include limits on the number of branches that can be set up within a particular country, foreign exchange controls, reserve requirements, and reciprocity requirements. Countries usually have limits on the number of branches of foreign banks in order to protect indigenous banks. Foreign exchange controls are used to control the flow of foreign exchange into and out of the country. These laws are very important to countries such as China and Vietnam, which need foreign exchange to continue their reforms and growth. Reserve requirements are set up in order to protect against costly bank failures or bail-outs due to a loss of capital and liquidity from bad loans or investments. Finally, most Asian countries require that the home country of a bank wishing to establish a branch in their territories grants one of their own banks reciprocal rights.

Although many regulations exist, the recent trend has been toward deregulation of the banking industry in Asia. However, it is still important to keep in mind that regulation runs on a continuum, from strict enforcement of regulations (China) to lax enforcement (Vietnam), and even enforcement by the bank's home country (Hong Kong). Therefore, when deciding where to set up, it is important to consider the regulations of the host country. They can have a major impact on a bank's profit-making potential and its ability to enter the market. Also, it is very important to understand that one must follow not only the law, but also the intent of the law.

Citibank, Bank of America, Standard Chartered, and ANZ Grindlays provide excellent examples of how banks can get into trouble abroad. Currently, these banks are involved in a major scandal in India involving allegations of securities fraud. According to Indian securities laws and regulations, public sector companies are not allowed to deal with brokers; however, this is legal for banks. Therefore, the public sector companies dealt with brokers via the banks. This allowed these companies to circumvent the law and invest in the stock market. While banks saw this activity as legal, the government did not. In addition, banks violated guidelines stating the investor must take the burden of risk when buying stocks. Because of the boom in the Indian stock market, banks were issuing guarantees on the investments. The ongoing investigation of this scandal has led to the relocation or dismissal of top management at all four of these banks. Government regulation, which was lax before this incident, is tightening in order to prevent this from happening again. As with the Bhopal disaster, foreign banks are shouldering more of the blame than their local counterparts despite the local banks' apparent involvement.

After taking into account all of the regulations and other environmental factors, the major US banks have chosen to offer a combination of services:

1. cross-border corporate finance and advisory deals with funding financial transactions between two countries;
2. capital markets trading of stocks and bonds;
3. treasury products deals with cash management, including hedging, derivatives, and bank and loan financing;
4. local banking which includes meeting the needs of the corporate and/or the consumer markets;
5. operating and trade services, including letters of credit and other trade financing and services.

Although US banks operate in countries throughout Asia, Japan is unique. It is an economic global powerhouse, and the present situation in Japan and its banking regulations merit special attention. Currently, Japan is experiencing a banking recession similar to the one that the US faced in the late 1980s. The primary reasons for this recession include bad real estate deals, the poor performance of the Japanese stock market, and a liquidity crunch caused by bad loans and investments made by the less regulated segment of the banking industry (a Japanese version of the American S&L crisis). As a result of these problems the Japanese government is trying to assist in the bail-out of the banks. Their plan calls for the establishment of a 'purchasing company' with a charter of ten years. For the first five years the company, which will have approximately 6 billion yen in capital, will buy the bad debts for a discount from the banks. The banks will thus be able to get the debts off their books, write off the loss on the sale of the loans and claim tax relief. This plan is only expected to be successful with the big banks, however, that can afford to write off the loans at a loss. There is speculation that the government will have to pump much more money into the banking system before the crisis is resolved.

Despite all of the efforts to help banks out of the recession, there are still obstacles that stand in the way of the recovery. The most notable of these is the system known as post office banking. In Japan many people deposit large savings at the post office because of the preferential treatment this form of banking enjoys. It is less regulated than a conventional bank and is allowed to offer higher interest rates. Therefore, the post office has an advantage when competing with more traditional banks. Because of this unfair advantage, there is a big controversy over the future of this system, and the debate is still unresolved.

In spite of all the problems that Japanese banks are having, US banks in Japan are holding their ground. However, before a bank chooses to set up an operation in Japan, there are some regulations to consider. First, all foreign banks must obtain a licence to operate in Japan. In addition, reciprocity must be granted by the home country of the bank wishing to set up an operation in Japan. Even when a bank gets approval to operate in Japan, there are limits on the number of branches that can be established. Finally, banks must report financial statements according to a fixed format, and the government reserves the right to examine the books, ledgers, account summaries, or the premises at any time.

If any of these rules are not adhered to, then the bank risks punitive actions by the regulatory authorities.

Appendix: US Banks Overseas

Historical view: 1913–73

The Federal Reserve Act of 1913, section 25

The first major piece of regulation by the US government to affect international US banking was the Federal Reserve Act of 1913, section 25, which made it possible for national banks to open branches overseas for the furtherance of the foreign commerce of the US. Prior to this Act, US banks were unable to even accept drafts arising from imports and exports. Following this legislation, banks began to replace representative and correspondence offices with branches. The first foreign branch opened in Buenos Aires in 1914. Most of the early branches were located in South and Central America, which were nearby markets for trade and suppliers of natural resources for US businesses.

First World War

During the First World War, European countries were unable to provide for their own needs, and could no longer supply their own overseas markets. US businesses were able to step in and meet these demands, and US exports accelerated. Consequently, US banks opened branches overseas to accommodate their customers and the number of branches grew from 26 in 1914 to 181 in 1920 (see Figure 4.1).

1919 Federal Reserve Act Amendment – Edge Act

In 1919, the Federal Reserve Act was amended to include the Edge Act, which authorised banks to establish subsidiaries for the purpose of engaging in foreign banking for deposits and investment activities. This gave US commercial banks broad latitude to function as multipurpose banks overseas and perform many activities which were still prohibited on American territory. However, the Edge Act was not fully utilised until the early 1960s, when Edge Act corporations became widespread.

1920s and 1930s

The boom in overseas business ended with the 1929 stock market crash and subsequent Great Depression in the 1930s. This period led to new restrictions on banking. The Glass-Steagall Act of 1933 prohibited US commercial banks from directly owning shares in the stock of industrial corporations. This would later weaken US banks' competitiveness *vis-à-vis* European banks, which were not restricted in this way.

Second World War and the 1950s

Prior to the Second World War, US banks were primarily engaged in the financing of trade. After the war, this broadened to include transnational lending. The war devastated European economies and, after the war, US government policy, especially as enacted through the Marshall Plan, was geared toward rebuilding Europe. A short-term currency crunch immediately after the war resulted from European customers' demand for US goods and a shortage of US dollars to buy them. This also resulted in the US dollar becoming the accepted major world trading currency. In the early 1950s, there were large deficits in the US balance of payments. US banks stayed home mainly because they were leery of exchange crises in Europe. Post-war US monetary policy was aimed at reducing this deficit and brought about the development of the Eurodollar market. The Eurodollar market was also instrumental in establishing US banks overseas: 'It is unlikely that the Eurodollar market would have achieved anything like its present size and importance in the absence of the expansion of the Eurodollar operations of foreign branches of US banks beginning in the early 1960s. We therefore regard the Eurodollar market in considerable measure as an extension of the US banking system' (Mathis, 1995: p. 7). Some other factors in the Euro-dollar market expansion were the desire by the USSR to hold dollar balances in Europe instead of the US, and the removal by Western Europe in December 1958 of the remaining foreign exchange restrictions on currency conversions.

1960s to 1973 international banking boom

There was an international banking boom in the period from 1960 to 1973. This era was characterised by political stability and confidence in trade; consequently trade flourished. There was a rapid growth of world trade and multinational companies. Many US companies expanded abroad, with US banks following in order to service them. By the 1960s many commercial banks had set up networks of branches and subsidiaries abroad so as to be able to operate in both foreign money and Eurocurrency markets. Many European subsidiaries of US multinational corporations found that it was convenient and often cheaper to get capital through local borrowing in Eurodollars than borrowing dollars in the US.

Restrictions on export of capital

There were several key restrictive US regulations in the 1960s which were aimed at stemming the export of American capital, at the same time as US corporations were expanding their international activities. The government tried to reduce US payment imbalances by decreasing US dollar flows abroad. The net effect was that those companies and individuals seeking dollars turned to sources outside of the US, which again increased the number of foreign branches of US banks to 160 in 1965 (see Figure 4.1). Domestic banks were restricted in the level of funds that could be loaned or invested abroad by the Voluntary Foreign Credit Restraint Program of 1965. This also helped to increase the number of foreign branches of US banks. Regulation Q of 1965 imposed interest ceilings on deposits in the US. The effect was that when domestic credit was tight and market interest rates rose above Regulation Q levels, banks turned to their European branches to attract deposits. In effect, it forced US banks to finance domestic loan demands from the Eurodollar market. Another factor in the expansion of US banks overseas during this time was 'the limited scope for growth opportunities in the U.S. resulting from [governmental] constraints on geographic and product powers' (Pecchioli, 1983: p. 52). During the 1969 credit crunch, banks that had never considered having foreign branches opened them in places such as London and Nassau. The Caribbean 'shell' branches offered exemption from US state and municipal taxes, and avoidance of double-taxation from foreign income. The expansion of branches under the Edge Act corporations allowed smaller banks to enter the international market without large investments during this period. Both the number of branches and the volume of assets increased dramatically following 1965. The number of foreign branches of US banks rose to 425 in 1970 (see Figure 4.1). 'As some of the banks were candid enough to explain, much of the business classified as international came about because of government rules rather than brilliant banking' (Mathis, 1995: p. 5).

The 1973 Arab oil embargo

In 1973, the world banking situation changed dramatically, due to the Arab oil embargo and the associated price hikes. This resulted in an increased supply of dollars held outside the US. The petrodollar recycling process, whereby banks lent OPEC surpluses to oil-importing countries, who borrowed heavily in the Eurocurrency market, caused a growth in the number of foreign branches of US banks and a huge jump in assets after 1973 (see Figures 4.2 and 4.3). The recycling process caused banks to significantly increase their exposure to deficit countries. The associated growth of balance sheet volumes impacted the level of capital adequacy and profitability and increased the level of international lending risks. The oil price hike caused higher inflation and interest rates and, in general, increased the volatility of world financial markets. The US government lifted most currency regulations at this time and the US dollar was allowed to float freely in foreign exchange markets. The deregulation of interest rates in 1974 reduced the US banks' reliance on overseas branches for short- and medium-term loans. This allowed offshore financing of investments. Banks were allowed to pay higher rates on deposits, but this cut into profits, forcing banks to rely on better management, and often resulted in riskier lending.

After 1973

Link to foreign policy

Another issue in US banking overseas is that of the link to US foreign policy. US banks played a prime role in several foreign crises at this time. An example of this was the freeze of US banks' multi-billion dollar financial dealings with Iran at the time of the seizure of American hostages in November 1979 and the freezing of an estimated $15bn in outstanding commercial bank claims on Poland when martial law was imposed there in December 1981 (Spindler, 1984: p. 16).

Movement into international markets

There was a second oil price shock in the late 1970s, but it did not have as great an effect on the world economy as the 1973 price hike had had. US banks moved into international markets to a huge extent in the 1980s, pushed by lower profits in traditional banking markets. The 1980s are considered the boom years of international banking.

Loans to LDCs

In the late 1970s and early 1980s, US banks made huge loans to developing countries. At the end of 1983, US banks had a total of $66.8bn in loans to Argentina, Brazil, Mexico and Venezuela alone (Kettell and Magnus, 1986, p. 71). Lending margins were cut to the extreme in order to build up assets, often at the expense of profitability. At the end of 1983, the seven largest US banks had lent 137% of their capital to the four countries mentioned above (*ibid.*, p. 10).

The beginning of the debt crisis in 1982

Competition increased and banks developed new financing techniques, resulting in new risks. In August 1982, Mexico unilaterally declared a temporary moratorium on its debt payments, with a balance of $80bn in foreign obligations. This was the beginning of the debt crisis, which lasted until the late 1980s. Many other LDCs were also unable to meet their loan obligations. Many major US banks were involved and were forced to restructure their loans. In an effort to reduce increasing risk, US banks shifted to other business areas, such as portfolio management and merchant banking, which involved actively buying and selling loans instead of simply creating and holding on to them.

Deregulation and technological changes in the 1980s

An emerging trend at this time was the deregulation of foreign exchange and capital controls around the world, which led to the formation of a global capital pool. Improved technology allowed for larger volumes of transactions and the development of innovative securities and financial instruments.

Disintermediation in the mid-1980s and 1990s

The effect of these changes was disintermediation, that is the removal of banks as intermediaries in accessing the capital markets. Banks had come under pressure and their credit ratings dropped. Their large corporate customers found that they could borrow more cheaply in open markets than the banks could themselves and they began to issue their own commercial paper. The direct consequences of disintermediation were heightened competition, reduced intermediation costs, and a mushrooming of new financing techniques, while more traditional forms of financing declined. Some of these new financing products were: mutual funds, which paid market rates of interest; mortgage-backed securities; interest rate and currency swaps; syndicated lending, whereby more than one financial institution provides financing; and consortium banking, whereby banks pool their capital and resources, usually for medium-term lending.

Pullback from international lending

The main beneficiary of these trends was the US investment banks, often at the expense of US commercial banks. This weakened the banks, and drove them into dangerous lending practices similar to those that had created the Savings and Loan crisis at the end of the 1980s. Many large and once aggressive US banks pulled back from international lending due to the disastrous performance of South American, Southeast Asian, and African loans and the heightened scrutiny of bank regulators, in order to concentrate on domestic problems. The lost capital financing was often replaced with lesser quality corporate real estate loans, which became a problem in the late 1980s when many loans went into default during the recession. The 1990s saw continued disintermediation, regulatory changes, new competition, and large exposures to bad loans at home and abroad. Banks retreated from international lending in an effort to restore balance sheets and capital positions. Banks reduced the number of branches both domestically and abroad. The industry suffered from overcapacity. There was increased permeability of markets and lower barriers to entry.

Location of foreign direct investment (FDI)

FDI of US banks

Figures 4.4 and 4.5 show the claims on foreign countries held by US banking offices and foreign branches of US banks from 1976 to 1992. The largest amount of claims on a single country are those on the United Kingdom, which peaked in 1982 at $72.1bn; Japan is the second largest, with a peak of $34.9bn claims in 1988. The claims for all foreign countries was also at its highest in 1982, at $438.8bn. Some of the trends in the last 15 years are as follows.

- The peak of international lending, as measured by claims on foreign countries, occurred in the period 1981–83, and has been declining since then.
- Claims on the offshore banking centres increased at the beginning of the 1990s.
- Claims on OPEC countries have been declining since 1983.
- Claims on non-OPEC developing counties have sharply decreased since 1984.

Risks

Banks face several types of risk when they expand internationally. One is currency risk, which is related to the vulnerability of a bank to losses resulting from an imperfect matching of claims and liabilities denominated in foreign currencies in the event of unanticipated changes in exchange rates. Another is country risk, which relates to the possibility that the political, social or economic events of a country might prevent debtors there from fulfilling their loan obligations. The third type of risk is liquidity risk, which is related to the risk of insolvency of the business itself.

France and the United Kingdom

Both France and the UK act as a relay station for US capital as it is transferred to other parts of the world. US banks are indirectly represented in many regions of the world. The UK acts as a relay station for Commonwealth countries and France for many African countries, whereas Japan has the same role for Southeast Asia and Brazil for South America.

Part II

Banking Competition and Integration

5

Financial Intermediation, Market Failure and Regulation

5.1 The nature of financial
intermediation and regulation
5.2 Asymmetric information and
regulation
5.3 Regulatory issues in EU and US
banking

5.1 The Nature of Financial Intermediation and Regulation

The existence of close supervision and complex regulation of banks in most countries suggests that there is something special about the banking sector *vis-à-vis* other sectors of the economy. Banks perform four major functions. First, they mobilise savings and provide liquidity insurance and risk-sharing by transforming illiquid assets into liquid liabilities. Second, they facilitate transactions, providing mechanisms of wealth allocation. Third, they facilitate risk diversification by bridging different portfolio preferences. And, finally, they lower transaction costs by monitoring loans and signalling.

In carrying out these activities, banks have to maintain some characteristics which differentiate them from non-financial institutions (Tirole, 1993). First, small depositors hold a relatively large part of banks' debts. Second, most of banks' investments are financed with external funds, and in particular debt, so that the debt–equity ratio of banks is much higher than that of non-financial companies. (However, much of the banks' debts are insured, and a straightforward comparison of debt–equity ratios of financial and non-financial institutions cannot be made without looking also at the asset composition.) Third, banks' insolvencies have repercussions on the operation of the payment system. And, finally, as already mentioned, banking is highly regulated, although the level of competition in banking is no less than in other, unregulated industries.

The debate on why banking firms should be different from commercial firms in relation to the need for regulation has mainly been centred on the importance of banks in the transmission mechanism of monetary policy, the provision of transaction accounts and the signalling of default risk information to financial markets. The strongest argument in favour of regulation is that banks transmit monetary policy changes from the central bank to the commercial sector of the economy through the stock of inside money and asset allocation decisions. In particular, the stock of inside money, which is created endogenously by the banking system, is considerably larger than the stock of outside (or high-powered) money, under the control of the central bank; thus, banking activities need to be regulated if the monetary authorities are to operate any control on the money supply. It has often been argued that an unregulated and competitive banking system would tend to produce too much inside money, thus creating an unstable financial environment. This potential problem constitutes the main rationale for the imposition of reserve requirements, portfolio investment restrictions, activity regulations, deposit contract constraints and the like.

This micro approach to banking regulation has, however, been criticised in the past, by eminent authors such as Patinkin (1961) and Fama (1980), who argued that this type of regulation is not needed to exercise control over the money supply. Further evidence provided by Saunders and Yourougou (1990) suggests that such regulations may have produced a more risky banking system, with a less efficient transmission of monetary policy. They also showed that a 'universal' bank portfolio, constructed as a hybrid commercial bank-commercial firm portfolio, reduces significantly the total risk and the interest rate risk exposures of the banking system.

In the US, the need for a micro bank regulation system to achieve money supply control has led to the formation of institutions which specialise in the holding of nominal financial assets and liabilities, with the duration of assets longer than that of the liabilities. As a consequence, the US banking system tends to be quite vulnerable to interest rate risk. Empirical evidence of this effect of the bank regulation approach to monetary policy is provided by a number of studies: Flannery and James (1984a, b) and Aharony et al. (1986) found a negative relationship between nominal interest rate shocks and bank equity returns, and as this effect becomes stronger the larger is the mismatch between a bank's assets and liabilities; Merton (1977), Brickley and James (1986) and Aharony et al. (1986) argued that there could be a positive relationship between bank equity returns and interest rate volatility, because of the protection given by limited liability and the mispriced deposit insurance contract provided by regulators. However, Buser et al. (1981) have counter-argued that with high interest rate volatility the probability of bankruptcy increases, and this will at least mitigate the latter effect. Three main types of regulatory measures are in place to secure deposits: deposit insurance, reserve requirement and solvency ratio. The deposit insurance is a safety net to minimise the damage in the event of bankruptcy of a bank; the reserve requirement assures a minimum of liquid capital relative to total assets, while the solvency ratio assures a minimum percentage of liquid assets relative to a bank's total number of outstanding shares (Baltensperger and Dermine, 1987).

Another characteristic which distinguishes banks from most non-financial institutions is that banks perform a role of intermediation. There are other financial intermediaries, such as mutual funds, investment managers, securities funds, pension funds and insurance companies. The reasons why intermediation is so necessary in financial markets are instrumental in understanding the nature of financial institutions. Financial intermediaries, like intermediaries in any other market, exist because financial markets are imperfect and incomplete (Vives, 1991). Instances of externalities and asymmetric information, with the associated problems of moral hazard and adverse selection, occur in several financial functions (Diamond, 1984; Leland and Pyle, 1977). A bank that is otherwise sound can be forced into closure by a panic run (Diamond and Dybvig, 1983), or by an information-based run (Jacklin and Bhattacharya, 1988; Postlewaite and Vives, 1987). Bank closures are costly and could be contagious with external costs for the local community and in general the real sector of the economy (Friedman and Schwartz, 1965). Even when they do not cause failures, asymmetric information between financial intermediaries and customers, whereby customers cannot observe the quality of the services provided, can cause loss of welfare. In fact, following Akerlof's (1970) seminal paper, the widespread perception of low-quality financial services could lead to a low level of intermediation. By ensuring a certain level of quality of services, regulation can thus enhance welfare.

Thus, another traditional justification for the regulation of the banking system is the need to ensure honesty and efficiency in the supply of credit, avoiding mishandling of funds, such as investing in fraudulent activities or taking excessive risk through an inappropriate diversification policy. Finally, banking regulation can also have the scope of preventing a too high degree of concentration in the industry, both in terms of size and power of individual institutions.[1]

Although the above arguments can apply to all financial intermediaries, whenever the concept of regulation is discussed in reference to the financial services industry, the banking segment is usually the central focus. Banks indeed are unique in the financial services sector because of the important function of transforming short-term deposits into long-term loans/obligations. More importantly, the role of banks in modern-day society regarding the transfer of payments is unquestioned. Unlike other segments of the financial services industry, banks hold a significant amount of psychological sway in the financial health of an economy. There is also the risk of contagion if other banks' ability to rescue failing banks leads to subsequent perceived failures of the rescuing institutions. It can therefore be argued that banks in general are subject to substantial systemic risk, and, hence, regulation is appropriate due to the externalities that exist between investors/depositors and banking institutions. The failure of a non-banking institution has less impact because of the ability to transfer portfolios at relatively low cost from one non-bank to another. The

[1] Structural and conduct regulation in relation to competition in banking are discussed in Chapter 6.

regulatory environment of non-bank institutions is designed to protect investors as opposed to systemic failure.

It is recognised that the level of contagion varies between different segments of the financial services sector, but it is also recognised that it is most significant in banks. Fama (1980) argued that if banks were solely engaged in the functions of (i) portfolio management and (ii) exchange and payments, then there would be no need for the extensive regulation of the industry. However, since banks are also involved in (iii) the conversion of illiquid assets into liquid liabilities, as well as (iv) reducing transaction costs via monitoring of loans and signalling, a regulatory framework becomes essential (Vives, 1991). The cause of market failure comes from functions (iii) and (iv) above, especially the vulnerability of banks to panic runs. In addition, with the diversification of banks' business towards riskier markets, insolvency risk and investor protection are now relevant issues also in banking regulation.

5.2   Asymmetric Information and Regulation

Examples abound of large-scale problems in the banking industry throughout this century. Some of them have been discussed in the previous chapters, but to recall just a few recent problems we can think of Japan, where in 1992 the banks were thought to hold some $500bn in bad loans;[2] the United States with the Savings and Loan debacle, discussed in Chapter 3, and the large number of bank failures (more than a thousand in the 1980s); and South America and Scandinavia, where large banks had recently to be rescued by the government, or failed.

There is a large body of literature which agrees that, when asymmetries in information are present, the existence of regulation and supervision may increase welfare, since it should decrease the informational asymmetry's problem (Chant, 1987). However, if banks recognise that reputation is crucial to their long-term survival, they may try to minimise the inefficiencies caused by the existence of asymmetric information and in this case a free-market solution may be optimal (Dowd, 1988).

Traditionally, market failure caused by imperfect information on the part of investors has been associated with non-bank financial institutions. However, today's banks often act as agents for investors, who delegate investment management functions to them. To establish the quality of their agent (bank manager), investors face the cost of acquiring information. If there is a large number of investors, a free-riding problem arises in the collection of information, since investors cannot keep information private. The consequence of this situation is the inability of investors to discriminate between low- and high-quality banks and thus market price of services which reflect the perceived

[2] See *The Economist*, 7 November 1992.

average quality of banks. These prices are too low for banks to offer high-quality services and thus either the 'good' banks will cease to supply the service, i.e. a problem of adverse selection arises since the quality of the agent is information private to the agent; or the 'good' banks will reduce the quality of the service provided, in which case we have a problem of moral hazard since investors are unable to monitor the effort of the agent. These problems can arise for any banking service which can be classified as a credence good, that is a good whose quality can never really be established. Many financial services are credence goods, since it is difficult to evaluate financial performance, even *ex post*, and it is often impossible to differentiate between incompetence and negligence on one side, and bad luck on the other side.

The problem becomes even worse when prices reflect average quality and this average quality is higher than the marginal quality. In this case, banks of quality ranking below the average have an incentive to enter the market, further lowering the quality of services supplied. The market solutions to these problems are signalling and incentives. High-quality banks may signal their quality to investors by, for instance, advertising the training of their managers, and investors will ask banks to share the risk of their investment by, for instance, requesting guarantees, so that bank managers have an incentive to act in the best interest of investors. The role of reputation is also thought to be very important in rectifying market failure caused by asymmetric information. However, the failure of Baring Brothers Bank in the UK at the beginning of 1995 shows that the incentives to cheat are high, even when an excellent reputation is at stake. In fact, improved reputation may lead to greater incentives to cheat, when it is the good reputation of a bank which allows too risky, or even irregular activities, to remain undetected for a long period of time, as in the case of another UK bank, Johnson Matthey.

Banking markets have often in the past proved inadequate to solve the problems caused by asymmetric information without regulation. There are two main causes for this inadequacy. Firstly, financial services may be credence goods and thus reputation may not sustain good behaviour, since investors are unable to judge the quality of services *ex post* as well as *ex ante*. Secondly, investors can be incorrect in their assessment of reputation, because their information is incomplete and thus they cannot evaluate quality accurately. Thus, there is an important role for regulation which imposes minimum standards, as a supplement to reputation.

5.3   Regulatory Issues in EU and US Banking

Whether banking supervision is necessary or not is an open debate, but in the absence of any strong evidence that the free-market solution is welfare-maximizing, we will take the view that some form of regulation is desirable. The questions then become what form this supervision should take; how close it should be; and whether it can provide an appropriate system of incentives.

Banks are usually highly regulated institutions; throughout the world, the competent regulatory authorities check on criteria such as the adequacy of the initial capital, prudential controls, the proposed methods of risk management and the suitability of directors, before granting a banking authorisation. Subsequently, a bank continues to be subject to ongoing supervision. The main objectives of such regulatory frameworks are:

1. to improve efficiency and create stability avoiding the negative consequences of panics;
2. to protect depositors and investors;
3. to facilitate the implementation of monetary policies by exploiting the money creation role of banks.

The last of these objectives is the most controversial, since financial liberalisation, with the institutional despecialisation and the increasing internationalisation and expansion of capital flows, and financial innovations have recently decreased the power of reserve requirements as a tool to control the money supply (Akhtar, 1983; Atkinson and Chouraqui, 1986; Baltensperger and Dermine, 1987; Chouraqui, 1992). Ironically the monetary authorities have often reacted to the increased difficulty in monitoring monetary aggregates by strengthening banking supervision to suit the methods and goals of individual countries.

As a consequence, banking regulation tends to differ significantly among different countries. This was also the case among EU member states, thus presenting a serious obstacle to competition across national borders.[3] In order to remove this barrier, two main solutions were available: harmonisation of laws, or mutual recognition and equivalence. The latter was preferred because it was quicker to implement and it was decided that only minimum financial regulations would be harmonised, leaving member states free to adopt stricter rules than others, or to legislate in areas not covered by the EU's laws (Strivens, 1992).

Regulation typically seeks to protect investors and depositors, as well as improve the operational aspects of the industry. Another important but more controversial aspect of banking regulation is in connection with the monetary policy management use of the banking industry. Monetary policy management is usually carried out via the reserve requirements imposed on banks whereby M1, which is made up of currency, demand deposits and other transaction accounts, is used to monitor the money supply in the economy. This important contribution of banks in aiding the management of monetary policy is being eroded, since innovation in financial markets creates difficulties in distinguishing clearly between monetary assets. Furthermore, deregulation of interest rates and banks' product offerings is altering the behaviour of monetary aggregates

[3] For an overview of banking law in the EC before the creation of the single market, see Coopers & Lybrand Europe (1987).

such that banks pay interest on monetary assets and non-banks also offer monetary-like assets. Additionally, the increasing globalisation of markets has increased the international effects of domestic policy through trade accounts and exchange rates.

The regulatory response of the US banking crises of the 1930s was the creation of the deposit insurance system. Other significant regulatory provisions pertaining to the banking industry in the US are summarised in Table 5.1. The deposit insurance system is more recent in Europe starting in the late 1970s (Vives, 1991). As mentioned earlier, the protection offered varies among European countries, from full to partial coverage, according to a predetermined limit of deposit or account(s).

The Federal Deposit Insurance Corporation Improvement Act of 1991 (FDICIA) was passed in order to strengthen the Bank Insurance Fund (BIF) as well as to protect US taxpayers. The recapitalisation of the BIF was paid for by healthy banks via increased premium payments. The goal of protecting the

Table 5.1   Significant bank legislation and regulatory provisions in the US since 1900

Federal Reserve Act (1913)
• Establishes the Federal Reserve System
Bank Act of 1933 (Glass-Steagall Act)
• Prohibits payment of interest on demand deposits
• Establishes the FDIC
• Separates banking from investment banking
• Establishes interest rate ceilings on savings and time deposit
Bank Holding Company Act (1956)
• Regulates formation of bank holding companies (BHC)
• Allows non-bank subsidiaries to operate across state lines
Bank Merger Act (1966)
• Establishes merger guidelines and denotes competition as a criterion
Amendment to Bank Holding Act (1970)
• Regulates one-bank holding companies
Depository Institutions Deregulation and Monetary Control Act (1980)
• Establishes uniform reserve requirements for all depository institutions.
• Phases out deposit rate ceilings by 1 April 1986
• Allows NOW accounts at all depository institutions
• Allows thrifts to make some commercial loans
Depository Institutions Act of 1982 (Garn-St. Germain Act)
• Allows the possibility of interstate and interinstitutional mergers
• Gives thrifts authority to make some commercial loans
Competitive Equality in Banking Act (CEBA) of 1987
• Limits growth of nonbank banks
• Changes definition of bank to include FDIC-insured institutions
Financial Institutions Reform, Recovery, and Enforcement Act of 1989
• Changes structure of thrift institution regulation
• Changes federal deposit insurance structure and financing
Federal Deposit Insurance Corporation Improvement Act of 1991 (FDICIA)
• Strengthens the Bank Insurance Fund
• Reduces taxpayers' exposure to losses caused by bank failure

taxpayer was achieved by reducing potential taxpayers' exposure to losses when banks become insolvent or fail. Unlike in the past, when bank regulators usually tried to protect non-insured depositors as well as being indecisive regarding closure of banks, the Act forces regulators to intervene earlier and more vigorously when it is perceived that an institution appears to be having problems. As a result, banks will be closed much earlier than in the past, at the least cost to the uninsured depositors and the BIF. Another aspect of the Act is that banks are now required to maintain higher capital-adequacy reserves and institutions that are unable to meet the new standards will face significant penalties.

The FDICIA has received mixed reviews from experts. By and large it has removed the regulators' discretionary powers. However, there is some concern that neither bank diversification nor the real riskiness of loans are sufficiently taken into account. In particular, it has been suggested that regulators should use more information about the quality of loans, and not simply rely upon the institutional standing of the borrower. The mechanically stringent requirements imposed by the Act are expected to further reduce banks' role as financial intermediaries. Depository institutions held about 57% of the financial sector assets in the mid-1970s. This share has fallen to just below 35% as of 1992. The regulatory forbearance and the increased premiums designed to strengthen the BIF will essentially lead to an increase in the banks' costs. Depository institutions will have to adjust the interest rates that they pay on deposits downwards, at a time when they have to compete for funds with non-bank institutions.

The positive aspects of the Act include the ability of banks to establish special subsidiaries under section 20 of the Glass-Steagall Act in order to conduct 'non-permitted activities', not exceeding 10% of the revenues of the subsidiary. In addition banks may also petition for exemption from states in order to bypass the restriction imposed by the McFadden Act.

The US Congress has tried to ease the various competitive disadvantages faced by banks in contrast to the various non-banks. Table 5.2 presents the market share of US commercial banks as financial intermediaries. Banks' share of the market has fallen by about 8% and other intermediaries have increased

Table 5.2   Market share of commercial banks

Years	1960	1989	1993
Commercial banks' share	34.2%	26.6%	20.4%

Source: Federal Reserve.

Table 5.3   Number of bank failures in the US, 1982–92

1982	1983	1984	1985	1986	1987	1988	1989	1990	1991	1992
42	48	79	116	138	184	200	206	168	127	122

Source: FDIC Annual Reports.

their respective shares. Table 5.3 shows the gradual increase in the number of bank failures since 1982.

As mentioned earlier, there are good arguments for the extensive regulatory environment of the banking industry. The other segments of the financial sector do not need such regulatory oversight because they do not face the substantial externality problems that banks face in the way of runs, hence regulation of non-banks is basically aimed at levelling the playing field for investors from the standpoint of imperfect information (Baltensperger and Dermine, 1989; Mayer and Neven, 1991).

Of all the various pieces of legislation pertaining to the banking industry, the deposit insurance and the existence of a lender of last resort has been the most contentious, due to the problem of moral hazard. The incidence of moral hazard arises because banks may assume too much risk, or artificially boost the interest rate paid on deposits. Investors and depositors also do not have the incentive to closely monitor the activities of banks. Of course various pieces of legislation are in place to help reduce the incidence of the moral hazard problem.

One aspect which has caused much debate recently is the issue of incentives in government and in particular how to provide formal incentive to a central bank (Tirole, 1994). The main problem stems from the fact that some aspects of a central bank's performance are measurable, while other aspects are not. Although it is tempting to conclude that incentives should then be given only on the measurable aspects, it has been discussed in the literature that this policy is likely to cause a misallocation of resources towards the measurable aspects (Holmstrom and Milgrom, 1991). Thus, central banks tend to be governed by informal incentives and, in particular: 'There are two main kinds of informal incentives (besides public service mindedness, and the ego): supervision by the political system (legislative, executive, or even the judiciary) and career concerns' (Tirole, 1993: p. 25). The consequences of these two types of incentives have been widely discussed both in the academic literature and in the popular press. Behind the political system's supervision lies the debate about the allocation of power between the central bank and the treasury, and how independent the central bank should be from political pressure. The incentives provided by career concerns may be even more problematic, especially at the medium and high career level, where a multitask framework is usually applicable. Although social optimisation may require officials to follow several goals simultaneously, their unique goal is being promoted and thus they 'may pursue a single mission even if given a composite one' (Tirole, 1993: p. 26), if high performance in just one task can give them the desired promotion.[4]

Two issues which have recently attracted much attention in the debate over the nature of banking regulation are the 'too-big-to-fail' phenomenon and the principal–agent problem for regulators. With respect to the first issue, regulators have shown reluctance to close large banking institutions because of possible

---

[4] For a more detailed discussion of more complex behavioural patterns see Tirole (1993a) and Wilson (1989).

financial disruption. Since, in this case, depositor and creditor claims become underwritten by the government, there is a likelihood of moral hazard. In fact, as the probability of closing down a large bank declines, large banks will be tempted into pursuing risk to a greater extent. This is one of the major problems in banking today and a solution has not yet been found. However, there are several relevant considerations that can be noted (Tirole, 1993). The central bank could closely monitor the borrowing of banks by becoming the 'bank of banks' in the strictest sense. The central bank would then constrain each bank's total borrowing and guarantee each transaction. Less drastic action could involve the regulator limiting the exposure of banks towards each other, so that the failure of one bank would not trigger the failure of another bank. Alternatively, there could be co-insurance on the interbank market, with the insurer being either a public or a private body.

With respect to the second issue, the principal–agent problem for regulators, in order for bank regulators to act in the best interest of the taxpayer (i.e minimise the cost of the deposit insurance), they must enact strict codes pertaining to the quality of assets held by banks, impose substantial capital requirements, and close down banks that are not meeting the aforementioned criteria. Unfortunately, bank regulators also face a dilemma in terms of protecting the reputation of their agency. One way is to artificially sustain a failing institution by pursuing regulatory forbearance instead of outright closure (Kane, 1989).

Legal scholars engaged in financial markets research have analysed numerous pieces of regulation from a technical perspective. Vives (1991) maintains that regulatory failure must be studied along with market failure. The justification for this position stems from the side-effects of the second-best principle. We cannot be certain that welfare can be improved through intervention, i.e. regulation, when the first best cannot be attained. Regulation via the law of unintended consequences has the potential to introduce new inefficiencies. It is, however, clear that given the concerns discussed above regarding the important role of banks in an economy, governments are obliged to guarantee the viability of the banking industry.

6

Deregulation and Integration

6.1 Deregulation and competition
6.2 Integration and competition

6.1 Deregulation and Competition

One of the main arguments in favour of deregulation is related to the alleged benefits that increased competition in banking should bring in terms of consumer welfare. It is common wisdom that, since deregulation should allow for greater competition, and thus lower prices, consumers should benefit from it. In banking markets, this argument often does not apply, because of the pricing behaviour of such markets. In fact, deregulated banks are likely to be rightly perceived as carrying greater risk. In addition, if consumers have to take advantage of 'cheaper' services, they lose the informational advantage of dealing repeatedly with the same bank, and this will also increase risk. Thus, what consumers gain in terms of lower prices, they may well lose in terms of higher risk, making an assessment of changes in consumer welfare extremely difficult.

More specifically, increased competition is often accompanied by lower stability. Entry restrictions are an attempt to slow down the increase in inter-bank competition and give the system more stability. Examples of increased instability due to relaxed barriers to entry are given by the US banking system, where commercial paper issues have increased sixfold in dollar value in the last two decades, without any regulatory control over this growth.

In Europe there have been several deregulatory tendencies in recent years. In particular, governments have deregulated in the areas of interest rates controls, required investment ratios, foreign banking, and permitted banking activities, as well as promoted innovation and modernisation in the organisation of financial markets; all this has caused an increase in price competition. In fact, in an environment where national regulation has been enforced in parallel with the norms emanating from the European Commission, national financial authorities have often encouraged competition at the expense of stability and investor protection. However, there has also been a move towards improving investors' information about the quality of financial institutions and products, which should have made the outcome more efficient.

More specifically, two regulatory channels have been used to affect the market structure of European banking. Firstly, structural deregulation has reduced entry barriers for both domestic and foreign competitors and has allowed increased capital movements internationally. Additionally, the reduction of functional separation and the elimination of the compulsory specialisation of banks has also had an impact on the structure of the banking industry by allowing banks to enter markets previously closed to them. Secondly, conduct deregulation, with the lifting of controls on loan and deposit rates among other measures, has been targeted towards increasing competition. The aim of these regulatory changes was to increase rivalry and lower profitability and thus to provide incentives for a restructuring of the banking industry.

These deregulatory tendencies have stimulated the expansion of banking activities towards new markets and new countries. European banking has thus become more diversified, both by services and geographically. The expansion of banking into non-traditional business areas has been one of the most important changes in the industry. The disappearance of legal entry barriers has created new business opportunities and ultimately improved efficiency. However, it has also created new doubts as to the desirability of functions of a very different nature within the same institution. A problematic area is the involvement of banks in stock market operations, which creates two main problems. First, it increases the risk, since the stock market activity is more volatile than traditional banking activities, and thus endangers depositors' funds. Second, there is a conflict between the department dealing with stock market investment and the departments organising loans and deposits (Canals, 1993). Many banks have indeed separated the two functions by creating affiliated institutions to carry out investment operations. This solution need not endanger efficiency, since the human skills required for commercial banking differ from the skills involved in investment banking.

A new institutional framework for EU banking

The EC Second Banking Directive completed the internationalisation process by giving banks recognition across the EU and allowing them to operate in foreign markets under the familiar regulations of their home countries. Competition is now on an international scale, with the main financial centres in different countries competing for business.

In designing a new institutional framework for the EU, there are two main models from which experience can be gained: the US Federal Reserve System (FRS) and the German Bundesbank. The American experience is particularly relevant, since in the first few years of the FRS, the individual reserve banks controlled their own discount policy and issued their own money in a system of fixed exchange rates. Gradually control over policy was then transferred to the Federal Reserve Board in Washington and its Open Market Investment Committee, consisting among others of the 12 representatives of the district reserve banks. However, regional conflicts continued to exist as long as policy implementation remained in the hands of the individual reserve banks. Smooth operation of the system only came about with the full centralisation under the Board of Governors and the Federal Open Market Committee. The ability to effectively administer monetary policy was also a significant factor favouring centralisation.[1]

While one would not argue that the Europe of the 1990s will go through the same experience as the US in the first few decades of this century, Europe can draw some lessons from the US (Eichengreen, 1992). In particular, the US experience suggests that the details of a close and efficient coordination of national central banks must be agreed in advance and no issue related to the implementation of such coordination should be left unresolved. For monetary unification to work, national central banks must be very closely coordinated. In fact, international stabilisation has the characteristics of a public good and thus there is no incentive for any individual national authority to bear its cost (Casella and Feinstein, 1989). An efficient solution is only achieved with transnational control. Although the European policy makers have recognised the need for central coordination, the Stage 2 proposals still leave room for some autonomy and thus possible inefficiencies. This is likely to cause conflicts between the newly created European Central Bank (ECB) and the national authorities, which will be trying to test their remaining power for independent action. To avoid this situation, the statutes of the ECB must explicitly delineate the hierarchy of authority and the boundaries of control.

It has been proposed that the future ECB should have a high degree of independence, along the lines of the German Bundesbank. This is based on the findings of empirical research which suggests that independent central banks have been more successful than dependent ones in keeping inflation low without destabilising the economy or hindering growth (Alesina, 1989; Grilli *et al.*, 1991).

Alesina and Grilli (1992) argue that the proposed institutional structure of the ECB is very similar to the structure of the Bundesbank. Banking regulatory control in Germany is exercised by two bodies: the Deutsche Bundesbank and the Federal Banking Supervisory Board. After the Second World War, the occupying forces closed down the Deutsche Reichsbank, which had been created in 1871 with the formation of the first German Reich. In its place, three state central banks were established in the Western part of Germany, with a central facility called Bank Deutscher Länder, which also issued notes. This system was similar to the US FRS and the state central banks had considerable independence. In 1957, under the new Central Bank Law, the Bank Deutscher Länder was replaced by the Deutsche Bundesbank, and the state central banks became mere branches of the Bundesbank. At present, the Deutsche Bundesbank consists of eleven state banks with 200 branches. Although the

---

[1] For more details on the history of the early years of the Federal Reserve System, see Eichengreen (1992).

Bundesbank is expected to support the German government's monetary policy and maintain the stability of the mark, it is in the main independent of the government.

The degree of independence of a central bank from the government is not easy to measure because of the many aspects involved in this relationship. There are at least two categories of independence recognised by the literature: political and economic (Grilli *et al.*, 1991). Political independence is achieved when the central bank can decide upon its economic policy objectives without interference from the government. One of the most important factors in achieving political independence is the tenure of the directors. Directors with short-term appointments are more likely to succumb to political pressure in an attempt to secure their reappointment (Alt, 1991).[2] The proposed term of office for the president of the ECB is the same as that of the governor of the Bundesbank – eight years. This is the longest fixed-term appointment of this nature in Europe, and even where the duration is not specified, as in Italy, France and Denmark, the average actual term is usually shorter, and sudden dismissal is possible. With respect to the two main decision-making bodies within the ECB, the Council and the Executive Committee, the proposed minimum term is five years: Executive Committee members will be elected for eight years, while the members of the Council will be the 12 governors of the EU national central banks; the statute of the ECB prescribes a minimum term of five years for any Council member.

The political independence of the ECB also derives from the degree of involvement of the government in monetary policy. The proposed statute gives a great degree of independence to the ECB, since it does not require approval of monetary policy decisions by the national governments or the EU. In addition, representatives of the EU cannot be part of the ECB's Council and furthermore cannot give instructions to any member of the ECB's Board. All these regulations are very similar to those of the Bundesbank.

The third factor determining a central bank's political independence is the explicit stating of the bank's objectives in its statute, so that when the government changes, the objectives of the central bank cannot be changed. The ECB statute states that the main objective of the bank is price stability – and this is again in line with the Bundesbank.

Economic independence has been defined as 'the ability to use without restrictions monetary policy instruments to pursue monetary policy goals' (Alesina and Grilli, 1992: p. 56). In this respect too, the proposed statute of the ECB is rather similar to that of the Bundesbank, since it would not permit the ECB to open lines of credit to EU or national public bodies, or to participate in the primary market for government bonds. Thus, according to the present proposals, the ECB will have a relatively high degree of both political and economic independence, although some conflicts between the ECB and the

[2] Short-term appointments also increase uncertainty about the conduct of monetary policy by the central bank (Alesina, 1989).

national central banks could arise if the mechanisms of control are not better specified.

6.2   Integration and Competition

Globalisation undoubtedly represents one of the most significant trends in the world economy in recent years, not just for the financial sector but for all major industries, to differing degrees. Global integration changes the competitive posture of firms and thus has a profound effect on the long-run structure of an industry, as well as on the strategic planning of individual companies (Porter, 1986).

In the financial sector, integration started as far back as the 1960s, but floating exchange rates and interest rates, and the consequent increase in the flow of capital between countries, accelerated this process (Pecchioli, 1983). New financial instruments were created to facilitate transactions which were mainly speculative in nature. A 24-hour currency market, which later also incorporated transactions in the short-term money markets, allowed financial activity to continue around the clock in the main world financial centres (Kohlagen, 1983). Futures markets also expanded worldwide, with new assets, such as government bonds and shares, being added to the foreign currencies. The major national stock markets were deregulated and modernised.

Establishing a single European Community market of over 320 million people by removing non-tariff barriers between the member states is expected to lead to substantial gains in economic welfare. Economic theory suggests that it should help in decreasing costs and prices. The greater dynamism of the competitive process should also stimulate trade, promote entry, new investments, cause restructuring and multinationalisation of firms, generate changes in location and foster technological progress. Eventually these changes may lead to increased growth and employment. At the level of resource allocation, Jacquemin (1982) identifies three effects of EU integration: (i) an improvement in production efficiency through the enlargement of the market; (ii) a reduction in monopoly power in national markets; and (iii) a possible greater range and diversity of some products and services, although in the long run this third effect may disappear. The other side of the coin is that there will also be costs of adjustment.

The traditional theory of integration, which originated from Viner's (1950) seminal contribution, assumes homogeneous products, perfect competition and constant returns to scale. In more recent years authors have recognised the need to incorporate product differentiation, imperfect competition and scale economies. These improvements make the theory more readily applicable to the empirical issues, since even after the liberalisation in Europe, intra-Community trade is still likely to be affected by extensive product differentiation, non-convexity in production, incomplete information and various forms of imperfectly competitive behaviour of both collusive and non-collusive types. The sources of these imperfections lie in the exogenous characteristics of the demand and costs functions, as well as in the strategies adopted by private and public agents. In fact, many of the potential gains in completing the internal market rely on the existence of these imperfections.

The economics of integration has long recognised the importance of imperfect competition. Viner (1950) had already mentioned economies of scale as a possible source of benefits from customs union. Similarly, other authors had underlined the importance of product differentiation for many internationally traded goods. For example, Johnson (1967) was already calling for general equilibrium models incorporating monopolistic competition.

Two types of approaches can be identified in the literature. The first one is concerned with the introduction of the imperfect competition features mentioned above into the traditional customs union theory. For example, Corden (1972) offers the first convincing attempt to show that exploitation of scale economies can be an important motive for such union and Pomfret (1986) analyses efforts to incorporate some missing pieces which could improve the theoretical framework, such as transport costs, tariffs outside the union and bargaining motives for preferential arrangements.

The second type of theoretical approach also views the international market as imperfectly competitive where economies of scale and product differentiation play a crucial role, but its focus is on the analysis of the conduct of trade and trade policy in the corresponding strategic environment where a relatively small number of economic agents make interdependent decisions. The names of Brander, Spencer Krugman, Grossman and Helpman are all well known in this area and have worked at models of imperfect competition that can be used for measuring the effects of suppressing trade barriers between member states. There are two types of models: partial equilibrium and general equilibrium models.

General equilibrium models of imperfect competition are quite rare and none has been applied to the European Community. Two recent papers are, however, particularly relevant for evaluating the effects of completing the single market. Goto (1988) develops a general equilibrium trade model under imperfect competition which incorporates labour market imperfection and variable elasticity of substitution. It shows that the opening up of trade can bring about several gains, including greater consumer satisfaction due to an increase in the variety of goods; decrease in monopoly power; technical efficiency due to the lowering of average costs; decrease in unemployment as a consequence of reduced imperfection in the labour market; and contribution to economic growth through the release of capital resources from the distorted sector. These findings fully support the conclusions of the European Commission's report on the benefits of a single market (Commission of the European Community, 1988). Harris and Kwakwa (1988) have used a dynamic general equilibrium model for a small open economy, which incorporates imperfect competition, scale economies, entry and exit dynamics and some labour rigidity, to analyse the effects of the 1988 Canada–United States Free Trade Agreement. They conclude that there are large gains in production from improvements in productivity achieved in the scale-economy-intensive industries through a process of rationalisation and that the adjustment costs imposed on the Canadian economy in terms of job losses could be small.

Partial equilibrium models under imperfect competition have also been applied to international trade. Several of them have used data on Europe to simulate the effects of various industrial and commercial policies on welfare (d'Aspremont et al., 1988). There seems to be agreement among them that more welfare gains would derive from full integration of the European markets rather than from a simple reduction in barriers to trade.

It is a well-known conclusion of the theory of oligopoly that oligopolistic firms will generally be better off if they collude than if they do not, and that a price war may have damaging consequences. However, open collusive behaviour is not allowed and, anyway, experience teaches us that collusive equilibrium is unstable because of the incentives to cheat. The concept of 'strategic behaviour' becomes thus central to the theory of imperfect competition. Following Schelling (1960: p. 160), a strategic move can be defined as 'one that influences the other person's choice in a manner favourable to oneself by affecting the other person's expectations of how oneself will behave'.

The European economies during the 1980s have been perceived as depending on such strategic relationships, the actors being firms which are endowed with varying powers and which behave so as to influence the actions and responses of their current and potential competitors and to anticipate the new conditions of the European single market. Many firms have had to cooperate with their competitors over common components and yet maintain keen competition at the final product stage. This they have achieved by erecting barriers against new players likely to enter the market; by merging in order to control products likely to be substitutes for their own products; by improving their bargaining position vis-à-vis suppliers and purchasers; and through other such strategic moves which influence the balance of forces in the industry (Stiglitz and Mathewson, 1986; Jacquemin, 1987).

Viewed in this way, competitiveness is not a series of simultaneous interactions between passive agents in which comparative advantages, market structure and competitor's behaviour are taken as given. Instead, it is a sequential game in which the application of new forms of organisation, the opening up of new markets and the introduction of new products and technologies continuously undermine the equilibrium and modify the rules of the strategic game. The completion of the internal market will have a different impact on the strategies to be implemented by firms depending on the type of structural environment of the different sectors. In this respect, three main types of structural environment have been identified by Buigues and Jacquemin (1988): fragmented, specialised and with volume as the main feature.

A fragmented structural environment is one where small firms predominate and only very few firms may hold a market share sufficient to enable them to exercise an influence in the industry; costs of entry and withdrawal are low; economies of scale are small; product and customer differentiation are high and change over time, so that many small firms can coexist with varying and unstable margins which tend to depend on the quality of their management. In industries with such characteristics, completion of the internal market should have a limited impact, unless the rules of competition change and there is a move towards large-scale production of standardised goods. Often factors such as local or regional differences in consumer tastes play an important role. Examples of such type of industries are breadmaking and some food processing in general, wooden furniture, leather.

Specialised structural environments are characterised by small firms existing alongside large ones; product differentiation is common, exploited and there are niches of limited size for very specific products, which explain the existence of small firms; several technologies may coexist and there is no dominant standard. Emerging industries are often of this type (e.g. lasers, medical equipment, microcomputers). These sectors tend to be affected by technological development which may alter the boundaries and nature of the activity. The fundamental choice for firms in these industries concerns the breadth of their product range and the geographical area to be served. Completion of the internal market may have a considerable impact on specialised industries, especially because a product or market niche is likely to expand with the size of the geographical area covered. So far, non-tariff barriers have hampered intra-Community trade and the removal of these barriers may encourage the dissemination and adoption of new technologies and new products.

In structural environments where volume is the main feature, market share is very important, since profitability depends on it. Thus, large firms predominate and the potential for differentiation is low (e.g. office machinery, data processing machinery, telecommunications equipment, basic chemicals). Some of these industries also depend on public contracts and have a very high level of R&D spending. They may benefit by the removal of some non-tariff barriers; however, they already tend to have a geographically expanded market.

The strategies employed in recent years by European firms point to a new trend. Firms have tried to concentrate on their main product line, withdrawing from marginal activities, in an effort to increase their geographical diversification rather than maintain product diversification in a limited geographical area. Mergers, takeovers and divestiture have been used to better exploit returns to scale, achieve larger geographical markets and greater division of labour within Europe. Cooperation arrangements can also achieve these goals, in so far as they promote synergies, avoid costly duplication, internalise spillover effects, encourage the dissemination of technological information, reduce the marketing time of new products or processes and allow a better distribution of risk among partners.[3]

[3] Recent studies have confirmed that cooperative behaviour can have positive welfare effects in industries characterised by R&D activities generating spillover effects. See Katz (1987) and d'Aspremont and Jacquemin (1988).

Integration and the EMS

The major goal of the EMS was to create 'a zone of increasing monetary stability in Europe'; according to a large number of studies, it has been relatively successful in achieving this aim (Cobham, 1989; de Grauwe and Peeters, 1989; Folkerts-Landau and Mathieson, 1989; Giavazzi and Giovannini, 1989a and 1989b; Giavazzi and Spaventa, 1989; McDonald and Zis, 1989; Padoa-Schioppa et al., 1987; Thygesen, 1988; Ungerer, 1989). Since 1978, inflation rates of member countries have declined substantially and, more importantly, the differences in inflation rates between countries have narrowed. There is also agreement that the disinflationary effect was caused by either the fixed exchange rate mechanism, or some 'imported credibility' effects, mainly due to the low-inflation reputation of Germany, or both (Collins, 1988; Dornbusch, 1991; Giavazzi and Giovannini, 1989a and 1989b; Giavazzi and Pagano, 1988).

However, the success of the EMS has been limited by its short-term focus on exchange rate stability and the limited power of its institutions. Moreover, the EMS was not designed to evolve into the EMU, since it has no institutional arrangement for coordinating monetary policy. Individual countries' monetary authorities are still independent. The large speculative movements which followed the liberalisation of the trade in financial services and the integration of capital markets are an indication that tighter economic policy cooperation and a firmer commitment to fixed exchange rates are needed. This is what the Delors Report set out to correct: according to this report, decision-making power over economic and monetary policy should be gradually transferred from the national authorities to a new independent European Central Bank, operating in a single currency area.

Recently, the EMS has come under increasing pressure and currencies like the Italian lira and the British pound have been outside the system for protracted periods. There is strong evidence that financial markets have not taken the view that exchange rates are now fixed and yield differentials remain quite substantial. This means that the convergence of inflation rates is not reflected by interest rates, giving some countries, like Germany, relatively low realised real interest rates compared to other countries, like Italy. If exchange rates remain fixed, this situation will create problems of financial instability, given the high debt ratio of a country like Italy.[4]

Three minimum conditions are thought to be necessary for the creation of a monetary union:

1. the complete convertibility of currencies;
2. the complete liberalisation of capital movements in financial markets which are fully integrated;
3. fixed exchange rate parities.

---

[4] For a discussion of these issue in relation to Ireland, see Dornbusch (1988) and Kremers (1990).

The achievement of these conditions requires coordination of the monetary policies of the member states, but it does not necessarily require either the creation of a European central bank or the adoption of a single currency. Nevertheless, the most accepted view is that a change in institutions and policies is needed to achieve EMU. To understand why this is so, we need to go back to the policies of the 1960s and 1970s.

For the most part of these two decades, it was believed that monetary policy should aim at a number of objectives, such as full employment, sustainable economic growth, price stability, and that, in a system of irrevocably fixed exchange rates, individual countries would simply move along the long-term Phillips, curve, i.e. the trade-off between inflation and unemployment. However, in the last decade, price stability has become the only direct objective of monetary policy: controlling inflation is the precondition for achieving other economic goals. Towards this goal, public confidence in the ability and commitment of central banks to control inflation, i.e. the credibility of the monetary authorities, has become essentially important. The Delors Report accepts this view and recommends a complete shift in regime, with changes in institutions and policies 'for economic, psychological and political reasons'. The adoption of a single currency and the creation of a single and independent monetary authority, with the power to design and implement a common monetary policy with the main objective of price stability, is therefore aimed at gaining the credibility of the private sector agents, given that monetary union is thought to be irreversible.

7

From Imperfect Competition to Contestability

7.1 Integration and competitive
behaviour
7.2 Entry and contestability

7.1 Integration and Competitive Behaviour

National banking markets worldwide are becoming increasingly integrated; it is not just the markets for syndicated loans, bond underwriting and other wholesale products which have been operating on an international scale for a quite long time, but also retail banking is becoming international business. As a consequence, the nature of competition in banking is also changing, together with the structure of the industry. How exactly these changes will take place, and the final configuration of the banking sector, will depend on a number of factors. There is agreement in the literature on the consequences of some of these factors, while other factors are much less well understood.

Efficiency and economies of scale and scope

Improved profitability, larger amounts of funds intermediated, lower prices and better quality services for customers are all signs of greater efficiency. It is, however, very difficult to determine empirically the existence of scale or scope efficiencies in banking. In his monograph on mergers among large banks, Revell (1987) examines various econometric studies, nearly all from the United States, of economies of scale and scope in banking. Although these results need to be interpreted with care, they seem to suggest that economies of scale and scope are small and elusive, and that they are exhausted at a modest size.

The existence of economies of scale in banking is indeed very difficult to assess. Even if it were found that larger banks had lower overall operating cost ratios, the significance of this finding would probably be upset by one of two factors. The first factor is the business mix that is important in interpreting operating cost ratios and gross earnings margins, as explained in Revell (1980). The interest margins and the operating costs are so much higher in retail banking than in wholesale – sometimes as much as twenty times higher – that it matters greatly which proportion of each type of business a bank has. The second factor is the cost dispersion among banks of similar size. Humphrey (1987) observed that the variation in cost among banks can be split into two categories: scale or cost economies across different sized banks, and cost differences among similarly sized banks. Using data on commercial banks, he showed that estimated cost economies are relatively small in comparison with existing differences in average cost levels.

The literature on scale efficiency in banking suggests the average cost curve has a relatively flat U-shape. This implies that very small and very large banking institutions tend to be less efficient than medium-sized ones (Humphrey, 1990). Although there is agreement on this general statement, studies disagree about the actual location of the flat bottom of the average cost curve, that is the range where banks appear to be most efficient. Studies which included in their samples banking institutions with under $1bn in assets locate the bottom of the average cost curve between $75m and $300m in assets (Berger et al., 1987; Ferrier and Lovell, 1990; Berger and Humphrey, 1991; Bauer et al., 1992). However, studies which include only banks with above $1bn in assets locate minimum average costs between $2bn and $10bn in assets (Hunter and Timme, 1986 and 1991; Noulas et al., 1990; Hunter et al., 1990). This contradiction in the findings suggests that a significant factor linked to bank size might have been omitted from these studies, or that the functional form used might be inadequate to incorporate the technologies of both small and large firms in the same model.

McAllister and McManus (1993) criticise in particular the commonly used translog cost function specification which, they argue, is not a good approximation when it is applied to banks of different sizes. In fact, the assumption behind the translog function is that the ray average cost curve is symmetrically U-shaped. This implies that, if small banks enjoy economies of scale, by imposing symmetry, it would always appear that large banks experience diseconomies of scale. Further, the translog approximation is also based on an average product mix; this badly reflects the reality of large banks which, especially in the last decade, have diversified their services away from the more traditional banking business. By using non-parametric estimation procedures and adding risk to their analysis, McAllister and McManus concluded that below $500m in total assets there appear to be increasing returns to scale for banks, and approximately constant returns from there to the upper limit of their sample, which was about $10bn assets.

The introduction of risk as one of the factors affecting efficiency is of particular interest. Diamond (1984) in his delegated monitoring model acknowledges the importance of the relationship between diversification and asset risk in the theory of intermediation. Since asset diversification reduces risk, it also reduces the amount of costly financial capital that an intermediary must hold. Theoretical models of financial intermediation suggests that this is the most important source of returns to scale in banking. This follows from the nature of the relationship between a bank and its creditors, which is characterised by asymmetry of information and moral hazard. Under these circumstances, bank deposits have the form of debt securities (Townsend, 1979; Gale and Hellwig, 1985; Williamson, 1986). Hence, a financial intermediary must have enough financial capital to minimise the probability that it will default on its debt and thus protect depositors and bond-holders from the risk associated with its asset portfolio. The diseconomy comes from the increased costs due to this financial capital being much more costly than alternative sources of finance, such as deposits. However, the need for expensive financial capital lessens with the reduction in risk. This reduction could come from an increase in the loan portfolio size which has been associated with a lower variance of returns, presumably because of diversification benefits (McAllister and McManus, 1993). In fact, up to about $1bn, the standard deviation of the rate of return falls very steeply as size increases and thus financial scale economies are enjoyed, due to the decrease of the average costs of running the fund.

A potential difficulty worth noting is that most scale economy studies do not use a frontier estimation method. In theory, scale economies apply only to the efficient frontier; however, if empirical studies also include data from banks off the frontier, scale efficiencies could then be confounded with differences in X-efficiency. In practice, this does not appear to be a significant drawback, since studies comparing scale economies on and off the efficiency frontier have found only small differences (Berger and Humphrey, 1991; Bauer et al., 1992; McAllister and McManus, 1993; Mester, 1993).

The evidence on scope efficiency is even more controversial than the scale efficiency literature. Three main problems have beset studies of economies of scope. Firstly, once again the use of the popular translog cost function specification is not appropriate when studying scope economies. Analysing scope economies involves making a comparison between the predicted costs of producing a given output mix by several specialising firms versus joint production by a single firm. If $C(.)$ is the cost function and $y = [y_1, y_2]$ the output vector, then $C(y_1,0) + C(0,y_2)$ is compared to $C(y_1,y_2)$. Since the translog cost function is multiplicative in output, it would predict zero costs for the two specialised firms. Even if we set a minimum level of each output, there is always the risk that setting any output sufficiently close to zero would yield predicted costs arbitrarily near to zero.[1] Alternative specifications found in the literature are the Box-Cox transformation to the outputs, which has encountered similar problems to the translog function (Pulley and Humphrey, 1993; Berger et al., 1987; Buono and Eakin, 1990), and the composite function, specifying the fixed-costs component separately from the cost-complementarities component, which appears to be the best behaved functional form (Pulley and Humphrey, 1993).

---

[1] Berger et al. (1987) provide a useful discussion of estimation problems of scope economies.

The second problem in analysing scope economies is the lack of data on banking institutions that specialise, since most banks seem to offer an entire array of services. This creates potentially very significant problems of extrapolation (Berger and Humphrey, 1991; Pulley and Humphrey, 1993; Mester, 1993). A more fruitful approach is to examine the combined scale and product mix effects of moving from one size class mean to the mean of the next larger size class by using expansion path subadditivity (Berger et al., 1987; Hunter et al., 1990; Berger and Humphrey, 1991; Hunter and Timme, 1991). This type of analysis also gives more interesting insights into banking efficiency, since it addresses the question of whether efficiency can be improved by changing simultaneously scale and product mix.

The third problem refers to the use of data on institutions which are off the efficiency frontier. Unlike in the case of scale efficiency, empirical evidence suggests that using data off the frontier can lead to a confusion between scope economies and X-efficiency. Both Berger and Humphrey (1991) and Mester (1993) found large discrepancies between scope economies on and off the frontier.

An interesting approach to scope economies is provided by Berger et al. (1993), who redefine scope economies in term of the output efficiency as well as input efficiency. They use the profit function, rather than the cost function, and under a given set of prices and other factors they examine whether a bank should optimally produce the entire array of products, or specialise in just some of them. Their findings suggest that in most cases it is optimal for banks to diversify into a wide range of products; there are, however, a few cases where specialisation appears to be more efficient.

X-efficiency in banking

Studies on the efficiency of financial institutions tend to relate to scale and scope efficiency. X-inefficiencies, or deviations from the efficiency frontier, have received very little attention, even if they could turn out to be a more important source of efficiency differences. In fact, differences in managerial ability to maximise revenue or control costs appear to be greater than the effect on costs of the choice of scale and scope of production. There is a strong consensus that X-efficiency differences across banking institutions are relatively large and dominate scale and scope efficiencies. It has been estimated that X-inefficiencies account for at least 20% of costs in banking, while scale and scope inefficiencies account for less than 5%, although the latter are easier to estimate (Berger et al., 1993).

There are major difficulties in choosing the best econometric procedure to use in estimating X-efficiency. The most difficult problem to overcome is to distinguish between two possible explanations of cost dispersion, namely X-efficiency differences from random error. Four different approaches in the literature attempt to distinguish between them. Each approach is based on different assumptions about the probability distributions of the X-efficiency differences and random error, and each estimation method arrives at different conclusions about the level of inefficiency. The econometric frontier approach assumes that X-inefficiencies are distributed as an asymmetric half-normal distribution, while random errors are normally distributed, both being orthogonal to the cost function exogenous variables (Ferrier and Lovell, 1990; Bauer et al., 1992; Pi and Timme, 1993). The thick frontier approach classifies deviations from the frontier in terms of their magnitude: deviations from predicted costs within the lowest average-cost quartile of banks in a size class are classified as random error, while wider deviations are considered to be X-inefficiencies (Berger and Humphrey, 1991, 1992a; Bauer et al., 1992; Berger, 1993). The data envelopment analysis approach simply assumes that any deviation from the estimated frontier represents inefficiency (Sherman and Gold, 1985; Parkan, 1987; Rangan et al., 1988; Aly et al., 1990; Ferrier and Lovell, 1990; Elyasiani and Mehdian, 1990; Fixler and Zieschang, 1991; Berg et al., 1991 and 1992; Grabowski et al., 1993). The distribution-free approach is based on the assumption that, while random error averages out over time, differences in X-efficiency are stable (Berger, 1991 and 1993; Bauer et al., 1992; and Berger and Humphrey, 1992b).

The average X-inefficiency has been found to lie between 20% and 25% of costs by most methods, apart from studies using the data envelopment analysis which find results ranging from less than 10% to more than 50%. More problematic is the fact that the rankings of individual banks do not correspond across methods, even if the measured average inefficiency is the same (Ferrier and Lovell, 1990; Bauer et al., 1992; Berger, 1993). Furthermore, the choice of inputs and outputs appears to change the results, and so does the choice of output measure employed, even if the estimation method is kept constant (Berg et al., 1991; Hunter and Timme, 1993).

The inconsistency in the results obtained from the above X-efficiency studies is most disappointing from a practical viewpoint. Since different methodologies give different results, it is virtually impossible to conclude which moves would improve the banking industry's efficiency, in terms of entries, exits and consolidations. Moreover, the large bulk of studies refer to US banks and only one (Berg et al., 1993), to our knowledge, compares X-efficiency across borders.

Comparisons of banking efficiency or productivity across countries would be particularly useful in understanding the cross-border consolidation and agreement policies of European banks. Unfortunately, such comparative analyses are virtually missing in the literature, with the exception of one study on the three Nordic countries, Finland, Norway and Sweden, (Berg et al., 1993). This study considers the relative efficiency of the banking industries of these countries, which constitute a region of minimum cultural barriers to entry. By using data envelopment analysis and Malmquist indices to measure productivity differences between banks from different countries, they found that:

(i) efficiency spreads were most important in Norway and Finland (the country with the largest number of banks) and least important in Sweden (the country with the lowest number of banks): although the temptation is to associate this result to the number of banks in each country, it must be noted that Norway has roughly the same number of banks as Sweden, and an efficiency spread as large as that of Finland; (ii) Sweden had also the highest share of banks on the efficiency frontier estimated for the Swedish banking industry, while Finland had the lowest share of banks on its frontier; (iii) most of the banks on the efficiency frontier estimated for the whole of the Nordic area were Swedish; (iv) the average Swedish bank was found to be more efficient than the average Norwegian bank, which in turn was found more efficient than the average Finnish bank; and (v) the largest Swedish banks were among the most efficient institutions, as was one large Finnish bank; no large Norwegian banks were on the Nordic area's efficiency frontier.

This type of comparative analysis between other national banking industries and individual banking intermediaries would certainly provide useful insights into present and expected structural changes. The globalisation of financial markets, and in particular the integration of EU markets, are expected to lead to more concentrated banking industries, where the most efficient institutions will play a major role. From the comparative analysis of the efficiency of different national banking industries, some interesting conclusions may also be drawn with regard to the effect on efficiency of regulation. If a country's banking industry is found to be consistently less efficient than another national industry, then this finding could suggest that the regulatory policies of the first country may need investigating.

Efficiency and bank mergers

In spite of the difficulties outlined above in measuring economies of scale and scope and differences in X-efficiency, efficiency improvements are often considered to be the main cause for mergers between banks, followed by the need for the rationalisation of the branch networks and the achievement of economies in technological investment. In both these last two areas, cost economies can probably be achieved by forming larger banks, although many of the technological economies can be achieved just as well by sharing.

The recent wave of large bank mergers in the US has once again sparked the debate on the efficiency implications of mergers, and in particular mergers between banks which are already large. The answer to the question of whether there is an efficiency improvement after a merger is very important for antitrust policy. In fact, great benefits may accrue to the customers and claim-holders from banks' improved efficiency, even if this means a more concentrated banking industry.

Most of the literature on bank merger efficiencies tends to simply compare pre-merger and post-merger financial ratios, such as the return on equity or assets, or operating costs over total assets (Rhoades, 1986, 1990; Linder and Crane, 1992; Cornett and Tehranian, 1992; Srinivasan, 1992; and Srinivasan and Wall, 1992). Most of these studies find that on average there are no benefits accruing from bank mergers. However, they tend to examine only the cost or input side. Studies which also analyse the revenue or output side find some benefits from mergers (Cornett and Tehranian, 1992; Spindt and Tarhan, 1992).

Studies based on financial ratios have been criticised for being too simplistic. Firstly, financial ratios can be misleading indicators of efficiency, since they do not control for product mix or input prices. For example, using a cost over asset ratio is equivalent to implicitly assuming that costs of production do not vary across assets or across locations. Secondly, it is impossible to distinguish between gains due to economies of scale and scope and gains due to X-efficiency. This of course limits the predictive power of these models.[2]

The first study to use an efficient frontier approach to determine the efficiency effects of bank mergers was Berger and Humphrey (1992b). By using a distribution-free approach, they found that: (i) there are no statistically significant average X-efficiency gains from mergers between banks with at least $1bn in assets each; (ii) since at this size they found diseconomies of scale, the total effect was a loss of efficiency which was statistically significant only in some cases; and (iii) there were no efficiency gains from mergers in which either the acquirer is more efficient than the acquired bank, or both banks are present in the same local market. These findings are quite interesting, since they go against the common beliefs about merger efficiency gains. In particular, the finding that no efficiency gains follow a merger between banks with market overlap, also supported by Srinivasan and Wall (1992), has implication for the present structural changes and indicates that mergers between banks operating in different geographical markets are more likely to create efficiency gains.

The article by Rhoades (1993) is very interesting in this respect. It analyses the efficiency effects of almost 900 horizontal (in-market) bank mergers. It has been often argued that horizontal bank mergers can reduce operating costs, not necessarily because of economies of scale, but because of the improved organisation of managerial and operational function. Rhoades distinguishes between cost reductions and efficiency gains. Cost reductions occur from consolidating back-office and other administrative operations and reducing employees and branches; however, if these cost reductions are accompanied by reductions in assets, then there is no efficiency improvement, but simply a decrease in the size of the operation. Concentrating on efficiency improvements only, Rhoades finds no evidence of improved efficiency following a horizontal bank merger – in spite of the fact that in his sample the acquiring banks were, on average, more efficient than the target banks, a situation which might be expected to lead to maximum efficiency gains.

[2] For a discussion of other methodological difficulties in these financial ratios studies, see Berger and Humphrey (1992b).

Shaffer (1993) follows a different and more forward-looking approach. Instead of trying to learn from past mergers, he simulates hypothetical mergers between pairs of large banks to estimate the potential contribution to cost reduction of scale economies, product mix economies, branch rationalisation and X-efficiency. This approach is certainly useful for decision-making in an environment which has changed remarkably over the past few years and is still changing. In particular, the increased pressure of competition has placed more emphasis on cost cutting, as shown by some aggressive cost-cutting measures in recent bank mega-mergers. Using a thick frontier approach, Shaffer finds that scale and product mix economies and some assumed closures of branches of the acquired bank would be likely to cut average total costs by less than 2%. On the other hand, the gains could be potentially large in terms of X-efficiency: if managerial efficiency can be transferred to the less efficient bank, a merger involving a bank in the most efficient quartile would have a predicted cost saving of around 21%; however, there could also be a loss of around 21% if, in a merger involving a bank in the least efficient quartile, the managerial inefficiency of such an institution spread to the merger partner. This suggests that the managerial talent of the merger partners is possibly the most important determinant of post-merger efficiency improvements.

Yet another different approach is provided by Fixler and Zieschang (1993), who use Tornqvist productivity indices for every bank in their sample to measure relative technical efficiency. There are a few interesting features in Fixler and Zieschang's study. Firstly, their index number approach considers technical heterogeneity, rather than a sub-optimal use of inputs, as the main reason for observed variations in productivity, and also facilitates a more detailed analysis of bank products. This compares well with studies based on the econometric and thick frontier and data envelopment approaches which are instead based on the assumption of homogeneous technology across institutions, with rare exceptions where limited technical heterogeneity is allowed for (Cornwell et al., 1990). Secondly, revenue effects are included through their output index, in addition to the more common cost effects in their input index. Previous studies have found that merger benefits tend to accrue from revenue, rather than cost effects and that the measured output efficiency differences tend in average to be larger than measured input efficiency differences (Berger et al., 1993). Their evidence is in line with other studies in supporting the view that there are no efficiency gains for the acquiring bank, which already tends to be 40–50% more efficient than average before the merger. However, although there are no considerable economies of scale to exploit, mergers can still boost the productivity and efficiency of the industry as a whole, since acquiring banks tend to maintain the same advantage in efficiency over other banks after the merger. This evidence suggests that usually the higher level of efficiency of the acquirer spreads over to the acquiree.

Mergers between banks and non-bank financial firms

There may also be other reasons for merging which are not related to efficiency improvements. There is the need to satisfy the growing requirements of large customers, which may themselves be growing through mergers and acquisitions. Historical reasons support this argument: large customers, first in railways and later in heavy industry, played an important role in the formation of both national banking systems and the large nationwide multifunction banks. In more recent times, the formation of multinational companies was the main factor in the development of international banking in the 1970s (Revell, 1987). Another reason is the need to match the size of other international banks and face foreign competition at home. There is no theoretical justification of why size should be a main advantage in competition. However, Rothschild (1947) suggested a military analogy: large armies usually succeed in defeating smaller ones. Like nations, large banks usually live peacefully for years, until something, such as the creation of a single European market, or major regulatory changes, upsets the balance of power within the competing group. To redress this balance, mergers and alliances are sought and in such an unstable environment sheer size can become important. However, these days banks, like armies, use highly sophisticated technical equipment and as long as a bank is large enough to buy and efficiently use this equipment, it may be in a position to compete effectively without growing any further.

Recently, banks have expanded through mergers and acquisitions into new business areas, outside traditional commercial banking, such as investment banking, insurance and real estate. While these mergers have been justified from a business diversification point of view and consequently have been seen as reducing risk, there is also a concern that some of these new activities could be riskier than traditional commercial banking and thus increase the overall risk of bank failure. This fear is well documented in the recent US experience of the 1980s, when firms in the savings and loan industry were allowed to expand into new activities. The expansion policies of many firms caused an increase in their business risk and many failures followed, with the consequent large losses of their deposit insurer. The same fate could be experienced by banks since they are in the same position, being protected by a deposit insurance that creates the same problems of moral hazard.

A solution has been suggested to decrease the moral hazard problem. In the structure of a bank holding company, banking subsidiaries could be 'protected' against the higher risk of non-banking subsidiaries by, for example, limiting the amount of financial transactions between the two types of business and by using collaterals (Greenspan, 1991). In this way, efficiency gains in managerial, operational and marketing functions could still be enjoyed without suffering from the adverse effects of an increase in risk. However, Boyd and Graham (1988) have argued that, unless the activities of banking and non-banking subsidiaries are fully separated by law, it would be almost impossible to avoid a situation where the resources of banking subsidiaries are used to finance non-banking subsidiaries. If they were separated by law, then the potential synergistic gains from the merger would disappear. In this latter case, it would be easier for the shareholders to achieve the same business diversification gains by buying shares in banks, insurance and real estate companies, and so on.

This controversy can only be solved by empirical observation. There are two types of analysis in the literature on this topic: some studies have analysed *ex post* the effects of already permitted non-banking activities on the risk of banking holding companies (Boyd and Graham, 1986; Wall, 1987; Brewer, 1989; Liang and Savage, 1990); other studies have simulated the effects of the expansion into currently prohibited non-banking activities (Litan, 1985; Kwast, 1989; Rosen *et al.*, 1989; Boyd and Graham, 1988; Boyd *et al.*, 1993). The evidence provided by the first group of studies is rather contradictory and appears to depend upon the period of estimation. They all use accounting data to estimate whether the risk of failure is increased by non-banking activities; however, they tend to aggregate all non-banking activities, making it impossible to isolate the level of risk of any one activity. For the period 1971–83, Boyd and Graham (1986) find no evidence of increased failure risk in banking holding companies with larger shares of non-banking assets in their portfolios. However, they find a statistically significant positive relationship between failure risk and non-banking activities during the subperiod 1971–77 and not between 1978 and 1983. During the period 1976–84, Wall (1987) found that, although the failure risk was higher for non-banking subsidiaries than for banking subsidiaries, the overall failure risk of the banking holding company either remained unchanged or declined slightly when it diversified into non-banking activities. A weak negative relationship between non-banking activities and risk is also found by Brewer (1989) during the period 1979–85.

Equally inconclusive are the findings of the group of studies which simulate the potential expansion of banking holding companies into non-permitted activities. Litan (1985) compares profit data for the banking industry and several non-banking industries in the period 1962–81 by calculating the coefficient of variation of earning for each industry and their correlation coefficient with banking. According to Litan's study, mergers between banks and non-banks tend to reduce the failure risk if the coefficient of variation for the non-banking industry is small relative to banking and the correlation coefficient between banking and non-banking earnings is negative. Unfortunately, Litan's use of aggregate industry data, rather than individual firm data, produces a downward bias in the estimated volatility of returns, and thus his findings must be considered with caution.

Other studies, based on individual firm data, suggest very small gains from diversification. Rosen *et al.* (1989) finds diversification gains up to, and no more than, a 4% share of real estate assets. Boyd and Graham (1988) find that the failure risk of banking holding companies decreases when they merge with insurance companies, but increases when they merge with real estate companies.

7.2   Entry and Contestability

Traditional theory of competition

Competition in the banking industry could be analysed by using the same theory which applies to any other industry. However, we need to be aware of the fact that structural regulation, a characteristic which is peculiar to the banking sector, may very much affect our analysis. This structural regulation does not so much control the efficiency of the production of banking services, but it controls the stability of the system. The supervisory philosophy derives from the banking crises of the 1920s and the Depression of the 1930s.

The working of the competitive market forces generally implies both a benefit and a cost for the society as a whole. The benefit derives from the elimination of the less efficient firms and the consequent efficiency gain. The cost is the bankruptcy cost for the society. Usually, the theory assumes that the social cost of bankruptcy is negligible, since it mainly falls on the shareholders. In the case of a bank, however, bankruptcy affects a large number of creditors and thus there are important externalities to bankruptcy. This is a notable factor both when the bankruptcy is the result of the competitive forces in the financial markets and when it is caused by very close links between banks and industry, as at the beginning of this century. This explains the supervisory policies of the last few decades and their dual goal of separating financial institutions from industry and sheltering banks, so that it is almost impossible for a bank to go bankrupt.

Bankruptcy is commonly the consequence of losses which can be caused by either systematic errors of management, or competitive interaction of firms in an industry with positive economies of scale, i.e. operating with decreasing average costs. In fact, in this latter case, which has been thought to apply to the banking sector, the theory predicts that an oligopolistic price war could drive some of the competitors out of the market. Structural regulations in the banking sector have for a long time avoided the consequence of this competitive mechanism. Italy is an extreme example of this. Since the 1930s, regulations have created rigid barriers to entry and thus the industry has behaved more like a monopoly than an oligopoly. Without the possibility of new entrants, collusion between banks has become an easy and profitable option.

Of course, in a situation where institutional regulations do not allow the free working of competitive forces, an efficient equilibrium may never be reached. Then a measure of performance of the industry is not based on the usual efficiency measures, but it is assessed against two types of indicators: (i) indicators relating to the structure, such as the degree of concentration and demand elasticity; and (ii) indicators relating to the behaviour of firms *vis-à-vis* competitors, such as the strength of a collusive agreement, or the speed of adjustment to rivals' moves. However, when there are large economies of scale, this approach can lead to contradictory results, since on the one hand an efficient scale of production is reached when a small number of firms are left in the market and on the other hand high industry concentration tends to lead to an equilibrium far from the competitive equilibrium. Costs thus tend to be higher than the minimum costs and consumer surplus is eroded; that is, an oligopolistic solution is reached.

As Stigler (1964) theorised, the behaviour of firms in an industry may be simply derived from the degree of concentration measured by a Herfindahl index: the larger the number of firms in an industry, the nearer the equilibrium is to a Cournot solution and the more difficult collusion becomes. In fact, oligopolistic competitors have unilateral incentives to break collusion agreements and thus, for a collusive behaviour to continue successfully over time, some form of control is required (Friedman, 1983). The cost of applying this control increases with the number of firms, and collusion becomes less likely as the number of participants increases. Furthermore, as Stigler has pointed out, with a large number of competitors it is more difficult for a firm to determine whether fluctuations in the demand for its products is due to its competitors' aggressive policies or not. Thus, such a firm is more likely to react to a downward turn of its demand by breaking the agreement.

The structural regulations of the Bank of Italy, for example, have been based on Stigler's theory, not so much in relation to the national market as a whole, but to local markets. The Italian national market has been divided into a large number of small local markets, for each of which the authorities have determined the number of banks necessary to stimulate the achievement of a Cournot equilibrium rather than a collusive one (Conigliani and Lanciotti, 1979; Lanciotti, 1983). The opening of new outlets has thus been limited in those areas with a high Herfindahl index, causing a reduction of industrial concentration and of the monopoly power of the banks operating in those areas.[3]

Contestability and banking

With the opening of the national EU banking markets, Stigler's oligopoly theory is not really adequate to explain the possible structural changes, since it refers to an oligopolistic market where there is no entry. It could only be applied to those services which may not be affected by integration, if they indeed exist. The freedom of entry of foreign banks into national markets makes the theory of contestable markets relevant (Baumol et al., 1982). Moreover, this theory is particularly appropriate for the banking industry because it is applicable to multiproduct firms.

---

[3] This is a rather simplified explanation of the theoretical basis behind the Piano Sportelli. Other variables were also used, such as the growth of deposits and an indicator of productivity. Furthermore, for large towns and cities, the adequacy of banking services for industry was also considered. For a more detailed explanation of the Bank of Italy's policy, see Banca d'Italia, *Piano Sportelli*, various years.

The main characteristic of a contestable market is that the behaviour of firms does not depend on the number of firms in the industry, but on the conditions of entry and exit. In very simplified terms, as long as entry is free and exit is costless, the incumbent firms, however large and apparently powerful, are forced to act almost as if they were in a perfectly competitive situation. This situation occurs because competition does not only refer to market forces inside the industry, but includes also potential competition and the transferral of resources from less profitable sectors. Transferral of resources in and out of a contestable market is assumed to be easy, since any entrant will face the same costs faced by incumbent firms and there are no sunk costs, i.e. the inputs acquired when entering the market can without cost be reallocated to other uses. In this situation, a potential entrant monitoring a market and seeing that the two incumbent firms which control the market have set a price above the sustainable, or average-cost, price will be able to transfer the necessary capital into this market, start operations, charge a lower price and take away customers from the incumbent firms. If the incumbent firms eventually retaliate and decrease their price below the entrant price, regaining their customers, the entrant can easily exit the industry and reinvest his capital elsewhere, since there are no sunk costs. This process of 'hit-and-run' competition ensures that product and service pricing is similar to that found in perfect competition, irrespective of the number of firms in an industry. Contestable markets tend to be efficient, since in particular the freedom of entry has two effects: it causes the exit from the industry of inefficient producers whose production costs are higher than potential producers; and the firms in the industry have to produce the quantity at which average costs are at a minimum to avoid the entry of potential competitors. It follows that firms will not earn any economic profits. If hit-and-run competition is not possible, the contestable solution breaks down and pockets of inefficiency can exist (Brock, 1983; Spence, 1983; Baumol et al., 1986; Schwartz, 1986).

This theory changes completely the way in which a firm's monopoly power is determined. In the traditional oligopolistic theory the extent of monopoly power was associated with the degree to which the total output of an industry was concentrated in the hands of a few producers. Various concentration indices have been defined over the years and used by antitrust authorities in many countries. The proposed merger in 1968 between Barclays, Lloyds and Martins, for example, was rejected by the Monopolies Commission because the assets of the business to be absorbed were deemed to be too large, as in the case of the rival takeover bids by Standard Chartered and Hong Kong and Shanghai Banking Corporation for the Royal Bank of Scotland, which were turned down in 1982. However, if there is contestability in the market, domestic concentration is not a good indicator of the degree of competition. It is the degree of freedom of entry for potential competitors that determines the monopoly power of the incumbent firms. Thus, in a country like the UK, where a virtual absence of legal prohibitions until the Banking Act of 1979 and the liberal attitudes of the Bank of England and the Treasury towards overseas banking institutions have brought about an exceptional degree of freedom of entry, the structure of the domestic banking industry might have had little to do with the level of competition.

There is a further reason why the growth of large banks does not inevitably inhibit competition. A large bank can be viewed as a multiproduct firm, facing different levels of competition in different markets. If the growth of a large bank is accompanied by product diversification, as is usually the case, it may not increase the monopoly power of the bank in any one specific market, but simply increase competition in the markets new to the bank. The bank may decide to enter a new market which is not too dissimilar to its existing ones, because it believes that there are profitable opportunities to be exploited in another market. In this case, competition will increase in this market. There is certainly evidence that firms operating in financial services have tended to avoid specialisation and have supplied more than one product or service.

One problem with applying the theory of contestable markets is that, even if potential entrants face the same costs as the incumbent firms, the size of capital needed by a potential competitor to set up in business in order to challenge the incumbent can be so large as to constitute an effective deterrent to entry. The proponents of contestable market theory reply that this problem does not exist if two conditions apply: firstly, financial markets enable competitors to gain access to capital at the same terms and costs faced by incumbents; and secondly, there are no sunk costs and thus heavy initial costs can be transferred into the production of another commodity or service. This is often the case in the supply of financial services: entry in a particular financial market can be free and exit from the same market costless. An example of hit-and-run competition can be found in the recent UK financial history in the supply of house mortgages. In 1979–80, UK clearing banks, US banks and other specialised financial institutions began to compete more aggressively with building societies in the mortgage market. Within three years, from 1979 to 1982, the size of UK mortgage lending by banks increased from £600m to £5000m. In the following years, the banks slowed down the rate of increase of their involvement in the mortgage market. Within the business strategy of a bank, it is fairly easy to vary the scale of involvement in different financial markets, especially if the staff skills required are fairly similar to the skills required in other areas of business.

Since the original formulation, the theory of contestable markets has evolved to consider situations when the costs of exit and entry are not negligible. Although there is not as yet a rigorous formulation, some interesting results have already been achieved by Eaton and Ware (1987) and MacLeod (1987), who have developed a model of sequential entry. According to this model, the potential entrant in an industry with n firms evaluates the benefits and costs of its entry and enters only if the profit gain is positive. Once part of the industry, all n+1 firms will then have to face the competition of another potential entrant; this process continues until n+k firms constitute an industry where entry becomes unprofitable. Since profits from collusion are always positive when the number of firms is equal to the efficient number under conditions of competition, positive sunk costs will cause too much entry in the industry (MacLeod, 1985). In fact, sunk costs only stop entry when the process of sequential entry is completed.

The main difference between perfect contestability and a model of sequential entry is that in the latter there is no risk of hit-and-run behaviour, since the 'run' phase is expensive. Thus a firm which enters an industry intends to stay in it, and will fight to do so if necessary. The behaviour of firms in this case resembles the traditional oligopolistic strategy, with the possibility of a price war. However, the probability of a price war decreases as sunk costs increase. With high sunk costs, the only reasonable behaviour is collusion, and thus potential entrants will expect to be able to gain collusive profits. This leads to the conclusion that the higher the sunk costs, the more likely is collusion, and thus the larger is the number of firms that are in a position to earn positive profits.

Sunk costs in banking

According to the theory of contestable markets, when analysing the structure of an industry with free entry and exit, it is important to access the nature of possible sunk costs, since the presence of such costs will affect the behaviour of the potential competitor, who needs to decide whether or not to enter the industry. Such costs are not just accounting, but economic costs, and they do not only refer to the costs that the bank may have to incur, but also to the costs that the public would face if the bank's operations were to fold. In theory, we would need to extend our analysis to the whole of the productive process, as well as factor markets and product markets, and the structural characteristics of the banking industry. Further, since sunk costs are only relevant to the analysis of competition, if there are too many firms in the market, an implicit assumption of the following analysis is that there is excess productive capacity.

In this section, there is no attempt to provide a comprehensive list of all possible sources of sunk costs in banking. However, some of the main sources of sunk costs will be identified. The first and most obvious possible source of sunk costs is capital investments, that is costs in goods and activities which will benefit the bank for more than one period of time. They include premises and equipment costs, but also other operating expenses such as R&D and advertising costs. Their evaluation is relatively simple. Usually, most of the costs of premises can be recovered; however, how easily and extensively will depend on the location of the buildings. In large towns and cities most costs may be quickly recovered; less so in rural areas. More problematic is the evaluation of equipment costs. Their incidence on total operating costs has grown remarkably in the last decade, with the introduction of increasingly complex computer systems and other electronic equipment. However, this equipment can often be leased and in this case sunk costs are most likely to be lower, increasing the level of market contestability. Furthermore, we need to distinguish between hardware and software costs, the first being more easily recovered than the latter. In fact, the hardware is not usually industry-specific and may thus be used for other purposes than banking. If it could be sold with the premises, then the costs of relocation would also be saved. The software, however, is often written for the specific operations of the bank and thus its costs might not be recovered. Advertising expenditures certainly constitute sunk costs, since any form of advertising is targeted to the specific bank or to its services. Coming into a new market may well mean high advertising expenditures for at least a few years, and these moneys would be lost if later the bank should decide to withdraw from that market.

The final category of investment costs mentioned above is R&D costs. Typically, most of the R&D activities take place at head office level; thus a bank opening a branch or a subsidiary in a foreign country need not directly employ R&D personnel in that country. However, starting to operate in a new market does usually involve market research and even development of new services, depending on the differences and similarities between the national and foreign banking markets. If these two markets are very different, then the need for R&D personnel in the foreign country may also be felt. Sunk costs in these activities are very difficult to access and will depend on the nature of the R&D. If the foreign branch or subsidiary is subsequently closed down, some services like retail banking will be discontinued and thus R&D expenses in this area are likely to be lost, unless the results can be applied to the home market. However, R&D expenses linked to services which can be offered in the foreign country from the home country can be considered as fully recoverable. For other categories of capital investment it is more difficult to determine which costs can be recovered, and to what extent, since this will depend on the efficiency of the secondary markets for the commodities involved.

A second main cost category is the cost of raising loan capital. We will argue that these costs can generally be fully recovered. To understand this, we need to look into the process of financial intermediation in which banks are involved. Financial intermediation carries a credit risk and an interest rate risk. If we assume for a moment that there is no credit risk, which we will consider later, and that our hypothetical bank is not taking any interest risk either, then it is easy to understand why there will be no sunk costs: since there is a perfect match between inflows and outflows, the bank's activities in this area can be closed down without any cost, simply by 'selling' the outstanding matched positions in the banking market.

However, even if interest rate risk is positive, we could argue that the expected sunk costs are zero. In general, when taking the risk, the bank knows that in any future period it will incur either a loss or a gain that will depend on the market rates trend, given a certain degree of mismatching between assets and liabilities. If, at any future date, the bank wants to withdraw from the market and thus sell its portfolio of credits and debits, it should on average be in a position to sell it at the market evaluation. There is no reason to believe that there should be a systematic difference between the bank's evaluation and the market evaluation of future interest rates. Thus, on average there should be no losses in this banking activity by exiting the market, unless there has been an error of evaluation by the bank. In this case, however, it would experience a loss anyway, even if it decided to continue its activity in the market.

The existence of sunk costs will also depend on the degree of specificity of the financial services and commodities supplied by the bank. Most of the 'products' of banking intermediation imply intertemporal agreements. Let us consider a loan with the associated operating costs and provisions to hedge credit risk and assume for simplicity that there is no interest rate risk, which we have already discussed in the previous section. Credit risk evaluation is highly subjective and this characteristic means that the loan is a commodity specific to the two parts in agreement. In practice, it is common that the bank has information on the customer which it does not share with the other operators in the market.[4] If this is the case, the bank may have to incur losses, should it need to sell the loans on the market. As such, the potential buyer will agree to pay a price which reflects the costs of concluding the transaction *ex novo*. If at time t, bank A has given a loan of amount K, charging an annual interest rate r and facing operating costs C_A and provisions P_A, after one year the repayment R would be:

$$R = (K + C_A)(1 + r) + rP_A \qquad (7.1)$$

If bank A needs to sell this loan to bank B, what price would B pay? First of all, B will discount the repayment R at the interest rate r and then subtract its operating costs C_B and provisions P_B, subjectively evaluated by each bank on the basis of the estimated credit risk.

Consequently, the maximum price, P, that B is prepared to pay is:

$$P = R/(1 + r) - C_B - rP_B/(1 + r) \qquad (7.2)$$

Substituting expression (7.1) into (7.2), we obtain:

$$P = K + C_A - C_B - r(P_B - P_A)/(1 + r)$$

The cost to bank A of selling this loan to bank B is thus:

$$C_B + r(P_B - P_A)/(1 + r)$$

Both the operating costs of bank B and the difference between the provisions of banks B and A are expected to be positive amounts because of the specificity of the loan mentioned above. In fact, bank B will not accept the loan on the basis of bank A's information alone, but will want to acquire new information, and thus its operating costs will be positive. Secondly, bank A is likely to have a lower evaluation of credit risk than any other bank in the market. This can be

[4] This applies, for instance, to the German industrial credit market, but also to a lesser extent to France and Italy. It is much less common in the United Kingdom.

justified by two considerations: (i) the relationship between the bank and its customer, especially if this is a long-standing one, would imply more trust from bank A than bank B; and (ii) if the market is efficient, a lower risk evaluation from bank B means that the borrower would have borrowed from bank B in the first place at a lower cost. Thus the difference in provisions ($P_B - P_A$) is also likely to be positive. This same reasoning can be applied to many other types of advances and customer services which imply an intertemporal agreement.

In general, we can say that sunk costs tend to be proportional to the level of commitment of the bank in the activity. So, for example, sunk costs are high in the case of financial services with positive set-up costs, such as the advisory service provided by merchant banks. In this case only the operating costs will be lost if the bank ceased activity. Conversely, there are no sunk costs linked to the holding of negotiable securities, where an active secondary market exists.

Empirical evidence

To date there have been only a few applications of contestable market theory to banking firms. A number of authors have argued that banking markets in the UK and North America do present the same characteristics of contestability. Davies and Davies (1984) offer several reasons why the UK banking market is nearly contestable; however, they provide no empirical evidence in support of this claim. Shaffer (1981a;b; 1982) and Nathan and Neave (1989), on the other hand, found some evidence that various North American banking markets possess characteristics of contestability.

The methodology employed by Shaffer (1982) uses the so called Rosse-Panzar 'H' statistics to measure the competitive nature of the banking market (Rosse and Panzar, 1977). The 'H' statistic is defined as the sum across all firms in an industry of their elasticities of total revenue with respect to input prices. As Rosse and Panzar showed, if a firm is a profit-maximising monopoly, 'H' cannot be positive. The intuition behind their proof is the following: for a monopolist, an increase in input prices will lead to an increase in marginal costs and thus reduce equilibrium output and consequently also reduce total revenue. In the case of perfect competition the 'H' statistic is unity because an increase in input prices increases both marginal and average costs but, since the increase in costs is passed on to output prices, equilibrium output for the individual firm remains unaltered. Output demand adjusts to the higher selling price and in the long-run total revenue rises by the same amount as costs. In a perfectly contestable market, the 'H' statistic is also unity, since the price behaviour is perfectly competitive even if there are only a few firms in the industry, or even in the case of a natural monopoly. The main problem in empirically estimating the 'H' statistic is that in theory only long-run equilibrium values should be used.

Shaffer (1982) checks that the observations are in long-run equilibrium by relating return on assets (ROA) and return on equity (ROE) to input prices: if the market is in long-run equilibrium, ROA and ROE should not be statistically correlated with input prices. He estimates the following revenue equation of a sample of banks in New York:

$$\ln TR = a + b(\ln PL) + c(\ln PK) + d(\ln PF) + e(\ln AST) + f(\ln MKT) + g[(C + D)/Dep] + h[(C + I)/Loan]$$

where: $\ln$ = natural logarithm
TR = total interest revenue
PL = annual wage, salary and benefits per full-time equivalent employee (unit price of labour)
PK = ratio of annual expenses of premises, furniture, fixtures and equipment to the balance sheet total of these items (unit price of capital)
PF = ratio of annual interest expenses to total funds (unit price of funds)
AST = bank assets
MKT = total market deposits in commercial banks
(C + D)Dep = ratio of cash and due from depository institutions to total deposits
(C + I)Loan = ratio of commercial and industrial loans to total loans

Using the above equation, Shaffer estimated the effect of input prices (PL, PK, PF) and other variables on equilibrium total revenue. The rationale for including variables other than input prices was to proxy other influences on revenue, such as economies or diseconomies of scale (AST); local demand for banking services (MKT); and different levels of correspondent banking activity and business mix ((C + D)/Dep and (C + I)/Loan). Shaffer's estimate of H = b + c + d = 0.318 suggests that there were competitive forces preventing monopolistic behaviour, even if competition was more potential than actual. Although neither perfect competition nor perfect contestability seemed to apply, a value of 'H' between zero and one suggests monopolistic competition. In this case, contestability theory approximates the actual banks' behaviour at least as well as theories of oligopoly.

The same methodology was applied to Canadian banks, trust companies and mortgage companies by Nathan and Neave (1989) and to the Japanese commercial banking market by Lloyd-Williams *et al.* (1991), with similar results. Nathan and Neave specified the following model:

$$\ln TRILL = a + b(\ln PF) + c(\ln PKB) + d(\ln PL) + e(\ln AST) + f(\ln BR) + gD6$$

where: TRILL = total revenue less provision for loan losses
PF = interest expenses/total deposits (unit price of funds)
PKB = premises expenditure/number of branches (unit price of capital)
PL = wages and salary expenses/number of employees (unit price of labour)

AST = total assets
BR = number of branches/total number of branches in the system
D6 = dummy variable worth 1 for the six largest banks and 0 otherwise.

Compared to Shaffer's study, Nathan and Neave's specification takes into account the effect of loan losses on reported bank profits, which has become much more important in recent years. Surprisingly, however, the loan loss effect does not appear to have a significant impact on their estimation of the 'H' statistics. Bank size is proxied by three variables: total assets to identify possible scale economies like in Shaffer's work; the relative number of branches operated by each bank; and the dummy variable to capture oligopoly behaviour at very large sizes. The results suggested that the dummy variable has no additional explanatory power and thus that the six largest banks do not exhibit significant revenue effects in addition to those explained by size. The values of H = 0.68 and H = 0.729 for the years 1983 and 1984 respectively rejected both the monopoly and the perfect competition hypotheses and led Nathan and Neave to conclude that 'since the effects of competition seem to be potential rather than actual, the banking industry seems to be well described by contestability theory' (Nathan and Neave, 1989: p. 586).

Contestability and regulation

The theory of contestable markets has profound implications for the regulatory arrangements of an industry. In an ideal perfectly contestable market, the best policy that any government can adopt is one of *laissez-faire*. This follows directly from the welfare properties of a contestable market. Firstly, companies in a contestable market do not earn more than the normal rate of profits; i.e. economic profits are zero even if there are only one or two firms in the industry. In fact, if incumbent firms were to earn positive economic profits, potential competitors would enter the industry, produce the incumbent's output at the same cost, sell it at a slightly lower price to the incumbent's customers and still make some profits. In other words, as soon as positive economic profits are earned by an incumbent firm in a contestable market, there is an opportunity for an entrant to 'hit' and, if necessary, subsequently 'run', after having earned above-normal profits.

The second welfare characteristic of a contestable market is the absence of any inefficiencies in production; that is, production will take place at minimum average cost. In fact, any unnecessary cost would give potential entrants the same profit opportunities than if incumbent firms were earning positive economic profits. Since the potential entrant faces the same cost conditions as the incumbent, an efficient entrant could sell his output at a lower cost and still earn positive profits.

The third welfare characteristic is that no output can be sold at a price which is less than its marginal costs. The argument here goes as follows: if incumbent firms sell some output, y, at a price, p, below marginal cost, it is possible for an entrant to sell a smaller quantity at a price slightly lower than the incumbent's and still make a profit. In fact, if p is below marginal cost, the sale of an output slightly smaller than y at price p would yield a profit higher than the sale of y at price p. Thus, there must be a price lower than p at which an entrant can undercut the incumbent firm and still earn as much as the incumbent.

The fact that price must always be equal to marginal cost has important consequences for regulatory and antitrust legislation. It follows that in a perfectly contestable market no cross-subsidy is possible; that is, firms cannot use unfair competition tools, such as predatory pricing. Thus, the regulator should not focus so much on pricing policies, but more on making sure that the industry maintains the characteristics of a contestable market. This is an important point which has often been misunderstood: the existence of a contestable market does not imply that there is no need of regulation. As Baumol and Willig (1986: p. 9) wrote: 'Contestability theory does not, and was not intended to, lend support to those who believe that the unrestrained market automatically solves all economic problems and that virtually all regulation and antitrust activity constitutes a pointless and costly source of economic inefficiency.' Indeed, there might be some markets which, being contestable, do not need intervention in order to function efficiently at zero economic profits, thus improving society's welfare. Furthermore, contestability theory rejects the idea that a large-sized firm must automatically squeeze the consumer and earn monopoly profits and thus must always require regulating. Intervention in a market which shows characteristics of contestability can be justified when competitive forces, actual or potential, are insufficient to reach a contestable equilibrium. That is, intervention should induce an industry where there is some monopoly power to behave in a contestable way, irrespective of the size and the number of firms in the industry.

The debate on contestable markets and regulation has mainly concentrated on the traditional antitrust legislation which affect most industries. In the case of banking, regulation takes a much more complex form and certainly goes beyond antitrust concerns. It follow that in a contestable banking industry, there is still need of regulation. Traditionally, regulation in the banking sector can be categorised into preventive regulation and protective regulation. Preventive regulation includes anticompetitive regulation, such as controls on market entry and restriction on price competition; capital adequacy, liquidity and interest rate risk regulation; the identification of permissible business activities; loan limits; and bank examination. Protective regulation includes deposit insurance and lender of last resort and emergency measures. Of all these regulatory measures, only anticompetitive regulation would work against the achievement of a contestable equilibrium.

Anticompetitive regulation in banking usually imposes limits on the competitive process with a view to both increasing the returns associated with any given level of risk, thus reducing the risk of failure, and restraining banks' own propensity for risk-taking. These limits are usually of two main types: controls on market entry, such as the imposition of licensing conditions, and restrictions on price competition, such as ceilings on rates payable on deposits, or restrictions on the payment of interest on demand deposits. However, it is generally recognised that market entry controls reduce efficiency and price competition restrictions can create distortions in the supply of financial services, often giving non-bank financial institutions an advantage over banks and encouraging financial disintermediation. Because of these problems, restraining the competitive process, which was a major focus of the legislation introduced in the 1930s, has become less important as an objective of the regulatory authorities, which now tend to be in favour of freer competition even in the banking sector. In this renewed environment, market contestability then becomes as important in banking as in other industries to determine the equilibrium industry structure and to guarantee efficient and welfare-enhancing behaviour.

PART III

The Future: Cooperation or Competition?

8

EU and US Banking after 1995

8.1　The future of EU banking
8.2　US versus EU banking
8.3　Concluding remarks

8.1　The Future of EU Banking

In the theory of international finance it is rather difficult to find an explanation of how in the European Union free capital mobility and fixed exchange rates can coexist with independent national monetary policies. With perfect capital mobility and fixed exchange rates in fact, interest rates in a smaller economy will essentially be determined by the prevailing rates outside the country. In effect, the central bank of this smaller country will be unable to carry out an independent expansionary policy without the risk of capital outflows and reserve losses. Recently there have been clear signs that the coordination of European monetary policies is not strong enough to avoid deep crisis in the ERM. Even if EMU is achieved, the stability of the system will depend on the relationship between the national banks and the central control.

On the regulatory side, there are two contradictory hypotheses. On the one hand, it seems that the authorities of member countries will retain the power to prevent the foreign acquisition of any of their banks. On the assumption that nationalism will not disappear with the advent of the single internal market, it is very likely that governments will use this power when one of their core banks is threatened. On the other hand, the European Commission is seeking some extension of powers in this matter. In particular, it is seeking the control of all mergers above a certain size. If this comes about, the national authorities will have lost their power to block the bank mergers that really matter, those between large banks. The only criterion that the Commission would employ would be the effect on competition within the single internal market, not within each country.

The situation would be further complicated if large companies were allowed to choose the status of 'European public limited company', and thus escape subjection to any national authority. The corollary would be that all banks in this category would have to be supervised by a central authority, which is probably the only way in which a completely level playing field could be assured. In this case the Commission would be even less likely to have any regard to national considerations in its attitude to mergers between pairs of large banks, one of which was a European plc.

All this is speculation, but it must be recognised that the power of national veto on the acquisition of a core bank is now a somewhat fragile instrument. Either of the above ways of extending the Commission's powers would bring nearer the day in which the EU banking system could start developing in the same way as every other national banking system, with the exception of that of the US, has developed in the past. We could then see the formation of a core group of pan-European banks through cross-border mergers. This would not be bad news for the consumer if the banking sector is contestable in nature.

Referring to the analysis of sunk costs in section 7.1 of the last chapter, there are at least two types of banking institutions with high exit costs, and which therefore violate a major characteristic of contestability: the German hausbank and the British merchant bank, both specifically active in industrial banking. The German hausbank has a very close and unique relationship with its corporate customers. Since it participates in the corporation's decision-making process, the hausbank knows its corporate customers better than any other banking institution, and is highly committed. Most of its activities in this respect are specific and thus, in the event of its exit from the market, it could only sell its output at a loss, as explained in the previous section. Similarly, a British merchant bank offers highly specialised services in corporate finance. In most cases a merchant bank acts as issuing house, with a high level of commitment. If it exits from the market before completion of an issuing operation, it would almost certainly be unable to recover the operational costs already sustained. It is therefore likely that for these two types of institutions, the contestable market hypothesis does not apply. We could then infer that the full integration of European banking will not necessarily mean greater competitive pressure for institutions specialised in industrial banking.

In between financial products with no commitment and others with high commitment, there are a number of operations which carry only partial commitment. Recently, the market has paid particular attention to the level of commitment incorporated in the individual operations which form some traditional banking activities, in particular lending. Some of the recent financial innovations represent, in fact, a restructuring of elements of traditional banking activities, which are combined in new ways to form new products with different levels of commitment. Examples of such innovations are securitisation and origination. Securitisation involves the separation, within a traditional lending operation, of the element with commitment (the guarantee) from the element without commitment (the security) and the sale of the latter on the secondary market. Thus, the guarantor bears the credit risk, but passes the interest rate risk on to a third party (Gardener, 1987). Instead, the activity of originating involves the bank buying the element carrying commitment from a multiproduct operation and then issuing on the primary market the part of a lending operation which carries no commitment. In this case, the bank from which the operation originates keeps the credit risk through a facility on the loan supplied by other institutions, or underwritten by the market (BIS, 1986; Federal Reserve Bank of New York, 1986). In both securitisation and originating, the bank bears the credit risk with the associated sunk costs. These are examples of how banking activities do often involve commitment. Different from securitisation, it is the sale on the secondary market of loans (or facilities) which incorporate an element of commitment. This, too, is a transaction which has become more popular in the last few years, in spite of the sunk costs associated with it. Although in theory such a transaction should not take place, because of the sunk costs of the seller, in practice it can be explained by the different positions of the seller and the buyer with respect to regulation and interest rate risk associated with the operation. These factors affect the equilibrium price and allow the sale to occur (Pavel and Phillis, 1987).

We can take the analysis further and divide the market for banking products into two areas: non-committed products and committed products. In the market for the first type of products, the conditions of contestability hold and thus banks are more likely to behave competitively. In the market for the latter products, the existence of sunk costs encourages collusive behaviour among an 'excessive' number of institutions. This would, for example, explain why large companies face relatively low costs of financial services, often too low to be justified only on the grounds of reputation, solidity and generally lower risk associated with them. In fact, two main factors make services to these firms a non-committed product: information on large corporations is usually more freely available to all financial operators, and the market tends to generally agree on the level of credit risk associated with this kind of company. In this case, according to our previous analysis, sunk costs are either zero or so low that they are irrelevant, and hit-and-run competition is possible. On the contrary, services to medium and small firms do usually involve high levels of commitment and thus present positive sunk costs. In addition, in the market for non-committed products, banks face the competition of a growing number of large non-financial companies. In fact, the introduction of innovative financial products which separate credit risk from interest rate risk has created an incentive for large companies to become more active in financial markets. Innovations have helped to break down many of the traditional lines of demarcation between market sectors. Some of the new financial instruments make it possible to unbundle the different elements which are combined in traditional banking transactions. Their use may thus enable a firm to adjust its exposure to changes in interest or exchange rates, while accepting a limited exposure to credit risk. As a result, it is possible for a firm, with some precision, to fine-tune exposure according to its objectives and expectations, to hedge existing positions or to open new ones.

The competitive environment has been exacerbated not only by the appearance of new non-financial entrants, but also by the process of integration. By analogy with the historical development of national banking systems in Europe, we could expect that the ultimate effect of a large increase in the size of the internal market would be a relatively small number of very large pan-European universal banks, although nobody would expect this to happen in the short space of a few years. This is the logical outcome of a process aimed at creating a free market in banking and other financial services, where financial institutions are allowed to reap to the full whatever benefits in size there may be. Such an outcome may be expected in the long run, but certainly is not likely to occur for as long as the power of veto of foreign control of core banks remains. A different solution must then be sought.

Following Buigues and Jacquemin's (1988) categorisation of structural environments described in section 6.2 of Chapter 6, we could argue that the banking industry has characteristics common to both an environment where volume is the main feature and a specialised environment, depending on the specific banking functions considered. In fact, for the supply of most traditional banking services size is important to compete efficiently, although, as we have previously noted, there is no evidence that there are still economies of scale to exploit. An example of this is retail banking. However, many of the functions of industrial banking have some specialised aspects which make the product non-homogeneous and the relation between supplier and customer specific, especially when the customer is a local small or medium-sized firm. According to the theory of integration, thus, banks involved in industrial banking should benefit from integration, which will open new markets for specialised products. However, we have also noticed that this tends to be an area where sunk costs are high, and consequently competition is not of a contestable type. This means that entry in this sector of the market may be difficult, due to collusive behaviour of existing banks. One way of avoiding some of these problems is to enter a foreign market by acquiring an existing local operator. This could well be the theory behind some of the cross-border acquisitions which have already taken place, such as the acquisitions by Deutsche Bank of the Italian Banca d'America e d'Italia and Morgan Grenfell, the British merchant bank.

If this proves to be the main theory behind the actions of the EU banking industry, we could then observe the formation, not so much of pan-European universal banks, but of pan-European specialised banks. The latter could be those which take either a product group focus or a client segment focus. While their managerial task will be made somewhat easier by the fact that they will not be burdened with a complex matrix of products and/or clients, they will also have less ability to rely on profits of one business area to support another during temporary crises. Nevertheless, their very focus will also be their competitive advantage, giving them flexibility in reacting to changes in demand. Pan-European specialised banks will be able to take advantage of market integration, because a European field of operations will enable them to build scale and diversify their business risk. The main skill in doing this will be to choose the right segment of the market and define its characteristics and parameters.

8.2   US Versus EU Banking

The current US banking structure remains fragmented and geographically confined. Although there are signs of a movement towards greater geographical diversification, or nationwide banking, the US banking system is still to some extent resisting universal banking. This compares with a proposed EU banking structure which strives to achieve geographical diversification and universal banking. However, the EU banking structure still varies substantially from one member nation to another, and universal banking, as practised in the EU, is rather localised; as such, cross-border banking still remains difficult to achieve. In terms of universal banking, the US authorities are proposing the so-called 'firewall' approach, while EU banks are following the German universal banking model. The firewall approach allows banks to participate in securities trading, while providing a structure that insulates banking activities from the greater risks of securities trading. The German model, on the other hand, allows banks to offer a full line of services, including some specialised banking services, such as mortgages.

These trends are a consequence of the different natures of US and EU banking regulation. US banking regulation is more rigid and restrictive than the proposed EU banking regulation in specifying the range of allowed financial activities (Table 8.1). The US continues to resist giving up its segmented financial system. This can be attributed partly to the age of the US system, and the fear of financial instability based on historical experience. In contrast, the EU legislation strives to foster competition by providing a context of universal banking. Instead of restricting specific banking activities, the EU regulations set minimum standards for conduct and minimum requirements for the financial indicators of stability.

A major policy difference between the US and the EU is the level of safety built into the financial system. The EU has proposed a very conservative safety net, while the US continues to maintain an extensive system of protection. The US financial services industry has been experiencing discontinuous changes due to advances in technology, government policy shifts such as deregulation, new entrants and new instruments. Some of these changes can be attributed to the pace of technological advancement and economic factors such as inflationary pressures and interest rate movements. In broad terms, the US financial services industry can be categorised into two segments, namely depository financial institutions and those that are non-depository. The depository institutions include commercial banks, savings and loan associations, mutual savings banks and credit unions. There have been a number of legislative changes related to depository institutions over the last two decades. Two in particular are noteworthy, namely, the Depository Institutions Deregulation and Monetary Control Act of 1980 (DIDMCA) and the Garn-St. Germain Depository Institutions Act of 1982. These Acts eliminated numerous regulatory limitations in terms of the management of depository

Table 8.1   Banks' permissible non-bank activities

	Securities underwriting	Real estate investment	Insurance business	Financial leasing	Fiduciary business
Belgium		R	R		
Denmark		R	F		
France			F		
Germany		S	F	S	
Greece	R	F	F	a	
Ireland		R	R		
Italy			F		
Luxembourg	S	F			
Netherlands	S	F			
Portugal		R	R	F	F
Spain		S	F	F	
United States	R	R	R	R	R
United Kingdom	S				

F   Forbidden
R   Legal restrictions or specific authorisation requirements
S   Limitations arising from comparatively heavy weighing in solvency and/or own-funds/fixed-asset
     requirements
a   Relevant legal arrangements under consideration.
Sources: Pecchioli (1987: p. 59); Dale (1992: p. 159).

institutions as well as revamping the nature of deposit and lending programmes offered to customers.

The US banking industry is unique in its structure. In other leading industrial nations, such as Germany, the UK, France and Canada, the banking industry is usually dominated by a few banks. In addition, these banks maintain branch networks that encompass their respective countries. The US banking system on the other hand is extremely fragmented in terms of the number of banks – over 12 000 – as well as in terms of geographical confinement. In addition, non-bank institutions, also referred to as consumer or limited-service banks, have been increasing their presence. These hybrid institutions have grown to become formidable competitors of commercial banks, in terms of the range of services offered. It is crucial to distinguish non-bank institutions from entities belonging to a traditional bank through the mechanism of a bank holding company. Non-bank institutions are typically finance arms of corporations and they usually include facilities for cheque-processing, ATMs, credit/charge cards, provision of capital, and the handling of certain depository transactions. From a legal standpoint, they enjoy unrestricted geographic spread as well as freedom in terms of product differentiation. Examples include department store finance operations, GE Capital and Ford Credit, as well as brokerage firms which offer a variety of services that traditional banks also provide and much more, such as real estate, insurance and securities services.

The process of deregulation can be examined from two perspectives, namely functional and geographic deregulation. Functional deregulation refers to the ability of institutions to offer a wider range of services. Deregulation of this type has allowed Savings & Loans to cannibalise some commercial bank activities; for example, they can invest up to 30% of their assets in consumer loans, as well as up to 10% in commercial loans. Additionally, state chartered Savings & Loans can invest another 10% of their asset base in loan participations. Geographic deregulation refers instead to the ability of banks to conduct interstate banking. The regulation in this area includes the Douglas Amendment and the McFadden Act, as well as numerous state laws that limit banks' ability to diversify geographically. This form of deregulation has been blamed for the failures of commercial banks, especially since the 1980s.

Furthermore, bank performance in the US is tied more closely to regional as opposed to national economic performance. Hence, banks seems unable to take advantage of the differences in the economic performance of the diverse areas in the country. The inability of banks to diversify their portfolio geographically has also been blamed for a significant number of bank failures. For example, bank failures were substantial in regions dependent on the oil, agricultural and real estate industries (Seballos and Thomson, 1993). Of course other reasons, such as the managerial ability of banks' top management, are also responsible for failures. Common problems pertaining to management include capital adequacy, ratio of non-performing loans, ratio of loans to total assets, as well as liquidity ratios. In addition to managerial incompetence, fraudulent activities also contributed to a number of bank failures. It has been estimated that about 35% of the failures of nationally chartered banks from 1980 to 1987 can be attributed to a certain degree to insider abuse or criminal fraud.

A common trend in the US and the EU has been the increasing openness of the financial system to international competition. Thus, the developments in US and EU banking should be assessed on an international scale. This greater degree of internationalisation should serve to diversify world economies from domestic problems or failures through scale and scope efficiencies. Furthermore, it should serve to diffuse losses caused by major financial disasters or failures across many nations. In respect of regulation, cooperation between national regulatory authorities in an effort to regulate international banking activity should ultimately result in a cohesive regulatory environment. One example of such cooperation is in the area of capital adequacy, which is helping to shape the domestic banking regulatory environment globally. Other initiatives include convergence of the multiple deposit insurance schemes worldwide.

8.3   Concluding Remarks

Critics of the current banking system in the US argue that restrictions that hamper the ability of US banks to compete effectively with foreign financial firms should be removed. For example, it is suggested that greater geographic diversification will help to enhance the safety of the banking system. The interstate commerce clause, which enabled the US to achieve prosperity and competitiveness in global markets, should likewise be applied to the banking sector (Heller, 1991: p. 15). In order to ensure financial stability and the integrity of the banking system, forced financial specialisation must also end (Pierce, 1991). It is no longer possible or even desirable to delegate certain financial activities to banks and exclude others from offering them. What specialisation occurs should be the result of economic forces, not a consequence of government directives. Market forces should ultimately determine the type of services currently provided by banking institutions. Geographically diversified banking should also be adopted in the US in order to maintain a competitive position globally and a healthy domestic financial system.

It is of course recognised that government oversight is needed to ensure monetary and financial stability. However, the regulatory environment must also be adapted to prevailing realities. Union-wide banking similar to that proposed by the EU would encourage financial stability by diversifying risk, at least geographically. Specialised banking allows for misallocation of resources and inefficiencies (Bentson, 1990: p. 210). The US banking environment remains the most regulated of the Group of Seven countries, as shown in Table 8.1. The disparity in permissible non-bank activities of institutions in the EU and the US is striking. For US banks to be able to compete internationally, it is very important that the regulatory environment in which they operate should be modernised. The equalisation of banking regulation will further increase the level of globalisation of the financial services industry as a whole, but in particular it will enable US banks to be potentially more competitive. Other advantages of universal banking include economies of scope and enhanced economic development when banks can offer corporations a wider array of services.

References

Adkisson, J.A. and Fraser, D.R. (1990) 'The ineluctable lure of lofty leverage', *Journal of Retail Banking*, vol. 12, no. 3, Fall, pp. 25–30.

Aharony, J., Saunders, A. and Swary, I. (1986) 'The effects of shift in monetary policy regime on the profitability and risk of commercial banks', *Journal of Monetary Economics*, vol. 17, no. 1, May, pp. 363–77.

Akerlof, G. (1970) 'The market for "lemons": qualitative uncertainty and the market mechanism', *Quarterly Journal of Economics*, vol. 84, pp. 488–500.

Akhtar, M.A. (1983) 'Financial innovation and their implications for monetary policy', *BIS Economic Paper*, no. 9, December.

Alesina, A. (1989) 'Politics and business cycles in industrial democracies', *Economic Policy*, vol. 4, no. 8, pp. 55–98.

Alesina, A. and Grilli, V. (1992) 'The European Central Bank: reshaping monetary politics in Europe'. In Canzonieri, M.B., Grilli, V. and Masson, P.R. (eds) *Establishing a Central Bank: Issues in Europe and Lessons from the US*. Cambridge: Cambridge University Press and CEPR.

Alt, J. (1991) 'Leaning into the wind or ducking out of the storm'. In Alesina, A. and Carliner, G. (eds) *Politics and Economics in the 1980s*. Chicago, Ill.: University of Chicago Press and NBER.

Aly, H.Y., Grabowski, R., Pasurka, C. and Rangan, N. (1990) 'Technical scale and allocative efficiencies is US banking: An empirical investigation', *Review of Economics and Statistics*, vol. 72, pp. 211–18.

d'Aspremont, C. and Jacquemin, A. (1988) 'Cooperative and noncooperative R&D in duopoly', *American Economic Review*, vol. 78, no. 5, December, pp. 1133–7.

d'Aspremont, C., Jacquemin, A. and Gabszewicz, J. (eds) (1988) 'Special issue on imperfect competition, international trade and European industry', *European Economic Review*, vol. 32, pp. 1419–1568.

Atkinson, P. and Chouraqui, J.C. (1986) 'The formulation of monetary policy: a reassessment in the light of recent experience', OECD Department of Economics and Statistics Working Paper, no. 32, March.

Ballarin, E. (1985) *Estrategias competitivas para la banca*. Barcelona: Ed. Ariel.

Baltensperger, E. and Dermine, J. (1987) 'Banking deregulation in Europe', *Economic Policy*, vol. 2(4), pp. 63–109.

Banca d'Italia, *Piano Sportelli*, various years.

Bank for International Settlements, *Annual Reports*, various years. Basle.

Bank for International Settlements (1986) *Recent Innovation in International Banking*. Basle.

Barry, G. *et al.* (1992) *Global Financial Deregulation.* Boston, Mass.: Blackwell Publishers.

Bauer, P.W., Berger, A.N. and Humphrey, D.B. (1992) 'Efficiency and productivity growth in the US banking'. In Fried, H.O., Lovell, C.A.K. and Schmidt, S.S. (eds) *The Measurement of Productive Efficiency: Techniques and Applications.* Oxford: Oxford University Press, pp. 386–413.

Baughn, W.H. and Mandich, D.R. (1983) *The International Banking Handbook.* London: Dow Jones-Irwin.

Baumol, W. and Willig, R. (1986) 'Contestability: developments since the book', *Oxford Economic Papers*, vol. 38, Supplement, pp. 9–57.

Baumol, W., Panzar, J. and Willig, R. (1982) *Contestable Markets and the Theory of Industry Structure.* Harcourt Brace Jovanovich.

Baumol, W., Panzar, J. and Willig, R. (1986) 'On the theory of perfectly contestable markets'. In Stiglitz, J. and Mathewson, F. (eds) *New Developments in the Analysis of Market Structure.* Cambridge, Mass.: MIT Press.

Bellanger, S. (1990) 'Regulation Must Recognize International Banking Realities', *The Bankers Magazine*, November/December, pp. 61–7.

Benston, G.J. (1990) *The Separation of Commercial and Investment Banking.* New York, NY: Oxford University Press.

Berg, S.A., Forsund, F.R. and Jansen, E. (1991) 'Technical efficiency of Norwegian banks: A nonparametric approach to efficiency measurement', *Journal of Productivity Analysis*, vol. 2, pp. 127–42.

Berg, S.A., Forsund, F.R. and Jansen, E. (1992) 'Malmquist indices of productivity growth during the deregulation of Norwegian banking, 1980–89', *Scandinavian Journal of Economics*, vol. 94, pp. S211–S228.

Berg, S.A., Forsund, F.R., Hjalmarsson and Suominen, M. (1993), 'Banking efficiency in the Nordic countries', *Journal of Banking and Finance*, vol. 17, nos 2–3, April, pp. 371–88.

Berger, A.N. (1991) 'The profit-concentration relationship in banking', Finance and Economics Discussion Series, no. 176, Board of Governors of the Federal Reserve System.

Berger, A.N. (1993) 'Distribution-free estimates of efficiency in the US banking industry and tests of the standard distributional assumptions', *Journal of Productivity Analysis*, vol. 4 (forthcoming).

Berger, A.N. and Humphrey, D.B. (1991) 'The dominance of inefficiencies over scale and product mix economies in banking', *Journal of Monetary Economics*, vol. 28, pp. 117–48.

Berger, A.N. and Humphrey, D.B. (1992a) 'Measurement and efficiency issues in commercial banking'. In Griliches, Z. (ed.) *Output Measurement in the Service Sectors.* Chicago, Ill.: University of Chicago Press and NBER, pp. 245–79.

Berger, A.N. and Humphrey, D.B. (1992b) 'Megamergers in banking and the use of cost efficiency as an antitrust defense', *Antitrust Bulletin*, vol. 37, Fall, pp. 541–600.

Berger, A.N., Hanweck, G.A. and Humphrey, D.B. (1987) 'Competitive viability in banking: Scale, scope, and product mix economies', *Journal of Monetary Economics*, vol. 20, pp. 501–20.

Berger, A.N., Hunter, W.C. and Timme, S.G. (1993) 'The efficiency of financial institutions', *Journal of Banking and Finance*, vol. 17, nos 2–3, April, pp. 221–49.

Bogen, J.I. and Nadler, M. (1993) *The Banking Crisis*. New York: Dodd, Meade & Company.

Boyd, J.H. and Graham, S.L. (1986) 'Risk, regulation and bank holding company expansion into nonbanking', *Federal Reserve Bank of Minneapolis Quarterly Review*, vol. 10, no. 2, Spring, pp. 2–17.

Boyd, J.H. and Graham, S.L. (1988) 'The profitability and risk effects of allowing bank holding companies to merge with other financial firms: A simulation study', *Federal Reserve Bank of Minneapolis Quarterly Review*, vol. 12, no. 2, Spring, pp. 3–20.

Boyd, J.H. and Graham, S.L. (1991) 'Investigating the banking consolidation trend', *Federal Reserve Bank of Minneapolis Quarterly Review*, vol. 15, no. 2, Spring.

Boyd, J.H., Graham, S.L. and Hewitt, R.S. (1993) 'Bank holding company mergers with nonbank financial firms: Effects on the risk of failure', *Journal of Banking and Finance*, vol. 17, no. 1, pp. 43–63.

Brewer, E. (1989) 'Relationship between bank holding company risk and nonbank activity', *Journal of Economics and Business*, vol. 41, no. 4, November, pp. 337–53.

Brickley, J. and James, C. (1986) 'Access to deposit insurance, insolvency rules and the stock returns of financial institutions', *Journal of Financial Economics*, vol. 16, no. 3, July, pp. 345–72.

Briscoe, S. and Johnson, C. (1993) 'The debate – Is the Maastricht path to EMU still feasible?', *The Business Economist*, vol. 24, no. 3, Summer, pp. 5–12.

Brock, W. (1983) 'Contestable markets and the Theory of Industry Structure: A review article', *Journal of Political Economy*, vol. 91, pp. 1055–66.

Buigues, P. and Jacquemin, A. (1988) '1992: Quelles strategies pour les entreprises européennes?', *Revue Française de Gestion*, June–August.

Buono, M. and Eakin, K. (1990) 'Branching restrictions and banking costs', *Journal of Banking and Finance*, vol. 14, pp. 1151–62.

Buser, A., Chen, A. and Kane, E. (1981) 'Federal deposit insurance, regulatory policy and optimal bank capital', *Journal of Finance*, vol. 36, no. 1, March, pp. 51–60.

Cable, J. (1985) 'Capital market information and industrial performance: The role of West German banks', *The Economic Journal*, March, pp. 118–32.

Canals, J. (1993) *Competitive Strategies in European Banking*. Oxford: Clarendon Press.

Casella, A. and Feinstein, J. (1989) 'Management of a common currency'. In de Cecco, M. and Giovannini, A. (eds) *A European Central Bank?* Cambridge: Cambridge University Press, pp. 131–55.

Cavanna, H. (ed.) (1992) *Financial Innovation*. London: Routledge.

Cecchini, P. (1988) *The European Challenge in 1992: The Benefits of a Single Market*. Aldershot: Gower.

Chant, J. (1987) 'Regulation of financial institutions – A functional analysis', Bank of Canada Technical Report, no. 45.

Chouraqui, J.-C. (1992) 'Financial liberalization and monetary policy: an overview'. In Cavanna, H. (ed.) *Financial innovation*. London: Routledge.

Clark, J.A. (1988) Economies of scale and scope at depository financial institutions: A review of the literature. Economic Review of the *Federal Reserve Bank of Kansas City,* vol. 73, September/October, pp. 16–33.

Clarotti, P. (1984) 'Progress and future developments of establishment and services in the EC in relation to banking', *Journal of Common Market Studies,* vol. XXII, no. 3, March, pp. 199–226.

Cobham, D. (1989) 'Strategies for monetary integration revisited', *Journal of Common Market Studies,* vol. 27, pp. 203–18.

Collins, S. (1988) 'Inflation and the EMS'. In Giavazzi, S., Micossi, S. and Miller, M. (eds) *The European Monetary System.* Cambridge, Cambridge University Press.

Commission of the European Community (1988) 'The economics of 1992 - An assessment of the potential economic effects of completing the internal market of the EC', *European Economy,* no. 35.

Committee of Governors of the Central Banks of the Member States of the EEC (1990) 'Draft Statute of the European System of Central Banks of the European Central Bank', manuscript, 27 November.

Conigliani, C. and Lanciotti, G. (1979) 'Struttura dell'offerta e dei tassi d'interesse nei mercati bancari italiani', *Bancaria,* November.

Cooper, K. and Fraser, D.R. (1986) *Banking Deregulation and the New Competition in Financial Services.* Cambridge, Mass.: Ballinger Publishing Company.

Coopers & Lybrand Europe (1987) *European Banking Law,* 2nd edn.

Corden, W.M. (1972) 'Economies of scale and customs union theory', *Journal of Political Economy,* vol. 80, pp. 465–75.

Cornett, M.M. and Tehranian, H. (1992) 'Changes in corporate performance associated with bank acquisitions', *Journal of Financial Economics,* vol. 31, pp. 211–34.

Cornwell, C., Schmidt, P. and Sickles, R.C. (1990) 'Instrumental variables estimation of a production function with cross-sectional and time-series variations in productivity levels', *Journal of Econometrics,* vol. 46, pp. 185–200.

Coxe, D. (1991) 'The Made-In-Japan Credit Crunch', *Canadian Business,* October, pp. 27–34.

D'Agostino, R.B., Belanger, A. and D'Agostino, R.B. Jr (1990) 'A suggestion for using powerful and informative tests of normality', *The American Statistician,* vol. 44, pp. 316–21.

Dale, R. (1992) *International Banking Deregulation.* Oxford: Blackwell.

Damanpour, F. (1986) 'A Survey of Market Structure and Activities of Foreign Banking in the U.S.', *Columbia Journal of World Business,* Winter, pp. 35–45.

Damanpour, F. (1988) Bank's financial condition and performance in the eighties, *Journal of Retail Banking,* vol. IX, no. 4, Winter.

Damanpour, F. (1990) *The Evolution of Foreign Banking Institutions in the United States.* New York, N.Y.: Quorum Books.

Danker, D.J. and McLaughlin, M.M. (1985) 'Profitability of insured commercial banks in 1984', *Federal Reserve Bulletin,* November, pp. 845–9.

Davies, G. and Davies, J.E. (1984) 'The revolution in monopoly theory', *Lloyds Bank Review,* Summer, pp. 38–52.

de Grauwe, P. and Peeters, T. (1989) *The ECU and European Monetary Integration.* London: Macmillan.

Dermine, J. (1990a) 'The specialization of financial intermediaries, the EC model', *Journal of Common Market Studies*, March.

Dermine, J. (ed.) (1990b) *European Banking in the 1990s*. Oxford, UK, and Cambridge, USA: Basil Blackwell.

Deutsch, B. (1991) 'A Conversation with Lester Throw, A Walk on the Dark Side', *Bank Marketing*, September, pp. 16–20.

Diamond, D. (1984) 'Financial intermediation and delegated monitoring', *Review of Economic Studies*, vol. 51, pp. 393–414.

Diamond, D. and Dybvig, P. (1983) 'Bank runs, deposit insurance and liquidity', *Journal of Political Economy*, vol. 91, pp. 401–19.

Di Cagno, D. (1990) *Regulation of Banks' Behaviour Towards Risk*. Aldershot: Dartmouth Publishing Company.

Dornbusch, R. (1988) 'Money and finance in European integration', in *Money and Finance in European Integration*. Geneva: EFTA.

Dornbusch, R. (1991) 'Problems of European monetary integration'. In Giovannini, A. and Mayer, C. (eds) *European Financial Integration*. Cambridge: CEPR and Cambridge University Press.

Dowd, K. (1988) *Private Money*. Hobart Paper no. 112. London: Institute for Economic Affairs.

Dugger, R. (1990) 'International Banking Competitiveness', *Secondary Mortgage Markets*, Winter, pp. 20–3.

Eaton, B. and Ware, R. (1987) 'A theory of market structure with sequential entry', *Rand Journal of Economics*, Spring, pp. 1–16.

Eichengreen, B. (1992) 'Designing a Central Bank for Europe: A cautionary tale from the early years of the Federal Reserve System'. In Canzoneri, M.B., Grilli, V. and Masson, P.R. (eds) *Establishing a Central Bank: Issues in Europe and Lessons from the US*. Cambridge: Cambridge University Press, pp. 13–40.

Eiteman, D.K. *et al.* (1992) *Multinational Business Finance*. New York, NY: Addison-Wesley Publishing Company.

Elyasiani, E. and Mehdian, S.M. (1990) 'A non-parametric approach to measurement of efficiency and technological change: The case of large US commercial banks', *Journal of Financial Services Research*, vol. 4, pp. 157–68.

Evans, R. (1993) Western Bankers' Strategies in China, *Global Finance*, April, pp. 62–6.

Fama, E. (1980) 'Banking in the theory of finance', *Journal of Monetary Economics*, vol. 6, no. 1, January, pp. 39–57.

Federal Communications Commission (1985) *Notice of Inquiry, in the Matter of Long-run Regulation at AT&T's Basic Domestic Interstate Sources*. Washington, DC.

Federal Reserve Bank of New York (1986) 'Recent Trends in Commercial Bank Profitability', Staff paper, September.

Federal Reserve Bulletin (1993) The Foreign Bank Supervision Enhancement Act of 1991, vol. 79, no. 1, January, pp. 1–2.

Federal Trade Commission (1985) *Final Order: In the Matter of the Echlin Manufacturing Company and Borg-Warner Corporation*. Docket Number 9157, Washington, DC, 28 June.

Ferrier, G.D. and Lovell, C.A.K. (1990) 'Measuring cost efficiency in banking: Econometric and linear programming evidence', *Journal of Econometrics*, vol. 46, pp. 229–45.

Fixler, D.J. and Zieschang, K.D. (1991) 'Pricing imputation problems in commercial banking: A production function approach', Working Paper, Bureau of Labor Statistics.

Fixler, D.J. and Zieschang, K.D. (1993) 'An index number approach to measuring bank efficiency: An application to mergers', *Journal of Banking and Finance*, vol. 17, nos 2–3, April, pp. 437–50.

Flannery, M. and James, C. (1984a) 'Market evidence on the effective maturity of bank assets and liabilities', *Journal of Money, Credit and Banking*, vol. 16, no. 4, November, pp. 435–45.

Flannery, M. and James, C. (1984b) 'The effect of interest rate changes on the stock returns of financial institutions', *Journal of Finance*, vol. 39, no. 4, September, pp. 1141–53.

Folkerts-Landau, D. and Mathieson, D. (1989) 'The EMS in the context of the integration of European financial markets', IMF Occasional Papers no. 66.

Friedman, J. (1983) *Oligopoly Theory*. Cambridge: Cambridge University Press.

Friedman, M. and Schwartz, A. (1965) *A Monetary History of the United States, 1867–1960*. Princeton, N.J.: Princeton University Press.

Gale, D. and Hellwig, M. (1985) 'Incentive-compatible debt contracts: The one-period problem', *Review of Economic Studies*, vol. 52, pp. 647–63.

Gardener, E.P.M. (1987) Structural and strategic consequences of financial conglomeration. *Revue de la Banque*, 9, pp. 5–16.

Gardener, E.P.M. (ed.) (1990) *The Future of Financial Systems and Services*. London: Macmillan.

Gardener, E.P.M. (1992) 'Capital adequacy after 1992: The banking challenge', Research Paper in Banking and Finance no. RP 92/11, Institute of European Finance, University College of North Wales, Bangor.

Gardener, E.P.M. and Molyneux, P. (1990) *Changes in Western European Banking*. London: Unwin Hyman.

Giavazzi, F. and Giovannini, A. (1989a) *Limiting Exchange Rate Flexibility*. Cambridge, Mass.: MIT Press.

Giavazzi, F. and Giovannini, A. (1989b) 'Can the EMS be exported? Lessons from 10 years of monetary policy coordination in Europe', CEPR Discussion Paper no. 285.

Giavazzi, F. and Pagano, M. (1988) 'The advantage of tying one's hands: EMS discipline and central bank credibility', *European Economic Review*, vol. 32, pp. 1055–74.

Giavazzi, F. and Spaventa, L. (1989) 'The new EMS', CEPR Discussion Paper No. 369.

Goto, J. (1988) 'International trade and imperfect competition: Theory and application to the automobile trade', The World Bank, mimeo.

Grabowski, R., Rangan, N. and Rezvanian, R. (1993) 'Organisational forms in banking: An empirical investigation of cost efficiency', *Journal of Banking and Finance*, vol. 17, nos 2–3, pp. 531–8.

Greenspan, A. (1991) Statement to the US House Subcommittee on Financial Institutions Supervision, Regulation and Insurance of the Committee on

Banking, Finance and Urban Affairs, US House of Representatives, 30 April, *Federal Reserve Bulletin*, June.

Grilli, V., Masciandaro, D. and Tabellini, G. (1991) 'Political and monetary institutions and public finance policies in the industrial democracies', *Economic Policy: A European Forum*, vol. 6, no. 2, October, pp. 341–92.

Gros, D. and Thygesen, N. (1990) 'The institutional approach to monetary union in Europe', *Economic Journal*, vol. 100, September, pp. 925–35.

Gual, J. and Neven, D. (1993) 'Banking', *European Economy*, no. 3, pp. 153–79.

Harrington, R.L. (1987) *Asset and Liability Management by Banks*. Paris: OECD.

Harris, R. and Kwakwa, V. (1988) 'The 1988 Canada–United States Free Trade Agreement: A dynamic general equilibrium evaluation of the transition effects', NBER/CEPR, mimeo.

Heller, H.R. (1991) 'Governing banking's future: A view from the Fed'; in England, C. (ed.) *Governing Banking's Future*. Boston, Mass.: Kluwer Academic.

Holmstrom, B. and Milgrom, P. (1991) 'Multitask principal–agent analysis: Incentive contracts, asset ownership, and job design', *Journal of Law, Economics and Organisation*, vol. 7, pp. 24–52.

Hultman, C.W. (1990) *The Environment of International Banking*. Englewood Cliffs, N.J.: Prentice Hall, Inc.

Humphrey, D.B. (1987) Cost dispersion and the measurement of economies in banking. *Federal Reserve Bank of Richmond Economic Review*, vol. 73, no. 3, May–June, pp. 24–38.

Humphrey, D.B. (1990) 'Why do estimates of bank scale economies differ?', *Federal Reserve Bank of Richmond Economic Review*, vol. 76, September/October, pp. 38–50.

Hunter, W.C. and Timme, S.G. (1986) 'Technical change, organizational form, and the structure of bank productivity', *Journal of Money, Credit and Banking*, vol. 18, pp. 152–66.

Hunter, W.C. and Timme, S.G. (1991) 'Technological change in large US commercial banks', *Journal of Business*, vol. 64, pp. 339–62.

Hunter, W.C. and Timme, S.G. (1995) 'Core deposits and physical capital: A reexamination of bank scale economies and efficiency with quasi-fixed inputs', *Journal of Money, Credit and Banking*, vol. 27, no. 1, pp. 165–85.

Hunter, W.C., Timme, S.G. and Yang, W.K. (1990) 'An examination of cost subadditivity and multiproduct in large US banks', *Journal of Money, Credit and Banking*, vol. 22, pp. 504–25.

Jacklin, C.J. and Bhattacharya, S. (1988) 'Distinguishing panics and information-based bank runs: welfare and policy implications', *Journal of Political Economy*, vol. 96, pp. 568–92.

Jacquemin, A. (1982) 'Imperfect market structure and international trade: Some recent research', *Kyklos*, vol. 35.

Jacquemin, A. (1987) *The New Industrial Organization*. Boston, Mass. and Oxford: MIT and Oxford University Press.

Johnson, H.G. (1967) 'International trade theory and monopolistic competition theory'. In Kuenne, R. (ed.) *Monopolistic Competition Theory: Studies in Impact*, New York: John Wiley.

Kahane, Y. (1977) 'Capital adequacy and the regulation of financial intermediaries', *Journal of Banking and Finance*, vol. 1, pp. 207–18.

Kane, E.J. (1989) *The S & L Insurance Mess: How Did it Happen?* Washington D.C.: Urban Institute Press.

Kapstein, J. (1992) 'Meeting BIS Standards Takes Its Toll', *Global Finance*, November, pp. 31–34.

Katz, M. (1987) 'An analysis of cooperative research and development', *Rand Journal of Economics*, no. 17.

Kennedy, S. (1973) *The Banking Crisis of 1933*. Lexington, Ky.: University of Kentucky Press.

Kettell, B. and Magnus, G. (1986) *The International Debt Game*. London: Graham & Trotman.

Khoury, S.J. (1980) *Dynamics of International Banking*. New York: Praeger Publishers.

Kim, D. and Santomero, A.M. (1988) 'Risk in banking and capital regulation', *Journal of Finance*, vol. 43, no. 5, December, pp. 1219–32.

Kim, S.H. and Miller, S.W. (1983) *Competitive Structure of the International Banking Industry*. Lexington, Mass.: Lexington Books.

Kindleberger, C.P. (1984) *A Financial History of Western Europe*. London: George Allen & Unwin.

Kohlagen, S. (1983) 'Overlapping national investment portfolios'. In Hawkings, R., Levich, R. and Wihlborg, C. (eds) *Research in International Business and Finance*, New York: JAI Press.

Kraus, J.R. (1991) 'For European Banks, U.S. Market Is a Ripe Plum', *American Banker*, March, pp. 2A–5A.

Kremers, J. (1990) 'Gaining credibility for a disinflation: Ireland's experience in the EMS', *IMF Staff Papers*, vol. 37, pp. 116–45.

Krummel, H.J. (1980) 'German universal banking scrutinised: Some remarks concerning the Gessler report', *Journal of Banking and Finance*, March, pp. 33–55.

Kwast, M.L. (1989) 'The impact of underwriting and dealing on bank returns and risks', *Journal of Banking and Finance*, vol. 13, no. 1, March, pp. 101–25.

Lackman, C.L. (1986) 'The impact of capital adequacy constraints on bank portfolios', *Journal of Business, Finance and Accounting*, Winter, pp. 587–96.

Lafferty Business Research (1990) *Financial Revolution in Europe*. London: Lafferty Publications.

Lanchner, D. (1993) Who'll Get the Business in France. *Global Finance*, July, pp. 52–5.

Lanciotti, G. (1983) 'Obiettivi e strumenti della vigilanza strutturale', *Bancaria*, December.

Lees, F.A. (1976) *Foreign Banking and Investment in the US*. New York, NY: Halsted Press.

Leland, H. and Pyle, D. (1977) 'Information asymmetries, financial structure and financial intermediation', *Journal of Finance*, vol. 32, pp. 371–87.

Lewis, A. (1992) 'Environmental Alignment: An Analysis of the Performance of the Banking Industry in the United States', *Journal of Strategic Change*, vol. 1, no. 4.

Lewis, A. (1993) 'The European Community and The Implications for the United States Banking Industry', *Journal of Strategic Change*, vol. 2.

Lewis, M.K. and Davis, K.T. (1987) *Domestic and International Banking*. Oxford: Philip Allan.

Liang, N. and Savage, D. (1990) 'New data on the performance of nonbank subsidiaries of bank holding companies', Staff Study, no. 159, Board of Governors of the Federal Reserve System.

Linder, J.C. and Crane, D.B. (1992) 'Bank mergers: Integration and profitability', Working Paper, Harvard Business School.

Litan, R.E. (1985) 'Evaluating and controlling the risks of financial product deregulation', *Yale Journal on Regulation*, vol. 3, no. 1, Fall, pp. 1–52.

Lloyd-Williams, D.M., Molyneux, P. and Thornton, J. (1991) 'Competition and contestability in the Japanese commercial banking market', Institute of European Finance, University College of North Wales, Bangor, Research Paper in Banking and Finance no. 91/16.

McAllister, P.H. and McManus, D. (1993) 'Resolving the scale efficiency puzzle in banking', *Journal of Banking and Finance*, vol. 17, nos 2–3, April, pp. 389–405.

McDonald, F. and Zis, G. (1989) 'The EMS: Towards 1992 and beyond', *Journal of Common Market Studies*, vol. 27, pp. 183–202.

MacLeod, W.B. (1985) 'Information, sunk costs and entry equilibria', Discussion Paper no. 596, Queen's University, Kingston, Ontario.

MacLeod, W.B. (1987) 'Entry, sunk costs and market structure', *Canadian Journal of Economics*, February, pp. 140–51.

Mathis, F.J. (1995) *Offshore Lending by U.S. Commercial Banks*, Bankers' Association for Foreign Trade and Robert Morris Associates.

Merton, R. (1977) 'An analytical derivation on the cost of deposit insurance and loan guarantees: An application of modern option pricing theory', *Journal of Banking and Finance*, no. 1, June, pp. 3–11.

Mester, L.J. (1993) 'Efficiency in the savings and loan industry', *Journal of Banking and Finance*, vol. 17, nos 2–3, April, pp. 267–86.

Mullineux, A. (1987) *International Banking and Financial Systems: A Comparison*. London: Graham and Trotman.

Murshed, S.M. (1992) *Analytical Models of North-South Interaction*. London: Academic Press.

Nathan, A. and Neave, E.H. (1989) 'Competition and contestability in Canada's financial system: empirical results', *Canadian Journal of Economics*, vol. 22, no. 3, August, pp. 576–94.

Noulas, A.G., Ray, S.C. and Miller, S.M. (1990) 'Returns to scale and input substitution for large US banks', *Journal of Money, Credit and Banking*, vol. 22, pp. 94–108.

Orr, B. (1990) 'Competing with Japanese Banks', *ABA Banking Journal*, September, pp. 39–42.

Padoa-Schioppa, T. *et al.* (1987) *Efficiency, Stability and Equity*. Oxford: Oxford University Press.

Parkan, C. (1987) 'Measuring the efficiency of service operations: An application to bank branches', *Engineering Costs and Production Economics*, vol. 12, pp. 237–42.

Patinkin, D. (1961) 'Financial intermediaries and the logical structure of monetary theory', *American Economic Review*, vol. 51, no. 1, March, pp. 95–116.

Pavel, C. and Phillis, D. (1987) 'Why commercial banks sell loans: An empirical analysis', *Federal Reserve Bank of Chicago Economic Perspectives*, May–June.

Pavel, C. and Rosenblum, J. (1985) 'Banks and non-banks: The horse race continues', *Federal Reserve Bank of Chicago Economic Perspectives*, May–June, pp. 3–17.

Pecchioli, R.M. (1983) *The Internationalization of Banking: The Policy Issues*. Paris: OECD.

Pecchioli, R.M. (1987) *Prudential Supervision in Banking*. Paris: OECD.

Pi, L. and Timme, S.G. (1993) 'Corporate control and bank efficiency', *Journal of Banking and Finance*, vol. 17, nos 2–3, pp. 515–30.

Pierce, J.L. (1991) *The Future of Banking*. New Haven: Yale University Press.

Pollard, A. *et al.* (1988) Banking Law in the United States. Butterworth Legal Publishers.

Pomfret, R. (1986) 'The theory of preferential trading arrangements', *Weltwirtschaftliches Archiv.*, vol. 122, no. 3, pp. 439–65.

Porter, M.E. (ed.) (1986) *Competition in Global Industries*. Boston, Mass.: Harvard Business School Press.

Postlewaite, A. and Vives, X. (1987) 'Bank runs as an equilibrium phenomenon', *Journal of Political Economy*, vol. 95, pp. 485–91.

Pulley, L.B. and Humphrey, D.B. (1993) 'The role of fixed costs and cost complementarities in determining scope economies and the cost of narrow banking proposals', *Journal of Business*, vol. 66, no. 3, July, pp. 437–62.

Rangan, N.R., Grabowski, H., Aly, H. and Pasurka, C. (1988) 'The technical efficiency of US banks', *Economics Letters*, vol. 28, pp. 169–75.

Revell, J.R.S. (1980) *Cost and Margins in Banking: An International Survey*. Paris: OECD.

Revell, J.R.S. (1987) *Mergers and the Role of Large Banks*. Institute of European Finance Monograph, University College of North Wales.

Rhoades, S.A. (1986) 'The operating performance of acquired firms in banking before and after acquisition', Staff Economic Studies, no. 149, Board of Governors of the Federal Reserve System.

Rhoades, S.A. (1990) 'Billion dollar bank acquisitions: A note on the performance effects', Working Paper, Board of Governors of the Federal Reserve System.

Rhoades, S.A. (1993) 'Efficiency effects of horizontal (in-market) bank mergers', *Journal of Banking and Finance*, vol. 17, nos 2–3, April, pp. 411–22.

Rosen, R.J., Lloyd-Davies, P., Kwast, M.L. and Humphrey, D.B. (1989) 'New banking powers: A portfolio analysis of bank investment in real estate', *Journal of Banking and Finance*, vol. 13, no. 3, July, pp. 355–66.

Rosse, J.N. and Panzar, J.C. (1977) 'Chamberlin vs Robinson: an empirical test for monopoly rents', Bell Laboratories, Economics Discussion Paper no. 90.

Rothschild, K.W. (1947) 'Price theory and oligopoly', *Economic Journal*, vol. 57, no. 227, September, pp. 299–320.

Saunders, A. and Yourougou, P. (1990) 'Are banks special? The separation of banking from commerce and interest rate risk', *Journal of Economics and Business*, vol. 42, pp. 171–82.

Schwartz, M. (1986) 'The nature and scope of contestability theory', *Oxford Economic Papers*, vol. 38 (supplement), pp. 37–57.

Seballos, L. and Thomson, J. (1993) 'Underlying causes of commercial bank failures in the 1980s' in Kolb, R.W. (ed.) *The Financial Institutions and Markets Reader*, 2nd edn. Boulder, Co.: Kolb Publishing Company.

Seth, R. and Quijano, A. (1991) 'In Brief Economic Capsules, Japanese Banks Customer in the United States', *Federal Reserve Bank of New York Quarterly Review*, Spring, pp. 79–82.

Shaffer, S. (1981a) 'Banking: competition or monopoly power?', Banking Studies Department, Federal Reserve Bank of New York, March.

Shaffer, S. (1981b) 'Empirical test for competitive conduct', Banking Studies Department, Federal Reserve Bank of New York, August.

Shaffer, S. (1982) 'A non-structural test for competition in financial markets'. In *Bank Structure and Competition*, Conference Proceedings, Federal Reserve Bank of Chicago, pp. 225–43.

Shaffer, S. (1993) 'Can megamergers improve bank efficiency?', *Journal of Banking and Finance*, vol. 17, nos 2–3, pp. 423–36.

Shelling, T. (1960) *The Strategy of Conflict*. Boston, Mass.: Harvard University Press.

Sherman, H.D. and Gold, F. (1985) 'Bank branch operating efficiency: Evaluation with data envelopment analysis', *Journal of Banking and Finance*, vol. 9, pp. 297–315.

Silber, W. (ed.) (1975) *Financial Innovation*. Lexington, Ky.: Lexington Books.

Spence, M. (1983) 'Contestable markets and the theory of industry structure: A review article', *Journal of Economic Literature*, vol. 21, pp. 981–90.

Spindler, J.A. (1984) 'Private Finance and Foreign Policy in Germany and Japan', *The Politics of International Credit*. Washington, D.C.: The Brookings Institution.

Spindt, P.A. and Tarhan, V. (1992) 'Are there synergies in bank mergers?', Working Paper, Tulane University.

Srinivasan, A. (1992) 'Are there cost savings from bank mergers?', *Federal Reserve Bank of Atlanta Economic Review*, March–April, pp. 17–28.

Srinivasan, A. and Wall, L.D. (1992) 'Cost savings associated with bank mergers', Working Paper, Federal Reserve Bank of Atlanta.

Stigler, G. (1964) 'A theory of oligopoly', *Journal of Political Economy*, vol. 72, February, pp. 44–61.

Stiglitz, J. and Mathewson, F. (eds) (1986) *New Developments in the Analysis of Market Structure*. Boston, Mass.: MIT Press.

Strivens, R. (1992) 'The liberalization of banking services in the Community', *Common Market Law Review*, vol. 29, pp. 283–307.

Sullivan, B. (1991) 'A Perspective on Banking and Global Markets', *The World of Banking*, September–October, pp. 5–7.

Sway, T. and Topf, B. (1992) *Global Financial Deregulation*. Boston, Mass.: Blackwell Publications.

Terrell, H.S., Dohner, R.S. and Lowery, B.R. (1990) 'The Activities of Japanese Banks in the United Kingdom and in the United States, 1980–88', *Federal Reserve Bulletin*, February, pp. 39–49.

Thygesen, N. (1988) 'The EMS: Introduction'. In Giavazzi, F., Micossi, S. and Miller, M. (eds) *The EMS*. Cambridge: Cambridge University Press.

Tirole, J. (1993) 'On banking and intermediation', Institut d'Economie Industrielle, Université des Sciences Sociale de Toulouse, Working Paper no. 31, December.

Tirole, J. (1994) 'The internal organisation of government', *Oxford Economic Papers*, vol. 46, no. 1, January, pp. 1–29.

Townsend, R.M. (1979) 'Optimal contracts and competitive markets with costly state verification', *Journal of Economic Theory*, vol. 21, pp. 265–93.

Ungerer, H. (1989) 'The EMS and the international monetary system', *Journal of Common Market Studies*, vol. 27, pp. 231–48.

US Congress (1984) *Effects of Information Technology on Financial Services System*. Washington, DC: OTA.

Vaubel, R. (1990) 'Currency competition and European monetary integration', *Economic Journal*, vol. 100, September, pp. 936–46.

Viner, J. (1950) *The Custom Union Issue*. New York: Carnegie Endowment.

Vives, X. (1991) 'Banking competition and European integration'. In Giovannini, A. and Mayer, C. (eds) *European Financial Integration*, Cambridge: Cambridge University Press, pp. 9–31.

Walter, I. (1988) *Global Competition in Financial Services*. New York: Ballinger.

Wall, L.D. (1987) 'Has bank holding companies' diversification affected their risk of failure?' *Journal of Economics and Business*, vol 39, no. 4, pp. 313–326.

Williamson, J.P. (ed.) (1988) *Investment Banking Handbook*. Chichester: John Wiley and Sons.

Williamson, S.D. (1986) 'Costly monitoring, financial intermediation, and equilibrium credit rationing', *Journal of Monetary Economics*, vol. 18, pp. 159–79.

Wilson, J.Q. (1989) *Bureaucracy: What Government Agencies Do and Why They Do It*. New York: Basic Books.

Zecher, J.R. (1984) 'Financial innovation in the 1980s'. In Federal Reserve Bank of St Louis, *Financial Innovation*. Boston, Mass.: Klywer-Nijhoff, pp. 151–75.

Index